ELECTION UMPIRES IN CAMEROON

ELECTION UMPIRES IN CAMEROON

A Comparative Analysis of the National Elections Observatory (NEO) and Elections Cameroon (ELECAM)

Dr. Mbamome Nkendong Divine
Dr. John Walah Mua

EXCELLER BOOKS®
A GLOBAL PRESS

Election Umpires in Cameroon

A Comparative Analysis of the National Elections Observatory (NEO) and Elections Cameroon (ELECAM)

Cover by Exceller Books

Print ISBN: 978-93-48892-86-7

First published in India in 2026 by Exceller Books,
An imprint of GE Group

Address: G1, Dream Apartment, Degree College Road, Belgharia,
Kolkata, 700056, India
www.excellerbooks.com

EXCELLER BOOKS®
A GLOBAL PRESS

In Memoriam:

August 1, 2006,
June 29, 2016,
July 4, 2020

Abstract

The study "Electoral Management Bodies and Voter Apathy: A Comparative Analysis of NEO and ELECAM" examines the relationship between electoral management bodies (EMBs) and voter apathy in Cameroon. EMBs in Cameroon, including the Ministry of Territorial Administration, the National Elections Observatory (NEO), and Elections Cameroon (ELECAM), have failed to achieve consistent voter turnout despite decades of democratic practice.

A comparative descriptive research design evaluates the factors contributing to voter apathy and assesses the impact of EMBs on electoral engagement. The study utilizes Rational Choice Theory, the Sociological Model of Voting Behavior, and Duverger's Theory as theoretical frameworks. Data were collected using purposive sampling techniques, including primary and secondary sources.

The findings reveal that EMBs in Cameroon lack autonomy due to significant dependence on the state, which leads to public distrust. Additional challenges, including insufficient polling infrastructure, partisan biases, and inadequate electoral communication, contribute to low voter turnout. Electoral flaws in Cameroon hinder democratic development, creating what has been described as an "autocratic democracy."

The study recommends revising ELECAM's legal framework to ensure greater independence, implementing internet voting to increase accessibility, and adopting an enhanced strategy for disseminating electoral information.

Keywords: *Electoral management, voter apathy, voter turnout, Cameroon, NEO, ELECAM*

List of Acronyms/Abbreviations

ACHPR: African Charter on Human and Peoples' Rights
ACHR: American Convention on Human Rights
CAR: Central African Republic
CPDM: Cameroon People's Democratic Movement
DGE: Directorate General of Elections
DRE: Direct Recording Electronic Voting Machines
EB: Electoral Board of Elections Cameroon
EBA: Extreme Bound Analysis
EC: Electoral Commission of Ghana
EISA: Electoral Institute of Southern Africa
ELECAM: Elections Cameroon
EMB: Election Management Body
GDP: Gross Domestic Product
ICCPR: International Covenant on Civil and Political Rights
IDEA: International Institute for Electoral Assistance
IEC: Independent Electoral Commission of South Africa
IFES: International Foundation for Election Systems
MINADT: Ministry of Territorial Administration and Decentralization
NDI: National Democratic Institute for International Affairs
NEO: National Elections Observatory
OECD: Organization for Economic Co-operation and Development
ONEL: Observatoire Nationale des Elections

Table of Contents

Chapter 1 | EMBs and Voter Apathy in Context and Appraoch: An Overview

The third wave of democratization in the 1990s prompted a surge in democratic elections across many developing nations. Elections provide a fundamental mechanism of democracy, allowing different interest groups within a state to express their preferences for political leadership through peaceful and structured processes. Iyayi (2006) argues that elections provide a legitimate medium for resolving claims to power and minimizing social conflict. Electoral participation, often measured through voter turnout, represents a critical indicator of democratic engagement and political legitimacy.

Citizens' participation in elections strengthens democracy by fostering accountability and reflecting the people's will. Dalton (1988) emphasizes that citizens' involvement in political processes ensures democracy remains viable and meaningful. Despite requiring minimal initiative, voting is the most widespread and visible form of political engagement. However, voter turnout has experienced a decline in most democracies (Blais, 2000; Gray & Caul, 2000), with significant variations observed across countries and over time (Lassen, 2005).

Higher voter turnout enhances political accountability. Elected officials, aware that their performance determines re-election, are incentivized to prioritize the public's best interests (Verge, 2009; Marin, 1997; Ferejohn, 1986; Fiorina, 1981; Barro, 1973). Voting, therefore, serves as a sanctioning mechanism, encouraging politicians to remain responsive to the electorate. However, this process requires competitive elections and robust voter engagement. When substantial portions of the population abstain, elections fail to promote accountability and legitimacy.

In developing democracies, credible elections play a critical role in promoting political stability and legitimacy. Following the Cold War, many African countries adopted multiparty electoral systems, acknowledging competitive elections as a cornerstone of democratic legitimacy (Mozaffar, 2002). Elections provide a framework for peaceful political competition and convey the people's will, thus supporting the legitimacy of political systems. However, political apathy—psychological disengagement and emotional detachment from civic duties—remains a significant obstacle to democratic participation. Voters' apathy, as a form of political disengagement, increasingly threatens both mature and emerging democracies.

Cameroon's political landscape is deeply rooted in its colonial history and post-colonial state-building efforts. Originally a German protectorate (1884–1919), Cameroon was divided into British and French mandate territories after Germany's defeat in World War I. In 1961, these territories united under a federal structure, which later transitioned into the United Republic of Cameroon in 1972. By 1984, the country was renamed the Republic of Cameroon (Eyongetah, 1974). Despite persistent authoritarian tendencies, Cameroon has managed to maintain relative political stability compared to its neighbors. However, security challenges such as Boko Haram insurgencies in the north and conflicts with Central African Republic (CAR) rebels in the east have posed significant disruptions to this stability.

The reintroduction of multiparty politics in the 1990s was a watershed moment in Cameroon's political evolution. Under pressure from domestic and international actors, the government allowed political parties to form and organize multiparty elections. Cameroon's political system remains heavily centralized despite these reforms, with the ruling Cameroon People's Democratic Movement (CPDM) dominating the political arena. Electoral periods are marked by intense mobilization, including rallies, door-to-door campaigns, and the distribution of party materials. However, the persistent decline in voter turnout underscores the significant challenge of voter apathy.

Understanding voter apathy in Cameroon requires an examination of the role of electoral management bodies (EMBs) in organizing elections and building public trust. EMBs, including the Ministry of Territorial Administration, the National Elections Observatory (NEO), and Elections Cameroon (ELECAM), have diligently worked to ensure transparent, fair, and credible elections. Despite their efforts, none of these entities has succeeded in reversing the trend of low voter turnout. This study examines the factors contributing to voter apathy in Cameroon and assesses the effectiveness of NEO and ELECAM in promoting voter engagement.

1.1. The Magnitude of the Paradox EMBs and Voter Apathy

Democracy relies on citizen participation, with elections as a primary channel for expressing political will. High voter turnout indicates public trust in the electoral process, while low turnout often reflects disillusionment and disengagement. In Cameroon, voter turnout has varied significantly over recent decades, with recent elections registering notably low participation rates. For instance, turnout during the 2018 presidential election dropped to 54 percent, down from 68 percent in 2011. Conflict-affected regions experienced even lower participation.

Declining voter turnout highlights widespread voter apathy in Cameroon. Apathy extends beyond disinterest in voting, revealing a more profound disconnection between citizens and the political system. Distrust in electoral management bodies, dissatisfaction with political parties, and perceptions of ineffective elections contribute to electoral disengagement. Citizens who view elections as manipulated or irrelevant are less likely to participate, undermining the legitimacy of elected governments.

Although ELECAM was established in 2006 as an independent electoral body, voter turnout remains low. Structural, legal, and operational challenges may undermine the effectiveness of EMBs. This study aims to explore these challenges, examining the legal frameworks governing EMBs, their operational shortcomings, and the factors influencing voter apathy in Cameroon.

1.2. Current Curiosities about EMBs and Voter Apathy

The study seeks to address one general research question and several specific sub-questions.

- What is the relationship between electoral management bodies and voter apathy in Cameroon?
- How does the legal framework governing EMBs in Cameroon affect their functional efficiency?
- What are the factors that contribute to voter apathy in Cameroon?
- What are the challenges that NEO and ELECAM have encountered in shaping voter behavior?
- What are the measures that NEO and ELECAM have implemented to increase voter turnout?

1.3. Research Objectives

The primary objective is to explore the relationship between electoral management bodies and voter apathy in Cameroon. Specific objectives include:

- Analyzing how the legal framework governing EMBs influences their functional efficiency.
- Identifying challenges faced by NEO and ELECAM in fulfilling their mandates.
- Examining the primary causes of voter apathy in Cameroon.
- Evaluating measures implemented by NEO and ELECAM to improve voter turnout.

1.4. Tempting Prompts on EMBs

- The following hypotheses guide the study:
- Restrictive legal frameworks hinder the independence and effectiveness of EMBs, leading to public distrust.
- NEO and ELECAM face similar challenges, including government interference, limited autonomy, voter apathy, and corruption.
- Electoral timing, communication strategies, political party dynamics, electoral laws, and registration processes influence voter turnout in Cameroon.
- The transition from NEO to ELECAM introduced changes to the legal, procedural, and operational frameworks, aimed at increasing voter turnout.

1.5. The Worth of Engaging a Study of EMBs

The study's findings offer valuable insights for various stakeholders, including academics, policymakers, and practitioners.

- **Academic Contribution:** The research enriches the literature on electoral management and voter behavior in Cameroon. By offering a comparative analysis of NEO and ELECAM, the study highlights vital challenges EMBs face in improving voter engagement. Future research may build on these findings to further explore voter apathy and electoral reforms.
- **Practical Value for Political Practitioners:** The study identifies the factors driving voter apathy, offering practical insights for

political parties, candidates, and civil society organizations seeking to mobilize voters. Understanding voter apathy dynamics can inform campaign strategies and encourage greater participation.

- **Policy Implications:** Policymakers may use the findings to design reforms that strengthen EMBs, enhance their independence, and improve voter engagement. Recommendations from this research can serve as a foundation for legislative changes aimed at enhancing electoral credibility and increasing voter turnout.

1.6. Scope and Limitations of the Book

17.1. Scope

The research focuses on electoral management bodies in Cameroon, specifically analyzing the roles of NEO and ELECAM in addressing voter apathy. The period under review spans from 2000 to 2022, encompassing the establishment of NEO in 2000 and the transition to ELECAM in 2010. This timeframe provides a comprehensive view of institutional efforts to enhance voter engagement.

1.7.2. Limitations

Reliance on secondary data for historical analysis may limit access to detailed primary sources. For consistency and focus, the study concentrates on national elections, excluding local elections. Additionally, restricted access to certain government records or proprietary information from ELECAM may constrain the research.

1.7. Definition of Key Terms

To ensure clarity, the following key terms are defined within the context of this research:

- **Elections:** A democratic process through which individuals are selected as executives or representatives in governmental bodies.
- **Electoral Management Body (EMB):** Organizations responsible for overseeing the election process, ensuring fairness and transparency.

- **Voter Apathy:** A lack of interest or motivation to participate in elections, often stemming from distrust in the political system or dissatisfaction with political options.
- **Voter Turnout:** The proportion of eligible voters who cast votes in an election. Voter turnout serves as a measure of public engagement in the political process.

The study is divided into six chapters, each addressing a specific aspect of the research topic:

- **Chapter One** introduces the study, including the background, problem statement, research questions, objectives, hypotheses, significance, scope, limitations, and definitions of key terms.
- **Chapter Two** reviews relevant literature, providing a conceptual and empirical foundation while identifying gaps and outlining theoretical frameworks.
- **Chapter Three** details the research methodology, including the design, area of study, target population, sampling techniques, data collection methods, and ethical considerations.
- **Chapter Four** presents data, analysis, and discussion of findings about the research questions and hypotheses.
- **Chapter Five** summarizes key findings, draws conclusions, and offers recommendations for policy changes and future research.
- **References and Appendices** include bibliographic references and supplementary materials.

Chapter 2 | What We Know and Think About Election Management

"However much we focus on the determinants of individuals' votes, it is their impact on the political system that matters in the end."

— *Lewis-Beck et al. (2008:4)*

2.1. Conceptual Review

A thematic approach is adopted in this study to review conceptual literature. The following concepts are of literary relevance to the research:

- Voter Turnout
- An Overview of Free and Fair Elections
- Assessment of Election Credibility
- Information and Voting
- Voting and Electoral Competition
- Determinants of Election Quality Perceptions

<u>2.1.1. Voter Turnout</u>

The topic of voter turnout often generates intense discussion. After elections, a frequent question arises: How many individuals turned out to vote? At times, turnout surprises observers by being unusually high. For example, many expressed astonishment at the long lines of people waiting under the scorching African sun during South Africa's first truly free and universal election. Conversely, turnout often surprises observers by being lower than anticipated. This frequent focus on low or declining turnout gives the impression that such trends dominate democratic elections worldwide.

One reason for this impression lies in the media's focus on turnout decline, as stable or moderately increased turnout needs more news value. The first national-level studies on voter turnout sought to explain its variations by examining lower-house elections in OECD countries. For instance, Jackman (1987) analyzed 19 democracies, Jackman and Miller (1995) studied 23, and Blais and Carty (1990), along with Powell (1986), focused on 20 democracies. These studies assessed factors such as the socio-economic environment, constitutional settings, and party systems (Blais & Dobrzynska, 1998, p. 241).

Low turnout garners significant attention because it fuels debates about the health of democracy. Commentators attribute low electoral participation to a symptom of weakened democracy, questioning its legitimacy or highlighting the underrepresentation of marginalized groups (Piven & Cloward, 1988; Teixeira, 1992).

However, evidence shows that turnout decline is not ubiquitous. Emerging democracies have recently witnessed increased voter participation (Norris, 2002, p. 12). Even in established democracies, declines in turnout appear modest. The IDEA voter turnout project estimated that turnout in 36 established democracies dropped by an average of 4 percent between the 1970s and the 1990s (ending in 1997). This represents less than half a percent decline per election, an amount difficult to distinguish from sampling error.

Period	**Established States (%)**	**All Other States (%)**
1945-1949	75	40
1950-1959	78	45
1960-1969	80	55
1970-1979	79	65
1980-1989	78	68
1990-1997	77	66

Table 2.1: Average Turnout in Decades for 39 Countries Since 1945

Source: IDEA Website (http://www.idea.int)

Instead of focusing solely on why turnout is declining, attention should be directed to why turnout remains stable. Among 21 countries holding elections continuously since 1945, most experienced less than 10 percent variation in turnout from their historical averages. Two-thirds of elections deviated by less than 5 percent. Notably, only five countries (Finland, et al.) exceeded this range, with Malta experiencing an upward shift, while others saw declines.

Country	Mean Turnout	Standard Deviation	b (Turnout on Time)	Standard Error of Estimate
Australia	94.591	1.842		
Austria	92.062	3.907		
Belgium	92.611	1.712		
Canada	74.588	4.199		
Denmark	85.591	2.52		
Finland	75.937	5.779	-11.0 (4.77)	
France	76.687	5.919	-10.9 (4.90)	
Germany	85.571	4.45		
Ireland	73.25	3.235		
Israel	80.4	3.135		
Italy	90.571	3.345		
Japan	71.35	4.591		
Luxembourg	89.833	1.992		
Malta	88.214	8.719	+23.5 (3.86)	
The Netherlands	87.562	7.545	-21.1 (4.15)	
New Zealand	88.579	4.059		
Norway	80.643	3.028		
Sweden	86.118	4.742		
Switzerland	56.643	11.05	-34.7 (2.59)	
The UK	76.4	3.602		
The USA	53.923	4.941		

Table 2.2: Mean and Standard Deviation for Turnout in 21 Countries (1945–1999)

Source: Data from the IDEA Website (http://www.idea.int) and Other Sources Time Is a Continuous Variable Running from 0 in 1945 to 1 in 1999

Turnout remains stable because voting tends to become a habit. Individuals participating in their first election are likely to vote in subsequent elections. Conversely, those who abstain in their initial voting opportunity generally continue to abstain. Studies in the United States (Miller & Shanks, 1996; Putnam, 2000) and Canada (Blais et al., 2001) have documented this trend, which is likely applicable globally.

The decision to vote mirrors party allegiance, often forming early in adulthood. Minor turnout variations within electorates mask significant changes among newly eligible voters. Over time, if younger cohorts vote less frequently than predecessors, turnout will decline. For example, a 4 percent decline over 20 years can deepen to an 8 percent decline over the following two decades due to generational replacement, bottoming out at a 10 percent total decline.

In light of this logic, answering the following two questions becomes essential:

- Why is turnout declining in so many established democracies?
- Does it matter?

Addressing these questions requires confronting three significant dilemmas. These dilemmas hinder political science research, but only some topics face all three dilemmas simultaneously as profoundly as voter turnout.

2.1.1.1. The Dilemmas

The first dilemma concerns the distinction between collective and individual actions. Turnout is a collective phenomenon arising from numerous individual decisions to vote or abstain. However, motivations to vote or abstain belong to individuals. Countries do not decide collectively that 82.5 percent of their citizens will vote, nor do they have the means to enforce such turnout. Instead, individual decisions cumulatively determine turnout levels. Decisions to vote often involve personal considerations such as convenience, weather, or whether the election outcome feels significant. Many of these motivations do not interest social scientists, as they are specific and cancel each other out. Therefore, explaining turnout levels by asking individuals why they voted or abstained is unlikely to yield comprehensive answers.

The second dilemma involves distinguishing causation from association. Following David Hume's idea of 'constant conjunction', social research often infers causation from correlations. For instance, if turnout decreases when societies become more atomized, researchers may assume that increasing individualism ('Bowling Alone', as Putnam describes it) contributes to lower turnout. However, turnout research suffers from the "small N, large V" problem. Elections occur infrequently in relatively few countries over short historical periods, yet many variables may explain turnout trends. Many of these variables exhibit one-directional trends, leading to positive or negative correlations with turnout trends. Consequently, isolating the specific causes of turnout decline proves challenging.

The third dilemma relates to distinguishing changes over time from changes across space. Individuals and collectives (e.g. countries or cities) behave differently over time and across contexts. For instance, individuals may vote in one election but abstain in another. Similarly, some countries may experience higher turnout in one election cycle and lower turnout in another. Social science research often assumes symmetry between differences across time and space. For instance, if individuals with characteristic 'x' consistently vote, researchers may conclude that instilling 'x' in the entire electorate will increase turnout. However, this reasoning often needs to be revised when applied across time. For example, changing all men into women will not be a practical solution for low turnout if women are found to vote more frequently than men. Much of what is known about voting behavior derives from cross-space comparisons, but most pressing questions about turnout pertain to changes over time.

2.1.1.2. Focusing on Over-Time Turnout Variations

Bernard Grofman (1992:36) argued in his essay, "Is Turnout the Paradox That Ate Rational Choice Theory?" that political scientists should prioritize explaining variations in turnout over time, emulating economists' focus on variables' temporal changes rather than their levels. While country-level studies often focus on turnout variations between nations, time-series analysis offers a more productive approach to understanding voter behavior.

For instance, if researchers suspect that countries moving elections to rest days achieve higher turnout, studying countries that change their voting days offers more direct insights than comparing countries with differing election days. Cross-sectional data provide value when time-series data are unavailable. However, with ample election data spanning multiple decades and countries, time-series analysis better isolates turnout trends.

Pooling data from multiple elections allows researchers to adjust for interdependence within countries while retaining enough observations to test over-time turnout models (Beck & Katz, 1995). However, the pooled analysis may still conflate over-space and over-time differences. Mis-specified models may result if over-space effects differ from over-time effects. Consequently, only deviations from country-specific means should interest studies on turnout change.

2.1.1.3. Turnout at the Individual Level

While turnout represents an aggregate-level phenomenon, voting decisions remain individual. Aggregating individual behavior into turnout data involves more complexity than simply summing individual tendencies. An electorate is not merely a scaled-up voter, just as an economy is not a scaled-up consumer. Despite this distinction, most research on voting focuses on individual behavior.

Survey research reveals that specific individual characteristics significantly increase voting likelihood. Older individuals, college-educated individuals, and those embedded in social networks (e.g. organizational memberships) demonstrate higher turnout rates. Conversely, younger, less-educated, socially isolated individuals are less likely to vote (Verba & Nie, 1972; Parry et al., 1990; Rosenstone & Hansen, 1993; Verba et al., 1995).

Education influences turnout through increased knowledge and earning capacity. Organizational memberships, meanwhile, foster turnout through mobilization. Members are more accessible to contact for political campaigns and more likely to respond to mobilization efforts.

Age is a significant variable. Younger voters often need to catch up with older cohorts in terms of education completion and organizational memberships. Consequently, younger voters exhibit lower turnout rates. Life-cycle effects suggest that as these individuals age, they gain characteristics that increase turnout.

Increases in the share of younger voters in the electorate drive turnout declines. For example, the baby-boom generation, reaching voting age in the late 1960s, coincided with many countries lowering the voting age from 21 to 18. This demographic expansion doubled the proportion of newly enfranchised voters, increasing the contribution of younger, less likely voters to turnout metrics.

As young voters mature, they often acquire characteristics that increase their turnout. However, this transition may take decades, and younger voters may never match older generations' turnout levels due to generational differences. Consequently, turnout declines driven by demographic changes may persist for decades.

2.1.1.4. Turnout at the Aggregate Level

Aggregate-level analysis requires examining how individual-level effects aggregate into broader turnout trends.

Three variable categories typically explain variations in turnout in established democracies: resources, mobilization, and motivations. Individual-level research often highlights resources and mobilization (Verba & Nie, 1972; Wolfinger & Rosenstone, 1980; Parry et al., 1990). Aggregate-level research emphasizes motivation-related factors, including the costs and benefits of voting (Merriam & Gosnell, 1924; Tingsten, 1937).

Individual rationality underpins the theoretical importance of motivation, though the "paradox of turnout" remains unresolved (Downs, 1957). Voters behave rationally but defy theories suggesting that voting costs outweigh its benefits. However, aggregate behavior aligns with rationality, suggesting broader patterns may obscure individual-level inconsistencies.

Institutional settings establish the costs of voting, which remain constant in the short term. Benefits fluctuate across elections based on party competition and policy stakes. Close elections likely to influence government policy motivate higher turnout by incentivizing voter participation and campaign mobilization efforts.

Resource and mobilization theories face challenges at the aggregate level. For example, even significant increases in college-educated individuals yield small turnout gains in established democracies. Similarly, increased group membership does not guarantee turnout gains due to inconsistent mobilization efforts during low-salience elections.

A notable exception lies in the electorate expansion. Increases in electorate size, often due to enfranchising new voters, directly affect turnout. New voters are more challenging to mobilize and tend to vote at lower rates, driving turnout decline.

Electorate expansion represents an aggregate manifestation of individual-level effects. For instance, new voters disproportionately influence turnout change. The aggregate effect of demographic replacement likely explains observed turnout declines in advanced democracies.

2.1.1.5. Variables that Directly Affect Turnout

Numerous variables influence voter turnout, including those directly related to election management bodies (EMBs). However, many other variables significantly affect voter turnout across different contexts. Recent studies document the proliferation of potential factors influencing turnout and expand research coverage.

For example, turnout tends to decline in larger political communities (Remmer, 2010, p. 2), under economic globalization (Steiner, 2010, p. 17), with higher levels of corruption (Stockemer et al., 2013, p. 60), and in ethnically diverse societies (Martínez et al., 2017, p. 23). On the other hand, terrorism increases attention to national politics, subsequently boosting voter turnout (Robbins et al., 2013, p. 28).

Earlier studies predominantly focused on economically developed democracies. Blais and Dobrzynska (1998:4) were among the first to collect data on a global scale from democratic elections. Later studies expanded to cover regions such as Latin America (Fornos et al., 2004, p. 36), post-Cold War Eastern Europe (Kostadinova, 2003, p. 17), Africa (Kuenzi & Lambright, 2007, p. 3), and Muslim-majority countries (Stockemer & Khazaei, 2014, p. 5). These studies typically utilized three categories of independent variables: socio-economic, institutional, and political (Geys, 2006; Blais & Dobrzynska, 1998, p. 10).

- Socio-economic variables include factors such as economic growth and urbanization.
- Institutional variables capture arrangements under which elections occur (e.g., the electoral formula).
- Political variables account for election-specific outcomes (e.g., the margin of victory).

Comparing results across studies reveals limitations in the literature. For instance, Blais and Dobrzynska (1998:20) identified economic development, literacy rates, population size, compulsory voting laws, minimum voting ages, electoral systems, the number of political parties, and competitiveness as significant predictors of turnout.

Subsequent research, such as Endersby and Krieckhaus (2008:5), confirmed some of these findings while emphasizing the importance of the context. Similarly, Martínez and Coma (2016:3) agreed with several conclusions by Blais and Dobrzynska (1998:11) but disputed the significance of variables like electoral systems and economic development.

A consensus remains elusive regarding the robust variables to include in a core turnout model. Studies continue to provide mixed evidence on predictors, with no universally accepted framework after over 50 years of research. As summarized by Remmer (2010:277):

> *"Draw[ing] on relatively small samples, differing sets of observations, divergent operationalization of turnout, and a wide array of theoretical models; the literature has mainly converged around relatively 'commonsensical' observations."*

2.1.1.6. Why a Meta-Analysis Is Not Enough

Meta-analyses are popular tools for evaluating lessons from literature by examining whether specific independent variables affect dependent variables. A meta-analysis combines findings from multiple studies and uses statistical procedures like "vote-counting" or "combined tests" to conclude.

2.1.1.6.1. Vote-Counting

This approach tallies significant results. Coefficients aligned with expectations count as 'successes'; those that deviate are anomalies. Higher success rates indicate robust associations between variables.

2.1.1.6.2. Combined Tests

Combined tests aggregate test statistics from included studies to determine variable significance. For example, Geys (2006:641) analyzed voter turnout using meta-analytic methods, identifying 12 socio-economic, political, and institutional factors significantly influencing turnout. However, Geys (2006:641, 653) noted the lack of a theoretical core model guiding variable selection.

Similarly, Stockemer (2017:712) reviewed 135 studies spanning from 2004–2013, identifying over 100 potentially salient predictors and analyzing 10 in depth. However, Stockemer concluded that no variable appeared omnipresent across studies. Variability in study designs and contexts explains inconsistent findings regarding predictors such as electoral closeness and proportional representation systems.

2.1.1.7. Limitations of Meta-Analyses

Meta-analyses face inherent constraints due to their reliance on sample-specific data. The ad hoc nature of robustness checks compounds uncertainty about meta-analysis results. Most studies test competing explanations by including a small set of additional variables in regression models.

However, the potential number of alternative variable combinations grows exponentially with the number of variables tested.

For example:

- Five variables generate 32 model combinations.
- Six variables generate 64 model combinations.
- Eight variables generate 40,320 model combinations.

As a result, even rigorous meta-analyses evaluate only a tiny fraction of potential predictors.

Furthermore, standard regression frameworks suffer from two fundamental limitations:

- Statistical significance often depends on variable inclusion/exclusion. Theories lack precision in defining appropriate empirical measures for variables (e.g., whether GDP or its log transformation is the best measure).
- Extreme Bounds Analysis (EBA): Extreme Bounds Analysis (EBA) addresses some limitations of meta-analyses by estimating all possible combinations of predictors to identify systematically robust variables.

An EBA model typically takes the following form:

$Y = \beta_i I + \beta M + \beta z Z + u$

Where:

- Y is the dependent variable (e.g. voter turnout).
- I is the core variable included in all models.
- M is the variable of interest.
- Z is the set of additional control variables.
- u is the error term.

Researchers test the robustness of variables by examining the distribution of their coefficients across models.

2.1.1.7.1. Leamer's Criterion

Leamer (1983:30) proposed that robust variables should retain the same sign across all models.

However, this stringent standard often excludes potentially meaningful predictors.

2.1.1.7.2. Sala-i-Martin's Criterion

Sala-i-Martin (1997:34) suggested a less restrictive approach, defining variables as robust if the majority (e.g., 90–95%) of their coefficient estimates share the same sign.

Both criteria offer trade-offs:

- Leamer's approach minimizes false positives but may exclude meaningful predictors.
- Sala-i-Martin's approach risks identifying false positives.

2.1.1.8. Institutional Predictors of Voter Turnout

Institutional variables significantly influence voter turnout. Table 2.2 summarizes key institutional predictors, their frequency in the literature, measurement methods, and results.

Frequeny	Indicator	No. of Ways of	Results	% Agree
		Measurement		
33	Compulsory voting	3	Positive (25);	84%
			Negative (5)	
19	Number of parties	10	Positive (10);	Mixed
			Negative (8)	
19	Proportional	2	Positive (10)	Mixed
	representation			
18	Concurrent/simultaneous	2	Positive (13)	Mixed
	elections			
13	Unicameralism	3	Positive (4);	Mixed
			Negative (1)	
9	Disproportionality	5	Positive (3)	Mixed
9	District magnitude	5	Positive (3);	Mixed
			Negative (1)	
8	Automatic (voluntary)	2	Positive (3);	Mixed
	registration		Negative (1)	
8	Legal voting age	3	Positive (1)	Mixed
5	Federalism	3	Positive (1)	Mixed

Table 2.2: Institutional Predictors of Voter Turnout

Source: Kaniovski & Miller, 2006

Compulsory voting demonstrated the most robust agreement, with 84% of studies reporting a positive relationship with turnout. However, other variables (e.g. proportional representation and the number of parties) yielded mixed results, suggesting that contextual influences may impact their effects.

2.1.1.9. Political Predictors of Voter Turnout

Table 2.3 summarizes political variables affecting turnout, including their frequency, measurement methods, and results.

Frequency	Indicator	No. of Ways of Measurement	Results	Positive	Negative	N	S	Mixed	%Agree
23	Closeness/competitiveness	5		3	9	9			45
11	Democracy	9		5	1	5			45
5	Previous turnout	1		4	1				80
4	Founding elections	1		3	1				75
3	Number of elections	3		1	2				67
2	New Democracy	1		2					100
2	Third election	1		2					100
2	Fourth election	1		2					100
2	Short-term majority status of Government	1		2					
2	Short-term margin of victory	1		2					
2	Short-term cohesiveness	1		2					
1	Recent threat to Democracy	1		1					
1	Second election	1		1					
1	Third or fourth election	1		1					
1	Fifth or sixth election	1		1					
1	Electoral volatility	1		1					
1	Voting share of the parties	1		1					
1	Frequent changes in executive	1		1					
1	Average strength of party group linkages	1		1					

1	Party polarisation	1		1					
1	Post-materialist party in parliament	1		1					
1	Prior democratic experience	1		1					
1	Terrorist attack	1		1					
1	Party replacement	1		1					
1	Two-party vote concentration	1		1					
1	Seat ratio – first to second parties	1		1					
1	Number pre-electoral coalitions	1		1					
1	Dispersions	1		1					
1	Opposition harassments	1		1					
1	Opposition ban	1		1					
1	Boycott	1		1					
1	Violence	1		1					
1	Party linkages	1							
1	Seventh or eighth election	1		1					
1	Decisiveness	1		1					
1	Short-term mean margin	1		1					
1	Authoritarian path	1		1					
1	Democratization path	1		1					

Table 2.3: Political Predictors of Voter Turnout

Source: Geys, 2006

Category	**Socio-economic**	**Institutional**	**Political**	**Total**
Variables	41	48	38	127
% of common variables	58 (24)	44 (21)	29 (11)	44 (45)
% of common variables measured differently	62 (15)	66 (14)	27 (3)	57 (32)
Variables mentioned	41	48	38	127
Variables included in EBA models	33	16	21	70

Table 2.4: Socio-economic, Institutional, and Political Predictors

Continuous predictors were log-transformed to reduce the effects of extreme values.

The closeness of elections was consistently identified as a significant factor in increasing voter turnout, underscoring its importance in motivating participation.

2.1.1.10. Conclusion

Explanatory variables influencing voter turnout can be broadly categorized into those explaining the decision to vote and those determining voting behavior. However, many variables influence both aspects, limiting the utility of strict categorizations.

Socio-demographic variables, institutional settings, and political factors all shape voter behavior. Nonetheless, inconsistencies in study findings highlight the need for more robust theoretical frameworks to model voter turnout.

2.1.2. An Overview of Free and Fair Elections

There is no universal definition of "free and fair" elections in international law. However, international norms provide vital guidelines to ensure democratic electoral processes. While domestic laws primarily govern elections, many countries adhere to international standards outlined in treaties, such as the International Covenant on Civil and Political Rights (ICCPR), as well as regional agreements, including the African Charter on Human and Peoples' Rights (ACHPR).

A genuinely democratic election must allow the free expression of the people's will. Violations such as gerrymandering, voter intimidation, and ballot manipulation undermine electoral integrity. As Autheman (2004:5) highlights, emerging democracies must develop robust electoral systems to build public confidence in their processes.

Some African states have faced significant challenges in meeting international standards for elections. For example:

- Nigeria (2007) and Zimbabwe (2008): Elections in these countries were heavily criticized for lacking credibility, pointing to the need for greater adherence to democratic principles.
- Ghana (2009) and South Africa (2009): These elections were widely praised for meeting international norms, demonstrating that credible and democratic elections are attainable on the continent.

The growing international interest in free and fair elections has ignited a global discussion regarding the defining characteristics of an ideal electoral process. At a minimum, credible elections must guarantee equal opportunities for all candidates, ensure the right to vote for eligible citizens and safeguard the transparency of vote counting.

A "free and fair" election should allow all eligible citizens to participate without unreasonable restrictions or interference. According to Goodwill-Gill (2006), terms like 'free' and 'fair' often lack precise legal definitions. However, the international community has developed benchmarks emphasizing transparency, accessibility, and integrity.

2.1.2.1. Key Elements of a Free and Fair Election

- Freedom from Coercion: Voters must be able to cast their ballots without fear of intimidation, violence, or retribution. Electoral violence and intimidation undermine democracy by deterring participation and creating a climate of fear.
- Equal Access: All eligible voters must have equal opportunities to participate in the electoral process. This includes ensuring accessible polling stations, accommodating voters with disabilities, and implementing measures to ensure all votes carry equal weight.
- Transparency: The electoral process, including vote counting and result verification, must remain transparent to allow stakeholders to monitor and verify its integrity. Election observers play a crucial role in providing independent assessments.
- Impartial Administration: Elections should be managed by an independent electoral management body (EMB) free from political interference. Such bodies must treat all candidates equitably under the law.
- Universal Suffrage: The right to vote should extend to all adult citizens without unreasonable restrictions. Universal suffrage ensures equal participation and representation within the democratic process.
- Rule of Law: Electoral laws must be clear, consistent, and upheld by an independent judiciary. Mechanisms should exist to address disputes and grievances that arise during the process.

2.1.2.2. International Standards and Treaties

While domestic law primarily regulates elections, several international treaties establish frameworks to promote free and fair elections. Key agreements include:

- The International Covenant on Civil and Political Rights (ICCPR): Article 25 guarantees citizens the right to participate in public affairs, vote, and run for office through genuine periodic elections.
- Universal Declaration of Human Rights (UDHR): Article 21 emphasizes the right to participate in government, directly or through freely chosen representatives. Although not legally binding, the UDHR has a substantial moral influence on electoral norms worldwide.
- African Charter on Human and Peoples' Rights (ACHPR): Adopted by the African Union, the ACHPR outlines fundamental rights, including democratic participation. It calls on African countries to uphold these principles during elections.
- European Convention on Human Rights (ECHR): Protocol 1, Article 3 mandates regular free elections by secret ballot to ensure the people's will is respected.
- The Harare Commonwealth Declaration (1991): This declaration commits Commonwealth nations to democratic political processes and the protection of individual rights.

While not permanently legally binding, these treaties encourage member states to adopt best practices for democratic governance. Countries that fail to meet these standards often face international criticism, sanctions, or the loss of aid from entities such as the United Nations and the World Bank.

2.1.2.3. Electoral Challenges in Emerging Democracies

Emerging democracies often struggle to conduct free and fair elections due to weak institutions, political violence, corruption, and resource constraints. Examples include:

- Nigeria (2007) and Zimbabwe (2008): The elections in these countries faced widespread accusations of voter intimidation, ballot tampering, and biased election administration.
- Ghana (2009) and South Africa (2009): The elections in these countries were celebrated as examples of African nations

adhering to democratic principles. Observers noted the peaceful environment and transparency.

- Kenya (2007): Allegations of vote rigging and non-transparent vote counting led to widespread post-election violence, highlighting the critical role of public trust in election integrity.
- Cameroon: Problems such as delayed voter registration, insufficient voter education, and alleged interference by the ruling party have undermined credibility. Separatist conflicts in Anglophone regions further complicate the process.

2.1.2.4. The Role of Election Observers

Election observers ensure free, fair, and transparent electoral processes. Independent observers, often from international organizations such as the United Nations, the European Union, or the African Union, monitor all stages of elections, from voter registration to the announcement of results.

Their assessments provide valuable insights into the process's integrity, increasing public confidence in election outcomes. However, their effectiveness relies on full access to the election process and the host countries' willingness to implement their recommendations. In some instances, governments restrict access, limiting observers' ability to conduct thorough evaluations.

2.1.2.5. Impact of Free and Fair Elections on Governance

Legitimate governance depends on free and fair elections. When citizens perceive elections as credible, they are more likely to accept the results and support the elected government. This acceptance is crucial for stability and effective policy-making.

By contrast, flawed elections often result in political instability. For instance, electoral fraud, disenfranchisement, and violence can erode trust in democratic institutions, leading to apathy, resentment, and, in extreme cases, radicalization.

2.1.2.6. Electoral Reforms for Strengthening Democracy

Many countries have implemented reforms to address election-related challenges, aiming to improve transparency, accessibility, and accountability. Key reforms include:

- Independent Electoral Commissions: These bodies ensure impartial election administration, handling voter registration, logistics, and vote counting free from political influence.
- Electronic Voting and Biometric Registration: Technological advances help reduce fraud and streamline the electoral process. For example, biometric registration prevents duplicate entries and improves identity verification.
- Legal Reforms: Updating electoral laws to clarify campaign finance rules, media coverage standards, and political party regulations ensures a level playing field.
- Civic Education Programs: Educating voters about their rights and the importance of participation helps reduce apathy and misinformation while promoting informed decision-making.
- Strengthened Judicial Systems: An independent judiciary is vital for resolving disputes and enforcing electoral laws fairly and promptly.

In summary, free and fair elections underpin democratic governance. Adhering to international standards and adopting robust reforms can strengthen election integrity, bolster public trust, and promote long-term stability.

2.1.2.7. International Observer Missions

Over the last fifty years, particularly since the end of the Cold War, challenges related to democratization and the role of elections within this process have become central to international affairs. There is a broad consensus that genuine elections are essential for establishing a government's legitimate authority and enabling citizens to hold their government accountable. The empirical record reveals an uneven global pattern in democratic development, with numerous countries achieving only limited progress (Chase-Dun, 2003, p. 49). Concurrently, international election observation practices have expanded, accompanied by a proliferation of observation organizations and the emergence of a professional community of election observers. By 2004, according to Kelly (2009), more than 80% of elections in non-established democracies underwent international observation. Although these observer groups generally employ compatible methodologies, many align their work with international standards based on several legal principles.

However, there still needs to be a single set of internationally accepted standards for assessing elections. This lack of uniform criteria has led to varied methods and assessment practices, which differ significantly in professionalism and approach. Several elections in the 1990s and early 2000s highlight the impact of differing observation methods on election assessments. In some instances, multiple observation missions analyzed the same election and reached conflicting conclusions. Additionally, Koelble and Lipuma (2008, p. 22) argue that some host countries anticipating contentious elections have engaged in "forum shopping"—inviting only those observer groups perceived to be sympathetic to their interests. This trend has led to charges of double standards and compromised integrity in regions such as Africa and the Commonwealth of Independent States (CIS) of the former Soviet Union. Such inconsistencies contribute to confusion over what constitutes a "free and fair" election and whether observer groups apply consistent standards during their assessments.

Recognizing these issues, international observation organizations initiated consultations to establish professional guidelines. These efforts culminated in October 2005 with the endorsement of the Declaration of Principles for International Election Observation and the Code of Conduct for Election Observers at the United Nations. The Declaration provides a shared definition of international election observation and sets broad guidelines for credible observation missions, including recommended mission size, duration, and scope. It also specifies critical conditions essential for effective observation missions, such as the host country's guarantees of access to essential electoral personnel and information. Hyde (2007, p. 9) notes that some endorsing organizations, especially inter-governmental bodies of member states, expressed reluctance to address electoral standards or assessment criteria, citing concerns about democratic legitimacy and national sovereignty. Additionally, some organizations doubted the feasibility of defining standards for democratic elections, including freedom of movement and the freedom for observers to issue public statements. Consequently, the endorsers should have expanded their focus to general principles for observation.

International law does not explicitly grant a right to observe elections or require any state to subject its electoral processes to international validation. However, the notion that national elections fall exclusively within the domain of domestic jurisdiction is increasingly challenged (Goodwill-Gill, 2006, p. 12).

2.1.2.8. The Principle of Transparency

Transparency is a foundational concept in discussions about democratic elections; yet, many do not scrutinize the basis for claims that election processes must be transparent. One might argue that transparency underlies other election-related rights. Merloe (2010) contends that citizens can only meaningfully participate in government and public affairs, as outlined in Article 21 of the Universal Declaration and Article 25 of the ICCPR, if government and public processes remain open to scrutiny. The public cannot ascertain whether the rights to be elected and to vote are safeguarded by governments that operate with transparency in their electoral processes.

The transparency principle in democratic elections does not solely rest on such deductions. However, they conclude that transparency exists within the broader spectrum of electoral rights embedded in treaties and state commitments regarding genuine elections.

Figure 2.2: Determinants of a Free, Fair, and Credible Election-Conceptual Framework
Source: Chigudu, 2012:27

Transparency in electoral processes is rooted in the freedom to seek, receive, and impart information—an integral aspect of freedom of expression within the electoral context. While a candidate or political party can theoretically seek election without sharing information with voters, and citizens can hypothetically vote without obtaining any information about candidates, such notions are impractical.

2.1.2.9. Determinants of a Free, Fair, and Credible Election

A free, fair, and credible election has become a central focus in advanced and emerging democracies. However, defining what constitutes the 'freeness' and 'fairness' of elections often remains the responsibility of observers, political parties, or supranational entities such as the Southern African Development Community (SADC), Economic Community of West African States (ECOWAS), European Union (EU), African Union (AU), or United Nations (UN). Chigudu (2012, p. 28) identifies four primary determinants of a credible, accessible, and fair election, as shown in figure 2.2 and discussed below.

These four determinants revolve around the central concept of a free and fair election, each attempting to influence the definition of electoral credibility. They interact through "political covalent bonds," which maintain stability within the electoral environment. Conflict may escalate into violence if these bonds break between any two determinants. Repulsive political forces between the core determinant of free and fair elections and the more minor determinants keep each element in constant motion.

2.1.2.9.1. Determinant 1: Incumbent Political Party (Ruling Party)

Ruling parties often strive to retain power indefinitely, resorting to various means to achieve this goal. Electoral losses by incumbent parties are frequently attributed to alleged electoral fraud perpetrated by opposition parties. The abuse of incumbency typically involves using state resources and facilities by the incumbent government to advance its electoral agenda. Holding the presidential office gives incumbents distinct advantages that challengers cannot easily replicate. For instance, incumbent presidents frequently enjoy privileges that accompany their status as heads of state and grant them substantial advantages in election campaigns.

In developing and developed countries, opposition parties accuse ruling parties of misusing state resources to secure political gains. In Africa, opposition parties often contend they are competing against the state itself. Although some African countries have enacted legislation to regulate state funding of political parties, few possess laws specifically addressing the use of state resources for partisan purposes. This gap suggests an area where further research and advocacy are needed. Some nations, recognizing the impact of incumbency in elections, have implemented legal frameworks that regulate the usage of state resources by political parties.

For instance, Zambia's Electoral Act No. 12 of 2006 and the Electoral Code of Conduct of 2006 prohibit using state resources for party campaigns except by the president and vice-president. Although this law grants certain privileges to the incumbent president and vice-president, opposition parties frequently express dissatisfaction, alleging that the ruling party exploits these privileges for partisan purposes. In Malawi, Section 193(4) of the constitution prohibits using state resources for specific party campaigns. Despite this prohibition, observers noted that during the 2009 election, President Bingu Wa Mutharika allegedly utilized state resources, including a helicopter and vehicles, for his campaign. Similarly, South Africa's Political Parties Act addresses state funding but lacks regulations governing incumbent use of state resources.

The Zimbabwe Political Parties Act also remains silent on state resource usage for political advantage. In Ghana, the Institute of Economic Affairs (IEA), an independent public policy think tank, criticized the New Patriotic Party (NPP) for abusing incumbency during the 2008 election when it was the ruling party (Ghana News Agency, August 14, 2011). The IEA, a non-partisan organization that promotes democracy in Ghana and Africa, emphasized the threat posed by incumbency abuse in Ghanaian elections. It advocated for legislation to regulate state asset usage by ruling parties during election years, calling for an equitable playing field in resource access and media representation.

The incumbency advantage issue is not unique to emerging democracies. Established democracies, such as the United States, have sought to address this issue through electoral laws. The Federal Election Commission (FEC) enforces the Federal Election Campaign Act, the Finance Law Act, the Presidential Election Campaign Fund Act, and the Bipartisan Reform Act of 2002. These laws set stringent guidelines requiring presidential candidates to disclose campaign expenditures and establish spending limits. Although these regulations provide detailed guidelines on campaign expenses, they lack specific provisions for incumbent expenditures. However, they restrict certain expenditures, such as using Air Force One, which the U.S. president employs for travel. Despite these provisions, sitting presidents, including Bill Clinton in 1996 and George W. Bush in 2004, reportedly used federal resources for re-election campaigns, enjoying privileges such as a large staff team and access to White House facilities.

This case underscores the need for additional research to explore how regulations can prevent incumbents from exploiting taxpayer funds for partisan purposes.

2.1.2.9.2. Determinant 2: Interested Parties

Interested parties encompass individuals or organizations directly or indirectly supporting incumbent or opposition parties. When an undesired party emerges as the election victor, supporters of the losing party may allege that the winner 'stole' the election or engaged in electoral manipulation. Interest groups, often called 'pressure groups' or 'non-governmental organizations', seek to advance specific sectional interests or causes without aiming to form a government. Interest groups typically organize around economic, professional, ideological, religious, racial, gender, or issue-based constituencies (Wilson, 1995, p. 22).

Wilson (1995) suggests that interest groups counterbalance majoritarianism by mitigating democratic tendencies that allow weak majority preferences to overshadow minority concerns. These groups often pursue unique benefits for their members, dispersing the costs across all taxpayers while concentrating benefits among a select few. This process can lead to what is known as "organizational sclerosis," where the accumulation of special-interest benefits lowers the general standard of living for society as a whole. In Britain, for instance, interest groups often target ministers and civil servants, given the concentration of power in the executive branch. In contrast, in the United States, interest groups focus on influencing Congress, often forming "iron triangles" with congressional subcommittees and bureaucratic agencies.

Interest groups advocate in various forms to shape public opinion and policy. While some have evolved into influential political institutions or social movements, others face accusations of manipulating democratic systems for narrow, self-serving objectives. Although most interest groups do not align with specific political parties, their policy stances often overlap with particular parties' positions. Interest groups should be empowered to oversee electoral processes (Ossome, 2011, p. 6). However, the political space available for interest groups varies significantly across countries, often limiting their operational effectiveness.

The significance of interest groups in a democracy cannot be overstated, as they help governments remain responsive to the electorate's needs and aspirations.

2.1.2.9.3. Determinant 3: Legal Framework

Every country operates under an electoral framework derived from its supreme law. Elections are thus conducted according to these sovereign statutes and guided by international electoral standards from bodies such as the Organization for Security and Cooperation in Europe (OSCE), the Office for Democratic Institutions and Human Rights (ODIHR), the International Institute for Democracy and Electoral Assistance (IDEA), and the SADC Election Guidelines (2004).

Before polling, each party typically agrees that electoral laws and guidelines are reasonable and that the playing field is level. If a party believes the conditions are unfair, it may choose not to participate and instead advocate for the necessary changes. However, if an election yields unfavorable results, opposition parties often claim that the legal framework was skewed to benefit the winners or disadvantage the losers. Even with strict adherence to the legal framework, some parties may reject the election outcome.

Evaluating the credibility of electoral processes involves determining which issues are pertinent to fairness. The boundaries of this assessment often need to be clarified. While it is crucial to go beyond the voting day and count, factors such as access to public media and boundary delimitation may be considered, whereas broader issues, like party funding and candidate selection, might not.

The primary standard for electoral indicators is to assess whether the rules are applied fairly and without partisan bias, rather than examining the inherent fairness of the system itself. Goodwin-Gill (1994, p. 22) argues that although states may seek particular outcomes, the methods used often vary in international contexts. While international standards remain universal, implementation methods do not.

The organization and administration of electoral processes are inherently complex. The extent of detail within legal frameworks varies across countries due to contextual factors such as the nature of the legal system and the trustworthiness of the election management body. A clear, simple, and comprehensive legal definition is essential to promote consistency, equity, and understanding.

For credibility within the electoral process, it is also crucial that all aspects of the electoral legal framework remain accessible to the public, with any changes being openly discussed and shared with relevant stakeholders. Generally, the legal framework aligns with international treaties and agreements supported by constitutional authority. Embedding fundamental electoral principles within the constitution can help safeguard electoral norms against potential manipulation by ruling parties. These norms often include the independence, composition, term of office, powers, and functions of the election management body; electoral systems; suffrage rights and qualifications; rights concerning political parties and candidacies; intervals at which elections must be held; and mechanisms for resolving electoral disputes.

It is essential to strike a balance between providing certainty and consistency within the legal framework while allowing the election management body sufficient flexibility to adapt to evolving circumstances.

2.1.2.9.4. Determinant 4: Electoral Contestants

A political party competing against a ruling party is defined as a contesting party. Contesting parties generally enter elections with skepticism and mistrust towards the ruling party, arguing that incumbents use state apparatus to their advantage and the detriment of the opposition. Consequently, if the incumbent wins, opposition parties often view this as a product of clandestine activities designed to outmaneuver the contestants.

2.1.2.10. Discussion

Free, fair, and credible elections ultimately depend on voters' perceptions, influenced by the four determinants outlined above. No single determinant can independently validate the credibility of an election; rather, it is the combined effect of multiple factors and perceptions that shapes public opinion regarding the election's integrity. The notion that personal preferences should establish an international standard to determine whether an election is "free and fair" is flawed, as this approach would undermine the very essence of democratic choice.

Elections represent a decision-making process between competing options, all presumed to merit public consideration. Electoral procedures aim to ensure that choices are freely made and accurately expressed. Predetermining the victory of any specific party as the sole acceptable outcome would render the processes of voting, candidacy, and free speech meaningless. Thus, claiming that elections can be considered free and fair only if opposition parties win lacks validity. While opposition parties should be free to critique and offer credible alternatives to government positions, their mere existence does not entitle them to power. Citizens retain the right to change their government according to their preferences, yet they are not obliged to do so.

Sweden provides a notable example. The same political party held the premiership and a cabinet majority almost uninterruptedly from 1932 to 1976, with one individual occupying the premier position for 23 years. Similarly, Canada's Liberal Party governed for approximately three-quarters of the time since 1896. Fundamentally, assessing electoral fairness based solely on political outcomes should be avoided. Criteria determined this way would likely provoke endless debates and fail to achieve broad acceptance beyond specific partisan or ideological groups.

As Huntington (1991, p. 10) notes, multiparty elections signal the end of dictatorship, and the early 1990s marked a period of significant political renewal in many Sub-Saharan African countries (Ayittey, 1992; Hyden & Bratton, 1992). According to Lindberg (2006, p. 12), the behavior of opposition parties can be analyzed in two specific ways:

- Participation of the Opposition: Opposition participation in free and fair elections may seem predictable, much like a boycott might be anticipated when a regime orchestrates a superficial election process. However, opposition parties sometimes participate in elections that lack fairness or legitimacy to pressure authoritarian rulers for concessions. They may also boycott legitimate elections to delegitimize the ruling regime when winning seems impossible. Opposition participation is classified into three levels: "near-total boycotts," when a leading opposition party does not contest, "partial boycotts," when only some participate, and "all contest," when all significant parties compete.
- Acceptance of Election Results by Losing Parties: When opposition parties participate, the question arises about when they accept the results. Losing parties may initially challenge the results to gain political leverage, especially from international bodies, and to undermine their opponents. Therefore, challenging official results should not automatically substantiate claims of irregularities. The relationship between credible elections and the acceptance of defeat by losing parties remains empirically ambiguous. Losers' acceptance is classified into three categories:
    - No: None of the main losing parties accept the outcome.

- Not initially/some: Some or all losing parties reject the outcome but accept it within three months, or if some parties accept while others do not.
- Yes, all immediately: All losing parties concede defeat immediately upon the result announcement.

2.1.3. Assessment of Election Credibility

Birch (2005) argues that elections represent one of the few governmental processes that voters are well-equipped to assess due to their broad participation and the heightened public attention they generate. Media coverage amplifies this attention, particularly regarding potential breaches of electoral integrity, keeping the public informed. Despite emphasizing electoral behavior within political science, Birch observes that conventional surveys rarely investigate voters' perceptions of electoral legitimacy and fairness. Assessing election credibility requires impartial observers lacking a vested interest in the outcome (Kan, 2005).

International organizations, such as the United Nations, have successfully maintained impartiality in election monitoring, as demonstrated in cases like Cambodia and Southern Africa. Conversely, superpowers with strategic stakes in election outcomes must respect the results and refrain from interference. While Ireland and the United Kingdom have historically shown restraint in Northern Ireland's elections, a similar approach has not been observed in countries such as Iran, Syria, Saudi Arabia, and Turkey, which have interfered in the electoral processes of other states.

Kan (2005) identifies several critical criteria for assessing election credibility, including transparency, freedom of choice, impartiality, and quality of the electoral process. The ruling authority must employ state resources strictly for governance rather than electoral purposes. The misuse of police or military forces to suppress opposition gatherings or critical media damages transparency and restricts freedom of choice. Such actions, as observed in Colombia during the 1980s, often lead to widespread voter dissatisfaction. Coercion and violence diminish voters' sense of meaningful participation.

Election Management Bodies (EMBs) uphold neutrality and impartiality and ensure that all parties and candidates receive equitable treatment. A perception of partisan bias within the election administration can erode public trust and confidence in the system and participating political parties (ACE, 2013).

- Inclusiveness: Inclusive elections provide equal opportunities for all eligible citizens to participate as voters and candidates. Any restrictions, such as age requirements, should be narrowly defined and legally justified. Authorities must identify and address barriers to participation, especially for marginalized populations like ethnic or religious minorities, women, youth, elderly citizens, and individuals with disabilities.
- Transparency: Transparency means that each stage of the electoral process is open to scrutiny, enabling stakeholders to verify its honesty and accuracy independently. Transparency aligns with citizens' rights to seek, receive, and share information, essential for informed public participation (Merloe, 2009). Transparent processes must remain accessible to the public and relevant stakeholders at all stages, including procedural information, voting, and the tabulation of results. Both non-partisan and partisan observers should be accredited to monitor all phases of the election and to provide public feedback without unreasonable restrictions.
- Accountability: Accountability pertains to the responsibilities of electoral stakeholders, including the government, EMBs, political parties, candidates, and security forces, toward the electorate. While elections offer a mechanism for citizens to hold their government accountable, accountability must also extend to the election process. Effective remedies should address violations of electoral rights, and election organizers must demonstrate administrative accountability. Legal frameworks should also provide avenues to prosecute criminal acts that infringe on electoral rights.
- Competitiveness: Competitive elections offer citizens equal and reasonable opportunities to compete for government positions. Competition is fundamental to elections that reflect the people's will. To ensure competitiveness, the legal framework must permit the formation of political parties and provide fair access to the ballot for parties and candidates. Parties and candidates should be able to campaign freely without intimidation, violence, or illegal influences on voters.

The Electoral Knowledge Network emphasizes that measuring election quality remains an evolving challenge. As election management professionals refine their skills, new technologies, social media, and private sector involvement continually influence the quality of elections. The introduction of electronic voting systems, internet-based voting, social media, public procurement processes, and private sector services has significantly transformed the way elections are conducted and evaluated. Assessing electoral quality entails evaluating adherence to international standards to ensure that election processes meet a baseline of integrity.

Various tools and methodologies exist for evaluating election quality, including observer methodologies, the electoral cycle approach, performance indicators, and election integrity assessments. For instance, the electoral cycle framework categorizes the election process into three primary phases: pre-election, election, and post-election, with specific components assessed at each stage. Both quantitative and qualitative scoring systems are used to comprehensively evaluate these phases. The resulting data inform election management professionals, political parties, candidates, voters, and observers, helping to refine and improve electoral processes.

The Measuring Electoral Quality Encyclopedia outlines established methodologies for evaluating electoral quality. While many of these methods are well-known, they are classified to illustrate their unique characteristics, differing methodologies, and the range of insights they yield. This topic also identifies critical national and international actors involved in measuring electoral quality and the approaches they employ.

2.1.4. Information and Voting

In a scenario of perfect information, where citizens possess complete and accurate information regarding candidates, voters would likely make choices based on three primary considerations:

- The proximity of the candidate's political position to their own
- The candidate's likelihood of being elected
- The candidate's perceived ability to implement policies effectively

This framework implies that voters prioritize candidates whose views align closely with their own, who have a realistic chance of winning, and who demonstrate competence (Downs, 1957). Voters may strategically support a second-best candidate who is more likely to win if they believe it optimizes their overall benefit (Cox, 1997).

However, the assumption of perfect information is rarely realistic. Gathering comprehensive details on every candidate's platform and success probabilities is often too costly. Consequently, voters frequently rely on heuristics—cognitive shortcuts—when making decisions. Party affiliation, for instance, offers a quick indicator of a candidate's ideology, particularly in direct contests between parties (Rahn, 1993; Lau & Redlawsk, 2001; Valdini, 2005; Shugart et al., 2005). However, party affiliation may not be sufficient in open-list or primary systems, where voters choose among multiple candidates from the same party. Here, voters may rely on cues like candidate names, implying gender, ethnicity, or social class (McDermott, 1997, 1998; Guell et al., 2015). In some countries, ballots include information about candidates, such as professions, residences, or birth years, enabling voters to infer policy positions and qualifications. Therefore, the amount and type of information available on ballots significantly affect voter choices under imperfect conditions.

The impact of additional ballot information remains ambiguous. More information might increase voter satisfaction and turnout by aiding the identification of candidates that closely match voters' preferences. Conversely, extra information may impose cognitive burdens, discouraging participation among some voters.

The net effect of providing additional candidate information depends on several factors:

- Need for Differentiation: When only one candidate per party is running, or a few well-known candidates dominate the ballot, additional information may offer minimal benefit. However, in elections featuring numerous unfamiliar candidates—such as local elections or down-ballot races—extra details may help voters make informed choices.
- Relevance of Information: The impact of specific types of information hinges on their usefulness for assessing candidates. Details about a candidate's profession or age provide valuable insights for voters, while superficial characteristics like eye color are unlikely to influence perceptions of political competence.
- Impact on Non-Voters: The potential for ballot information to mobilize non-voters depends on their awareness of these cues. Occasional voters might be influenced by additional information if they encounter it during an election cycle, whereas habitual non-voters may remain less responsive. Disseminating sample ballots to all eligible voters ahead of an election, as practised in some jurisdictions, can enhance voter awareness and engagement.

2.1.4.1. The Effect of Information Election Turnout

According to the literature, including more information on the ballot increases voters' satisfaction with the election system. This is a significant result, as higher satisfaction with the election system likely increases the overall consent with democracy among the voters and thus the legitimacy of democratically elected governments. As noted above, a second channel may exist towards the same end, which can further increase the relevance of meaningful information on the ballot. If individuals are happier with their choices and believe they can influence the election outcome, they may also be more likely to go to the polls and vote. In this case, the eventually elected government will possess a more extensive mandate and more authority in its actions (see Nadeau and Blais, 1993 and Anderson et al, 2005). Given the theoretical discussion in the previous section, however, it is not clear per se whether including more information on the ballot leads to an increase in actual voting, as the additional complexity may turn off individuals who want to spend as little time on the choice of candidates as possible. Answering this question is, therefore, an empirical task for further research.

2.1.5. Voting and Electoral Competition

Open democracy conceptualizes electoral competition as the degree to which challengers and minority parties can hold incumbents accountable by mounting credible campaigns. This serves as a further indicator of the accessibility and responsiveness of a democratic system to the people. Incumbents at every level of government have historically enjoyed high reelection rates thanks to their ability to deliver valuable constituent services, high starting name identification, access to the media and other in-kind campaign resources, and the ability to raise significant campaign contributions from influence-seeking individuals and special interest groups.

As campaign costs rise, challengers find it increasingly difficult to raise the necessary resources to overcome incumbents' institutional advantages and credibly compete for public office. Although low electoral competition does not necessarily signal a lack of representation, incumbent reelection rates that significantly exceed the voter approval of their elected officials may indicate a systemic bias towards status quo interests and a less open electoral system.

Studies examining electoral competition generally focus on how competition affects the behavior of representatives (for example, Key

1949:16; McDonald and Samples 2006:34) or how it affects voter turnout (Cox and Munger 1989:22; Blais 2006:43; Endersby, Galatas, and Rackaway 2002:3). A more petite body of research examines the effects competitive elections may have on voter attitudes (Brunell 2008:65; Brunell and Buchler 2009:80). Bowler on his part was interested in whether voters are aware of electoral competition, and whether campaign activity associated with competition affects voters' perceptions and attitudes about elections. He demonstrated that congressional campaign activity corresponds with perceptions that the election in a person's district is close. He also found that when voters are exposed to more excellent campaign activity, they appear more attentive to campaign news. However, competitive elections may not have uniformly positive democratic effects. Exposure to competition also corresponds with greater dissatisfaction with election choices.

2.1.5.1. How Do Voters Perceive Electoral Competition?

Are voters aware of how close elections may be, and does campaign activity affect other perceptions about elections? The strategic voting literature assumes not only that voters are aware of how close things are but that these perceptions are accurate and acted upon (for example, Downs 1957:12; but see Green and Shapiro 1994:4). A large body of work also documents that turnout in elections (Blais 2006:20) and instances of strategic voting (Cox, 1997; Karp et al., 2002:18) both correlate with how close an election is. Blais's (2006:21) extensive review of the voter turnout literature found that electoral competition is associated with increased turnout (see also Franklin 2004:5). Still, this effect can be caused by the mobilization efforts of elites rather than mass behavior being affected by actual awareness of how close an election is (Cox and Munger 1989:19). There are reasons to expect that voters may not be particularly aware of district-level electoral competition, and it may have limited effects on attitudes and behavior. Campaigns compete for attention in an environment where people generally pay little attention to politics (Converse, 1962:13) and people have limited information about politics (Delli Carpini and Keeter (1997:22). Ferejohn and Fiorina (1974:40) provide a model of the decision to vote as a choice being made under uncertainty about how close an election may be. Voters must sort between information about the national contest and the reality of their local race when evaluating electoral competition in their district. Perceptions of electoral competition may also be inaccurate, as people are biased toward overestimating how close elections are (Uhlaner & Grofman 1986:4). It is an open question, then, how voters are affected by electoral competition. We may expect that they assume elections are competitive. Thus, regardless of campaign spending before the vote, perceptions of the closeness of a race can be independent of how much money is spent on the contest. Conversely, even if perceptions of closeness tend to be inaccurate, they may be responsive to variations in campaign activity.

District-level competition may affect how people view an election's closeness and their interest and attitudes about it. Studies have demonstrated that spending corresponds with greater exposure to campaign ads (Kenny and McBurnett 1997:40), and campaign spending has been shown to decrease the likelihood that people would see something positive about incumbents (Coleman and Manna 2000:23). Exposure to campaign ads has been found to make citizens more interested in an election and more familiar with candidates (Freedman, Franz, and Goldstein 2004:47). Chong and Druckman (2007:180) also demonstrate that democratic competition stimulates deliberation and generates greater attention to issues.

However, do these patterns mean that campaign activity makes voters more optimistic about the election? Most campaign expenditures in the US House races are dedicated to advertising, and research demonstrates that most congressional candidates running ads in 2006 (the election examined here) went negative (Druckman, Kifer, and Parkin 2009:14). Higher spending may increase the chances that voters are exposed to information, both positive and negative. Although some literature reviews (Coleman and Manna 2000:34; Lau et al. 1999:22) show that negative ads do not have pervasively detrimental effects, others show that negative campaigns may correspond with lower political efficacy, less trust in government, more negative public mood (Lau, Sigelman, and Brown Rovner 200:37), demobilization, and increased cynicism (Ansolabehere et al., 1994). Research also demonstrates that people dislike politics and want to avoid it (Hibbing and Theiss-Morse 2002:43). Active campaigns may thus adversely affect attitudes about the election since they are a visible manifestation of the sort of politics many people disdain.

We propose that people experience electoral competition through campaign activity and that this activity is best measured by campaign spending. For example, a low-spending contest may be closed without active advertising campaigns, and such a race may have a limited effect on voter awareness and perceptions. People experience electoral competition through radio and television ads, direct mailing, billboards, signs, phone calls, and other campaign activities. Campaign spending serves as a measure of the level of campaign activity in a specific geographic area, and it is associated with candidate vote share (Jacobson and Kernell 1983:32; Pattie, Johnston, and Fieldhouse 1995:18), changes in vote intentions in the US House races (Jacobson, 1990), and the variation in voter turnout in gubernatorial (Patterson and Caldeira 1983:84) and the US House races (Gilliam 1985:8), as well as in other elections (Matsusaka and Palda 1999:5). Active campaigns have thus been shown to affect voter behavior. Here, we test how they influence perceptions of elections. In short, competition in the form of campaign expenditures can affect whether voters think their House contest is close and affect their interest in the race. We suggest that campaigns may focus greater critical attention on candidates and lead people to pay attention to the contest. If people dislike politics, visible political campaigns may sour their attitudes about the election. We test whether greater exposure to political campaigns reduces satisfaction with elections.

2.1.6. Determinants of Election Quality Perceptions

Within the emerging literature on perceptions of election quality, three primary explanations shape citizens' views on electoral quality: institutions, partisanship, and electoral irregularities. The main objective of this paper is to evaluate these competing explanations and jointly explore their relative salience.

2.1.6.1. Institutions

Only recently have scholars begun to assess the institutional sources of citizen perceptions of election quality. While there have been significant strides, the perception-based literature is deficient in two primary ways.

First, the literature has not effectively assessed the influence of electoral commissions (formerly known as electoral management bodies (EMBs)) on citizens' evaluation of election quality.

Second, the literature does not focus on various election-related institutions, especially within emerging democratic contexts. In examining the impact of EMBs, the perception-based literature can be divided into two main groups. One set of studies failed to assess the influence of EMB performance in their assessment of perceptions of election quality (Rose and Mishler 2009:13; Moehler 2009:45). For instance, Mishler and Rose (2009:33) assess the sources of citizens' election quality perceptions in the context of Russia, and although they highlight the importance of partisanship and other socio-demographic factors, they do not examine the impact of citizens' evaluations of EMB performance.

A second set of studies, while focusing on EMB performance, only examines a single dimension. As a result, these studies cannot reflect the complex relationship between EMB performance and citizens' election quality judgments. Birch provides the most recent cross-national study on the institutional correlates of election quality using data from twenty-eight elections in Organization for Economic Co-operation and Development (OECD) countries (2008:12). She identifies autonomous election administration, proportionality of elections, and public financing of political parties as institutional factors that structure confidence in electoral processes. Regarding election administration, her findings indicate that citizens living in countries with autonomous EMBs are more likely to consider elections illegitimate. Birch's findings contradict the existing empirical and theoretical literature that associates autonomous EMBS with a greater likelihood of free and fair elections (Hartlyn et al., 2008:30; Pastor, 1999:5). She attributes these counterintuitive results to the fact that formal legal independence may not reflect the actual independence of the institution. Although this review accepts Birch's justification, there remains a lack of consensus on the impact of EMB autonomy on citizens' election perceptions.

A promising series of studies in the American context has also pursued a dimensional assessment of EMB performance. Hall et al (2009:14) focus on EMB capacity by exploring citizens' evaluation of poll worker performance in the 2000 US elections. Interestingly, citizens who rated poll worker performance as excellent had greater confidence in the elections. Similarly, research by Alvarez et al. (2008:3) shows how citizens' evaluation of the credibility of voting technology has direct, positive implications for their confidence in elections.

Despite the new attention to electoral management bodies, the inadequate treatment of the multiple dimensions of EMB performance has left gaps in the literature. This review distinguishes in this sub-section between citizens' evaluations of EMB capacity and EMB autonomy and probes the impact of these evaluations on citizens' perceptions of election quality. Autonomy is conceptualized here as an institution's ability to make decisions independent of the control of the executive and other state and society actors. On the other hand, capacity connotes an institution's ability to implement its constitutionally mandated function effectively and efficiently.

A second shortcoming of perception-based literature is its limited institutional scope. Although electoral management bodies are the primary arbiters of elections in many emerging democracies, there are other pivotal election-related institutions that the existing scholarship has overlooked. These election-related institutions include the police (and other security forces, such as the military), the courts and election tribunals, the media, international and domestic observers, as well as other independent and state-based institutions. In this paper, I assess five election-related institutions crucial for understanding elections within the African context: police, military, judiciary, anti-corruption agencies, and the media. The selection of these institutions is rooted both in theoretical and empirical literature.

First, Diamond (2002) regards the impartial treatment of rival candidates and parties by the courts, police, and military as an essential part of electoral fairness in transitional settings. Specifically, within Nigeria's context, scholars underscore the importance of the police and other security agencies (Bratton 2008:20; Okoigun 2000:48), as well as courts and election tribunals (Fall et al. 2011:108-158), as pivotal institutions worthy of focused examination.

2.1.6.2. Partisanship

In addition to the import of institutional factors, other studies have examined the impact of partisanship on perceptions of election quality (Moehler 2009:79; Alvarez, Hall, and Llewellyn 2008:40; Birch 2008:10; Rose and Mishler 2009:58). Partisanship is represented as either an ingrained ideological attachment to a political party (Goren, 2005:206) or an affiliation with the winner or loser of the electoral contest (Bratton et al., 2005:41; Anderson and LoTempio, 2002:99). Regardless of the dominant method through which citizens are affiliated to political parties, this attachment structures their perceptions of election quality. Partisanship provides a perceptual frame for interpreting information regarding the quality of elections. Those affiliated with the winning party are more inclined to believe that the success of their party was legitimate, while those affiliated with the losing party search for evidence to show that their favored candidate or party was short-changed. In a recent cross-national analysis of citizens' perceptions of election quality in Africa, Moehler (2009:80) considers affiliation with the electoral winner. She finds that relative to all other factors, winner status has the most significant influence on evaluations of electoral integrity in both substantive and statistical terms. Similar research by Alvarez et al. (2009:40) shows that, within the American context, partisanship significantly impacts citizens' confidence in the accuracy of the vote count and tabulation for the US presidential elections in 2000 and 2004. Republicans, compared to Independents and Democrats, were most likely to display confidence in the elections because their candidate won.

The main limitation of the political orientations thesis is that it needs to test the impact of electoral institutions effectively. The empirical models used in these studies are underspecified and incapable of accurately adjudicating the relative significance of alternative sources of citizens' election perceptions. For instance, Mehler's (2009:52) assessment of the determinants of electoral integrity in Africa fails to control citizens' evaluation of any election-related institutions. To overcome this shortcoming in the literature, I test the relative importance of citizens' partisan status while maintaining other critical institutional determinants.

2.1.6.3. Electoral Irregularities

The literature approaches the link between electoral irregularities and perceptions of election quality in two main ways (Lehoucq, 2003:27). The current literature focuses predominantly on four types of irregularities: vote buying, intimidation, violence, and ballot rigging (Collier and Vicente, 2008:9; Bratton, 2008:47).

First, some studies employ indirect measures of electoral irregularities that do not effectively capture the phenomenon's extent and make it difficult to understand the causal effect. For example, Birch uses an aggregate measure of corruption perceptions and assumes that in countries where political corruption is pervasive, citizens are more likely to consider the administration of elections to be corrupt (Birch, 2008:30). While this might be the case, a more direct approach that taps into citizens' own experience with and perceptions of electoral irregularities may more clearly highlight how electoral irregularities shape popular opinions on the election.

Another group of studies relies on micro-level data to assess citizens' perceptions of and experiences with electoral irregularities (Collier & Hoeffler, 2008; Alvarez, Hall, & Hyde, 2008; McCann & Domínguez, 1998; Schaffer, 2007; Schedler, 1999; Bratton, 2008).

Bratton thoroughly examines citizens' perceptions of electoral irregularities in the context of the 2007 Nigerian election campaign period (2008). Nigerians who experience threats of violence are less likely to vote in the upcoming elections or support the ruling party. Those offered material benefits in exchange for their votes exude greater partisan loyalty but are no more likely to participate in elections than those not provided. Although existing studies directly examine citizens' experience with electoral irregularities and deal with the consequences of electoral behavior, surprisingly, none directly test these experiences' effect on citizens' perceptions of election quality. Nevertheless, these studies are instructive because they identify various potential causal pathways between experiences with election irregularities and evaluations of election quality. For instance, if we build upon Bratton's (2008:32) findings regarding the impact of intimidation, we expect that citizens who experience irregularities may score the elections poorly, not only because of their experience but also because they were deprived of their constitutional right to participate in the elections. This review then goes on to see whether citizens believe that the presence of electoral irregularities influences the overall outcome of elections. Undoubtedly, irregularities occur, but it is essential to see which types of matters and to what extent experience or perceptions of electoral irregularities factor into the overall perceptions of election quality.

2.1.7. How Do Citizens Assess Election Quality?

In addition to outlining the primary sources of citizens' evaluation of election quality, I propose specific mechanisms through which citizens construct their election quality perceptions.

First, citizens are generally capable of making informed and relatively accurate assessments of the legitimacy of election processes in their country. Similar assertions have been made in the existing literature (Birch 2008:39; Pastor 1999:12; Banducci and Karp 2003:10).

This research goes forward by specifying how citizens formulate their election judgments.

- Directly, through experience with various stages of the electoral process, such as voter registration, political party campaigns, polling activities (queuing, casting a ballot, and observing the poll station count), and experience with EMB staff (permanent and ad hoc), security officials, and members of political parties.

- Indirectly, through information from the media (TV, radio, newspapers, and the internet), political parties, civic organizations, popular discourse, and face-to-face conversations.

Citizens further combine their assessments from multiple pathways to construct their overall assessments of election quality. When attitudes are formed through direct experience, they are more reliable but limited in scope. For instance, a voter may assess the impartiality of EMB staff working on election day when she votes, but may need to gain first-hand knowledge of the impartiality of other EMB staff working in different regions of the country. However, even at this level, citizens' evaluations can be biased by:

- Prior performance evaluations of institutions in previous elections,
- Partisan affiliations, and
- Social and demographic attributes, including education, cognition, and ethnicity.

Attitudes constructed through indirect information about electoral processes have a greater scope and allow citizens a more comprehensive assessment of the elections. Yet, generating a clear picture through this channel depends on:

- The availability of information,
- The accuracy of information, and
- Citizens' willingness to seek out information on elections.

Availability and reliability of information on elections are usually a function of a free, independent, vibrant media environment that produces high-quality information with broad coverage throughout the country. In such an environment, opposition parties will have more opportunities to publicize fraud and electoral malpractice, while journalists are watchdogs and whistleblowers during the election. Finally, indirect channels also depend on citizens' willingness to seek information. Following empirical studies emphasizing the effect that greater access to media has on voting behavior (Conroy-Krutz 2009:20) and political attitudes (Bratton et al. 2005:39), it is contended that citizens with greater access to media will be more informed about various aspects of the elections and thereby more likely to develop accurate assessments of the quality of elections.

In sum, three competing explanations for the sources of citizens' election quality evaluations, election-related institutional performance, partisanship, and experience with electoral irregularities have been reviewed. The process through which citizens construct their election quality judgments has also been outlined.

2.2. Empirical Review

This research also includes an empirical review of related and relevant literature.

This empirical review touches on the following empirical issues:

- Independence of Electoral Management Bodies and
- Levels of Public Trust

Lethbridge (2019:2) defines independence as the autonomy to act without undue external influence, but being accountable for the acts of commission or omission.

This implies that an independent institution has sole authority to make decisions affecting its operations, though it should still be answerable and accountable for its actions. The independence of any EMB is crucial in the election management process and must be upheld at all levels (van Ham & Garnett, 2019:26).

Kerr and Luhrmann (2017: 33) studied public trust in elections and considered the role of the autonomy of election management bodies in enhancing public trust in them. In the working paper, the researchers analyzed cases from various countries where EMBs have been accused of manipulating election results in favor of incumbents or sitting presidents. They noted that as multiparty elections became more globalized, the regime's legitimacy became greatly dependent on the conduct of EMBs in the entire election process. The paper said that the 2007 election in Nigeria faced legitimacy questions because the EMB did not demonstrate autonomy during the electoral process. The citizens lost faith and trust in the government led by Umar Yar'Adua because they felt that the electoral commission and its head did not demonstrate autonomy while conducting the elections. The researchers also analyzed the Russian and Rwandan elections, arguing that they were manipulated but did not result in any public outcry. The study's findings showed that election manipulation led to a decline in public trust, as citizens would not trust EMBs that served the interests of one political party. The researchers concluded that there was a need for election management bodies to instil trust among the people by adhering to the rules and regulations that ensure their independence.

James, Garnett, Loeber, and van Ham (2019: 20) studied the determinants of electoral integrity in several countries. He noticed that most scholars who have researched this topic focused more on the organizational traits of the public.

Organizations mandated to implement elections overlooked one crucial aspect of electoral management. The researchers aimed to determine the percentage of electoral bodies operating independently worldwide. Their findings indicated that 72% of the responding countries had autonomous electoral management bodies. In comparison, 21% were government bodies, and 7% reported neither being government nor autonomous bodies (James et al., 2019:10). In the same research, 23% of the EMBs were identified as part of the judicial branch of government and did not operate independently. This meant that they were subject to manipulation to serve the interests of the sitting administrations, further declining the public's trust in these bodies. Their recommendations included the need for governments to ensure the independence of EMBs to enhance the public's trust in these bodies and their ability to manage elections transparently and honestly. The researchers, however, focused solely on electoral management as the primary determinant of electoral integrity. In a study on electoral manipulation in Africa, Van Ham & Lindberg (2015:2) noted that although multiparty democracy has gained roots in Africa, most African countries face challenges related to the manipulation of elections. The researchers noted that African governments are synonymous with manipulating elections using different strategies. For instance, they stated that the most commonly used mechanisms for controlling the outcome of an election include voter intimidation and intimidation of the opposition to such an extent that they shy away from participating in the competition. Additionally, governments have mastered manipulating electoral management bodies through intimidation or denial of resources, thereby facilitating their own interests. The researchers also discovered that the method and level of manipulation depend on the availability of resources and potential costs related to the varying tactics and the political context within which elections take place (Van Ham & Lindberg, 2015: 25). The study also analyzed elections in several African countries, and their quality was unfavorable.

For instance, their findings indicated that, in most countries, the autonomy of electoral management bodies was highly compromised due to the actions of incumbent governments. Most governments denied the EMBs sufficient resources to carry out their duties, rendering them weak and not independent. The researchers recommended that the autonomy of EMBs be guaranteed so that the public can trust the legitimacy of elections and the governments being elected.

According to Ntaganda (2015: 6), who studied the management of electoral processes in Burundi, following the signing of the Arusha Accord in 2000 that ended the civil war in the country, the legislation in the state provides an adequately sturdy base for the supervision of free and fair elections. However, like any African country, Burundi faces significant challenges related to the country's election management. The country's electoral body, NIEC, operates in an atmosphere that is not independent. Also, the electoral body lacks the political will and consensus of political parties in the country to agree on election rules. This has eroded the public's confidence in the county's electoral process's ability to conduct a free, fair, and credible election. The researcher also noted that the electoral management bodies in Burundi have faced various challenges that have led to their disability to run a free and fair election. Part of these challenges includes government interference in the affairs of the NIEC, thereby curtailing its independence as an election management body.

Makulilo (2015: 13) analyzed the independence of Tanzania's EMBs and noted that they experience several challenges, most related to their independence. The federal structure adopted in Tanzania implies that the country has in place two EMBs to manage elections, both on the mainland and on the islands of Zanzibar. The two EMBs (NEC & ZEC) have distinct functions with separate structures determined by some legal structures.

The researcher, however, notes that the two bodies face serious challenges relating to their independence. For instance, most Tanzanians believe that the commissions are not impartial and autonomous. Despite apparent legal guarantees and freedoms from political interference, the appointment process of commissioners for these bodies, especially on the mainland, cannot guarantee their independence. For example, the president of the mainland is responsible for appointing the commissioners of the NEC, a fact that cannot ensure that they remain independent. Besides, the NEC relies entirely on the executive branch for financial and logistical issues, undermining its independence (Makulilo, 201:118).

The researcher also notes that the Tanzanian constitution has limited requirements for appointing commissioners, with the only requirement being on the island of Zanzibar, where the president must choose from a list of seven names proposed by the opposition. The overreliance on the government for funding and other budgetary issues has undermined the autonomy of these bodies and, in turn, affected their ability to manage free and fair elections in the country. According to Aywa (2015: 12), Kenya has held numerous elections since independence, with most of them having historical records of irregularities. The country suffers from the problem of negative ethnicity, which is a crucial determinant of electoral politics, the first-past-the-post electoral system, and the design of constituencies based on ethnic divisions. EMBs have, in the past and better history of Kenya, been the objects of deep-seated mistrust because of the perceived absence of political independence. Aywa (2015:19) notes that citizens' trust in the electoral system before the 2007 election was relatively low. The then Electoral Commission, ECK, had exceptionally low and limited rankings among the people, and the public did not trust it to deliver a credible election. The aftermath of the bitterly disputed election resulted in post-election violence that has been described as the worst in the country's history.

The researcher also noted that the ECK was not a purely independent commission and would sometimes serve the government's interests of the day, thereby increasing the chances of manipulating the results.

In his analysis of the independence of EMBs in Kenya, Aywa (2015: 20) also noted that following the promulgation of the 2010 constitution, an independent commission in the name of IEBC was formed to solve all election-related challenges that existed before. According to the research, IEBC was supposed to be purely autonomous, and Kenyans were optimistic about it. Among the critical institutional core values governing the operations of IEBC is independence. "We shall conduct our affairs free from undue external influence" (The Constitution of Kenya, 2010). Independence in public institutions refers to the extent to which the institution can undertake its functions and mandates without interference or conflict of interest originating internally or externally. However, it should not be free from being held accountable for its omissions or commissions, which calls for due transparency and accountability of the public institutions to the other party (Aywa, 2015:22). For healthy and democratic elections in a country, there must be an independent EMB which operates on its own free from manipulation of any kind from any arm of the government (The Constitution of Kenya, 2010). The issue of IEBC independence has been discussed for a long time, and recognition of external interference has been noted. The problem of IEBC's lack of independence from political leaders has been hotly debated, and numerous factors have been pointed out. There is a need to allow IEBC to perform its roles effectively (Tumo, 2017: 45). Where citizens and other stakeholders in election management processes perceive a lack of independence, distrust in these institutions exists, and they retaliate, making the whole electoral system questionable.

Aywa (2015:24) also posited in his study that the independence of IEBC cannot be claimed solely because of the several actors who determine the outcomes of the elections. The electoral justice chain emerges from different parties where its sole powers are not clearly defined, thus bringing challenges to its independence (Collette Sebastian, 2015:23). The IEBC is not accessible from the undue influence of the executive arm of the government because it was evidenced in the process of procuring the BVR, where the IEBC made its decision, which the executive outlined. This is also concurred by AFRI Cog (2017:5). Another concern about the independence of the IEBC arises on the grounds of its autonomy over the courts. Constitutionally, the IEBC is mandated to determine the electoral boundaries and settle the disputes arising from the elections or nominations of the candidates in the political parties. Although it is mandated to make election decisions, it is subject to petitions and can be challenged in court. This implies that the IEBC should generally obey and comply with the court regarding its election operations and management processes.

2.2.1. Stakeholders' Engagement by Electoral Management Bodies and Public Trust Levels

Stakeholder engagement refers to the involvement of different parties that have an interest in various operations by an institution to enhance institutional role performance (Baugh, 2015: 4). James et al. (2019) studied the determinants of electoral integrity in several parts of the world and posited that electoral integrity was crucial in nurturing public trust in the management of elections in the globe. The researchers observed that, in addition to the independence of EMBs in election management, stakeholder involvement was also a crucial determinant of the levels of public trust in an election management body. Their findings revealed that electoral management bodies that prioritized the opinions and contributions of all stakeholders in managing elections did well in earning public trust. According to the study, the idea of centralization worked well in countries that adopted it, with over 60% reporting.

They improved public relations because of the centralization of the duties of the electoral bodies. Thus, this pointed to the crucial role of stakeholder engagement in the management and operation of elections in most states. Olugbemiga and Olugbemiga (2014: 21) conducted a study on 'the state and election administration in Nigeria' and noted that the country's history indicates a lack of stakeholder involvement in the electoral process. This led to a decline in public trust in the process. The researchers analyzed the state of elections in Nigeria since its independence and noticed a history of authoritarian rule. The West African nation had struggled with a series of coups, in which the military would overthrow the government and seize control of the country's leadership. The military rules were purely autocratic and frustrated any efforts by the country to adopt democracy. However, the researchers also noted that after the country transitioned to a pure democracy, the challenges of a lack of stakeholder engagement persisted, with people increasingly feeling left out of electoral management. The state's capture of the EMBs has severely impacted election management in the country, with public outcry directed towards the state, which is accused of manipulating the electoral body and the election outcome. The research findings indicate that the public has lost trust in the EMBs in the country because of open interference by the state. Kerr and Luhrmann's (2017:88) study also supported the findings of this study by arguing that the Nigerians' protest in March 2010 against the country's electoral body meant that they had lost trust in the body and how it managed elections. Its lack of autonomy and stakeholder involvement meant that the body had become a state organ serving the state's interests and not the public. This was not per its mandate as enshrined in the constitution. According to Sekaggya (2015:7), the electoral management body in Uganda has been perceived adversely by the election stakeholders in the country, some of whom have called it President Museveni's rubber stamp for staying in office.

This is because the commission needs to allow room for stakeholder engagement, as the media, political parties, especially the opposition, the international community, and the public are denied opportunities to participate in the formation and operation of the commission. In the last four elections, Ugandans have engaged in elections with limited freedoms, including media freedom, freedom of assembly, speech, and expression, thanks to the efforts made by the executive that runs the affairs of the EMBs in the country. This has eroded the public trust in the autonomy of the electoral commission to carry out an independent, accessible, and fair election. According to Sekaggya (2015:18), this decline in public trust has increased public mistrust of the government and its operations. However, the country's electoral management challenges have been due to the lack of stakeholder engagement in election matters. The researcher also noted that the commission relies on the executive for funding to facilitate the updating of voter registers and initiating voter sensitization exercises. Makulilo (2015:46) analyzed the independence of electoral management bodies in mainland Tanzania and the island of Zanzibar. In his study, the researcher noted that the Constitution of Tanzania did not allow the EMBs to engage other stakeholders in composing the electoral bodies and managing elections. For example, according to Makulilo (2015:47:7), the mainland Tanzania and Zanzibar island presidents handpick the commissioners of NEC and ZEC, respectively. The only attempt at involving other stakeholders in the process is in Zanzibar's requirement that the president receive seven names proposed by the opposition from which s/he can pick one. Due to the lack of funding, the electoral management bodies need to be more effective in managing voter registers and the election process. The NEC, for instance, needs more resources to digitize its records and ensure regular register updates as required by law. In Zanzibar, although the register is digitized, the ZEC faces challenges in updating the register due to the law that requires an individual to reside on the island for three years before being allowed to vote. Despite efforts to draft a union constitution that ensures EMBs have total autonomy, the country still needs assistance with the EMBs' ability to engage relevant stakeholders in electoral management processes. The researcher, however, did not exclusively analyze the influence of stakeholder non-engagement on public trust in electoral management bodies.

Owuor (2016: 14) studied the reforming of elections management and supervision in Kenya, using the IEBC as his case study. The research involved administering questionnaires to relevant stakeholders in the management of elections, including political parties, the judiciary, the IEBC, CSOs, and the Registrar of Political Parties. The researcher employed purposive sampling to identify individuals and organizations with extensive expertise and knowledge in running elections. The researcher also used direct observation to supplement data from experts and knowledgeable stakeholders. The study's findings indicated that, despite the numerous reforms initiated in election management in the country, the role of stakeholders remains diminished due to the constant interference of the executive in IEBC matters. This interference has led the commission to function as part of the executive, overlooking the contributions of other vital stakeholders to the management of the elections. In turn, public trust in the IEBC has dwindled, leading to violent incidents at every election. According to IEBC (2017), a stakeholder refers to an individual who has some interest or stake in the operations of the IEBC. They are categorized as either primary stakeholders or secondary stakeholders. They include the electorates, political parties, media, and the public, among others, who will likely be met during registration. Stakeholders require and expect transparency, fairness, and equity, among other core values. Based on the most recent studies, the stakeholders' engagement and managing the electoral process involve meeting their expectations. This means they are facilitated with sufficient support to participate in their full capacities in election processes with enough feedback and information (IEBC, 2018). For instance, in a forum held by the Maendeleo Policy Forum (2016) in Nairobi, Kenya, participants reiterated the critical role played by EMBs in managing elections in Africa. The forum participants, which included academics from Kenya and other African countries, as well as the Chairperson of the Electoral Commission of Ghana, ascertained the need for African countries to adopt necessary measures at the institutional and management levels to transform elections into crucial assets. There was also a need for countries like Kenya to adopt efficient and robust institutions and mechanisms to underpin credible polls. The forum also underlined the countries' need to promote electoral integrity and enhance social inclusion and cohesion. The participants also proposed that EMBs find ways to promote and encourage internal democracy within the political parties to strengthen electoral integrity. The need to engage all stakeholders in the management of elections was also mentioned as a critical determinant of electoral integrity in African countries.

KHRC's (2015:11) study revealed that the electorate is a critical stakeholder in electoral management. The electorates participate in the election process as voters, who expect to be informed about the various methods in advance. It includes voter education programs through dialogues, participation, and feedback on the inquiries raised. This provides the grounds for an electorate's instrumental involvement in the electoral process, thus building citizens' trust in the election management body. According to previous studies, civic education and voters' awareness campaigns, limited participation, and electoral prudence have been diminishing greatly (Owuor, 2016; Sekaggya, 2015; Erlich & Kerr, 2016;

Kerr & Luhrmann, 2017). Another essential stakeholder in determining the election outcome is the justice sector. This sector deals with interpreting the laws that regulate and govern election outcomes. The justice sector needs to be able to formulate, implement, and monitor or evaluate the applicability of various legal frameworks to instill justice in election management, thereby enhancing citizens' trust in the outcomes generated (KHRC, 2015; Maendeleo Policy Forum, 2016).

2.2.2. Professionalism of Public Institutions and Public Trust Levels

Lethbridge (2019: 25) defines professionalism as acting under the institutional norms and the core values guiding institutional operations and the law. This involves observing the critical metrics of integrity, transparency, and accountability, with strict adherence to the institutional code of conduct. A professional organization must, therefore, consider the issues of accountability and transparency as the critical determinants of openness and public trust (Buhl & Hilkenmeier, 2017:8).

In a study titled "The South African National and Provincial Elections: The Integrity of the Electoral Process," Schulz (2014:30) noted that the major component of free and fair elections in any democracy is compliance with the rule of law, which is both the outcome and the process of measuring the actual meaning of governance. The researcher also posited that for any government to be described as legitimate, it is necessary to maintain the credibility of an election and ensure that it is conducted professionally and fairly. The findings of the study were also supported by OECD (2013:5), which highlighted that citizens' trust levels in public institutions are determined by the extent to which they believe that the institutions in question observe the legal norms, the order and the rules, which are put in place to govern their operations. The citizens are sure that the concerned institutions are aware of all the laws, regulations, and legal norms that are in place to guide their operations (OECD, 2013:6). There exists a strong correlation between the citizens' trust in the government and its institutions and their confidence in the independent judicial system that maintains the integrity of various institutions set in place (OECD, 2013:6). Ntaganda's (2015:13) study on the electoral management in Burundi indicated that the electoral management body in Burundi (NIEC) did not act professionally. The study revealed that the body has more than once proved partisan and serves the interest of the ruling party led by President Pierre Nkuruziza. The researcher also noted that the government put much pressure on the EMB to act according to instructions, limiting its independence and ability to act professionally.

This is typical of most African countries, where EMBs are forced to dance to the incumbents' tunes, restricting their freedom and capability to practice professionalism. Schulz-Herzenberg, Aling'o, and Gatimu (2015:30) studied the integrity of the 2013 electoral process in Kenya and used the 2013 election management by the IEBC as a benchmark for determining electoral integrity in Kenya. The 2013 elections proved a big challenge for the EMB because, for the first time, Kenyans were voting for many leaders, as provided for in the 2010 CoK. To restore and maintain public confidence in the commission and the election, the IEBC needed to ensure its independence and professionalism. This included, but was not limited to, guaranteeing technical and logistical arrangements and demonstrating efficiency and impartiality in the registration of voters and the actual voting process. Nonetheless, the commission faced severe trust issues when it seemed to follow an order from the executive on the process of ordering biometric voter registration (BVR) kits for the 2013 exercise. The commission went to court to seek directions on the BVR kits contract and the election date.

The researchers argue that this, coupled with the commissioners' lack of experience in handling a general election, contributed to a decline in public trust. Some people felt that the commission had acted unprofessionally and against the spirit of the 2010 constitution, which called for establishing an independent commission to oversee matters related to elections in the country (Article 88, CoK, 2010).

Ellena, Vickery, and Reppell (2018:20) analyzed "the effective management of election disputes and violations." She found that the credibility of acceptable and stable elections is crucial, setting a growing focus on the efficiency of resolving disputes and violations throughout the election cycle. Therefore, EMBs must devise mechanisms to withstand new forms of political manipulation that have become increasingly sophisticated. The researchers also noted that electoral bodies in most developing countries lack professionalism, and the incumbents tend to use them as vehicles for extending their regimes without necessarily winning an election. They also use the courts to legitimize their stay in office way beyond their time and against the public's will. The EMBs should, therefore, put in place mechanisms to ensure that they always act professionally in managing and resolving disputes arising from an election process. According to the researchers, doing this will enhance the election's credibility and improve the public's trust in these institutions. Kerr & Luhrmann (2017:49) also concur with these assertions by arguing that an independent EMB must act with much professionalism, especially when carrying out its duties as a way of increasing or resurrecting the dwindling trust of the public in the bodies' capability to conduct free and fair elections. AFRI Cog's (2017:9) report on the 2013 general election in Kenya noted severe concerns about the management of the elections by IEBC.

The report also noted gaps in accountability and transparency, exemplified by the commission's inability to openly state which register was utilized in the elections. Another issue was the inability of the commission to enhance the efficiency of its electronic results transmission system. The public interpreted these issues as the traits of an IEBC under the control of the executive arm of administration, and one lacking professionalism. The lack of a legal framework for election management that integrates the participation of key stakeholders throughout the process suggests a commission that is already manipulated and serves the interests of the government of the day. The study also recommended that the EMBs in Kenya learn from past experiences and strive to avoid past blunders to restore public confidence in these electoral governance institutions. The findings of this study concurred with those of Aywa (2015) and Owuor (2016), who called for the involvement of all stakeholders and the need for EMBs to act professionally when handling election matters.

Kagwanja (2017:22) authored a research paper that called for the devolution of election management in Kenya after the nullification of the August 2017 presidential election by Kenya's Supreme Court, which Uhuru Kenyatta, the incumbent president, won. According to Kagwanja (2017:23), the nullification of the presidential results exposed the tantalizing liberal notion of autonomous electoral management bodies as a threat to the stability of delicate nations. The paper also argues that the ineptness of IEBC led to the unfortunate event, which he recommends can be solved by devolving election management. According to the researcher, IEBC had demonstrated unprofessionalism and an inability to run a fiercely contested election freely and fairly. Devolving election management will thus enhance the commission's ability to tackle issues arising from a fiercely contested election, such as the 2017 election.

The constitution provides for the IEBC's independence and advocates for the commission's professional conduct in all its undertakings.

According to a report by Ace (2019:4) on electoral management, the legitimacy and credibility of an electoral process greatly depend on the integrity of the process. The integrity of an election can be improved by ensuring that the systems and technology used in running the election conform to the tenets of practical technology. Electoral management bodies can utilize electoral technology in almost all facets of an election (Ace, 2019:8). Technology is used in registering voters. In contrast, the EMB utilizes electoral technology to build and maintain a voter register with all the personal details of an eligible voter.

Furthermore, the EMB can utilize electoral technology to identify voters during the voting process. This helps check the voter's eligibility before allowing them to participate in a voting exercise. Ace (2019) also discovered that EMBs can utilize electoral technology to track the registration of parties and candidates and the registration of systems. The technology is also used to delimit boundaries, facilitate electronic voting and counting, tabulate and transmit results, and publish and announce results. However, according to Cheeseman, Lynch & Willis (2018:45), the process of utilizing electoral technology, especially when conducting general elections, must be handled with a lot of care and professionalism to ensure that the credibility and legitimacy of an electoral process are always upheld. Other scholars recommend exercising maximum caution when using electoral technology in elections that are highly emotive and characterized by manipulation and violence. Electoral technology failure before, during, or after an election can be a significant source of public distrust in an electoral management body. The failure of transparency, openness, and accountability on the part of the electoral management body and the contracted company led to a decline in public trust in IEBC's ability to oversee a free, fair, and transparent election. The events that followed, including the cancellation of presidential polls, indicated that the electoral technology used in the electoral process was questionable and contributed to a decline in public trust in IEBC (Abraham, 2019).

2.2.3. Electoral Environment and Level of Public Trust Levels

According to Bhasin (2019: 12), the electoral environment refers to the conditions or surroundings that follow the preparations for a significant or minor election in a given country. These conditions can affect the behavior or conduct of electorates, leaders, contestants, and election management bodies. Furthermore, legislators' behavior, particularly how they adhere to the party line to maintain a cohesive or unified party record, clearly represents the tension between governability and representativeness. According to Shomer (2016: 31), the electoral environment can improve or disadvantage an EMB and, in the process, lower the chances of it performing as per its code of conduct. The electoral climate refers to the surrounding conditions or setting before, during, and after an electoral cycle. The electoral environment can influence an election's outcomes and impact the public's perception of the management capability of an EMB. Past studies on the influence of the electoral environment on the level of public trust in EMBs indicate that the environment plays a critical role in shaping the degree of confidence. For instance, a study by Jinadu (2014: 5) noted that electoral management in West Africa has extensively relied on the environment and the surrounding setting. According to the survey, among the challenges that EMBs in most West African states face are the ever-rising cost of elections, dispute adjudication issues, and an unfavorable environment, which are ranked as the highest priorities. The study looked at the gains and reversals made by EMBs in Sierra Leone, Nigeria, Ghana, Cape Verde, and Benin and discovered that the key challenges facing them revolve around environmental issues as well as ethical values and the political economy (Jinadu, 2014: 7). The electoral environment comprises both the internal and external environment. The internal environment encompasses the factors within IEBC that either strengthen or weaken its ability to supervise an election efficiently. The external environment comprises the analysis of the opportunities and threats facing IEBC in its electoral management. According to Bhasin (2019: 8), environmental scanning involves examining the strengths, weaknesses, opportunities, and threats that a specific organization faces, which can impact its ability to achieve its set objectives. Environmental scanning is a crucial part of the business process, as any establishment must monitor anything that can negatively impact consumers and their businesses. A study by Kerr and

Luhrmann (2017) indicated that public trust in election management in most parts of Africa was partly a factor of the electoral environment surrounding the electoral cycles. The study conducted experimental studies in which macro and micro-level controls were held constant to measure public trust in EMBs. The findings of the experimental studies indicated that in an environment where most of the electorates were affiliated with the ruling party or the party that won elections, the public's trust in the EMB was positive. This is opposed to the regions where their candidates did not win the election. This meant that the existing ecological setup played a crucial role in inculcating public trust in the electoral management body. The study, however, should have considered the influence of professionalism on the level of public trust in the EMB. The proposed research will consider this one of the determinants of public trust in the Kenyan EMB. ISFED (2019: 5) analyzed the impact of electoral management initiatives to improve the Georgian electoral system. It was discovered that, irrespective of the initiatives to improve the electoral system, the system remained the same. The investigation also notes that the pre-election environment is usually influenced by violence threatened against political leaders and several attempts to extort them using private clips. There is also the problem of state authorities' slow response to such issues, as well as the unfavorable media environment. The media environment also raises concerns due to the cancellation of media interviews because of legal disputes (ISFED, 2019: 7). The study recommended the timely adoption of appropriate legal arrangements, support of bills by parliament in a timely and efficient manner, and establishment of government agencies and authorities to act swiftly to avert violence before, during and after the electoral process.

According to a study by Jena (2017), African states can hold free, fair, and transparent elections by ensuring consistent adherence to electoral rules by state parties that are signatories to these rules. The EMBs must maintain an impartial approach to electoral management to ensure that the environment favors a positive outcome. The study also revealed that Ethiopia and Lesotho encountered specific electoral challenges, notably violence, intimidation, inflation, unreliable voter registers, and insecure ballot boxes (Jena, 2017:12).

2.2.3.1. Election Administration and Electoral Reforms in Cameroon Constitutional Background

The Constitution of the Republic of Cameroon provides for the election of the President by a majority of votes cast through direct, equal, and secret universal suffrage. The President of the Republic is elected for a seven-year term. In April 2008, the Constitution was amended to remove term limits on re-election to the office of the presidency. The Constitution describes the powers of the executive, the legislature, and the judiciary. It provides that legislative power shall reside with the Parliament, composed of the National Assembly and the Senate. The National Assembly and the Senate are elected for five years, and members are eligible for re-election. However, the Senate was yet to be established when authoring this report.

Parliament votes on laws, and the President enacts them by decree. The Constitution provides a Constitutional Council, which must be established when authoring this report. In the meantime, the Supreme Court has been assigned the role of the Constitutional Council in addition to its ordinary judicial functions. Specifically, the functions of the Constitutional Council regarding elections, as outlined in Articles 46 to 52 of the Constitution, are as follows:

- To ensure the regularity of presidential and parliamentary elections and referendums.
- To address claims or disputes regarding the regularity of the elections, which are referred to by the following:
- Any candidate or political party participating in the election in the constituency concerned;
- Any person acting as a 'government agent at the election';
- The President of the Republic;
- The President of the National Assembly, or
- One-third of the members of the National Assembly.
- To adopt and proclaim the results of the election.

According to Article 50 of the Constitution, rulings of the Constitutional Council are legally binding and not subject to appeal. Concern has been expressed that the powers of the Constitutional Council to announce election results detract from the powers of ELECAM as an independent electoral management body.

2.2.3.1.1. Election Administration

The 2006 law (as amended) establishing ELECAM provides that it shall be an 'independent' body and a 'moral entity' with 'managerial autonomy.' According to the Law, ELECAM must 'organize, manage and supervise elections and referendums.' In this respect, 'it shall be vested with the requisite powers to perform its duties.' ELECAM was established following the recommendation by the Commonwealth Observer Group for the Cameroon Presidential Election 2004 that Cameroon should have an independent election management body. ELECAM functions through the Electoral Board (EB) and the General Directorate of Elections (GDE). The EB comprises eighteen members (including a chairperson) and performs mainly supervisory duties, while the GDE (headed by a Director-General) manages and organizes elections. According to ELECAM's website, the EB is the 'policy-making organ' while the DGE is the 'executive organ.' Section 18 of the 2006 law affirms that the General Directorate of Elections shall be responsible for the organization and management of the poll under the supervision of the Electoral Board. Section 6 distinguishes this from the EB's role: to ensure compliance with the electoral law for all stakeholders to guarantee regular, impartial, free, fair, transparent and credible polls.

2.2.3.1.2. Appointment of Electoral Board Members and the Director General

According to the 2006 law as amended, members of the EB shall be appointed from 'independent personalities of Cameroon', reputed for their stature, moral uprightness, intellectual honesty, patriotism, neutrality, and impartiality. They are appointed by Presidential decree upon consultation with political parties represented in the National Assembly and civil society. The tenure of EB members is four years, renewable as appropriate, and expires in the situations of non-renewal of mandate, resignation, or death. Members' mandate may also be terminated in cases of physical incapacity, serious misconduct (notably the breach of oath), and where a penalty is imposed for a felony. The Director General of the GDE and their deputy are also appointed by Presidential decree for a five-year term, renewable as appropriate upon consultations with the electoral board. Their appointment may be terminated in circumstances like those of board members. Section 2 of the 2006 law prohibits ELECAM members from seeking or receiving 'instructions or orders from a public or private authority while performing their duties.' Section 3 provides that ELECAM members are immune from prosecution, investigation, arrest, or detention in performing their duties.

The Yaoundé-based headquarters of ELECAM serves as the central office for managing elections. ELECAM branches are responsible for election management duties at the local level and are directly answerable to the Director General of Elections. These branches comprise:

- 10 Regional Delegations
- 58 Divisional Branches
- 360 Council Branches

2.2.3.1.3. Electoral Commissions

The 2006 law, as amended, provides for the following Commissions (chaired by representatives of ELECAM), which are charged with responsibility for various aspects of the electoral process:

- Commission for the Revision of the Register of Electors
- Commission for Supervising the Establishment and Distribution of Registration Cards
- Local Polling Commissions
- Divisional Supervisory Joint Commissions
- Council Supervisory Commissions
- National Commission for the Final Counting of Votes

2.2.3.1.4. Voter Registration

The registration process commenced in August 2010 and officially ended on 31 August 2011, as required by law under Section 37 of the 1992 law as amended. To register on the voters' lists, Cameroonians had to go to the office of the ELECAM Council Branch in their electoral constituencies or contact the Joint Revision Commissions conducting mobile registration within institutions, markets, neighborhoods, and villages. In this election, the voter list was partly inherited from the previous parliamentary election in 2007. Voters who registered after 2007 were added to the list using new software provided by the United Nations Development Program (UNDP). The software is currently owned by ELECAM and was used to register an additional 2.7 million voters, bringing the total number of registered voters to 5,067,000. The total number of voters at the closure of the voter registration was said by ELECAM to be 7,525,122, which still needed to be consolidated. Voters are required to meet a set of criteria because they will be included in the voter register, and their registration cards will be issued. The following were the conditions potential voters had to meet to be included in the voter register.

- They must be a Cameroon citizen in the country or the Diaspora.
- They must have Cameroonian nationality by birth, or must have been naturalized as a Cameroonian, or must have been resident in an administrative unit for at least six months.
- They must be twenty years of age.

The potential voters would be disqualified because of the following:

- The conviction of a felony, even by default.

- The sentence of imprisonment without a suspension of more than three months.
- The sentence of imprisonment with a suspension of more than six months.
- Being the subject of a warrant of arrest.
- Being an undischarged bankrupt adjudicated by a Cameroonian court or a foreign judgment enforceable in Cameroon.
- Being an insane person [sic] or person of unsound mind.

Once potential voters meet the set conditions, they are entered into the voter register, and a permanent registration card is issued in their name. ELECAM was responsible for the distribution of registration cards. However, upon observation, it was noticed that not all voters received their cards. In addition, some members of political parties claimed that multiple cards were issued to some voters. Registration cards that were not delivered were sent to polling stations, and some were collected on polling day. The introduction of Law N°. 2011/013 on 13 July 2011 provided for Diaspora voting. Under Section 2 (1), Cameroonians residing abroad would be entered on the registers of electors opened at diplomatic representations and consular posts in their countries of residence or attachment.

A National Identity Card was the required identification for voting and was mandatory under Law N°. 90/042 of 19 December 1990. To encourage Cameroonians of voting age to register before the upcoming elections, the government waived the fee for obtaining these cards for the 2011 voter registration process. According to Section 32 of the 1992 Act, as amended, a registered voter should be issued with a voter's card that must indicate their 'full name, date and place of birth, filiation [sic], occupation, residence or place of abode.' In practice, and for the 2011 election, voters were given a receipt upon registering and a date to collect their voter's card.

2.2.3.1.5. Candidates' Eligibility and Nomination

Any citizen of Cameroon not younger than 35 may be eligible for nomination to be President if they possess complete citizen rights. The law requires anyone aspiring to stand in a presidential election to declare their candidature through a declaration bearing their authenticated signature. Such a candidate may either be nominated by a political party or stand as an independent. An independent candidate must be presented by at least

300 dignitaries from all regions, with 30 signatures from each area from members of parliament or the Chamber of Commerce and Agriculture, municipal councilors, or first-class chiefs. Nomination papers must be submitted to ELECAM — the body responsible for approving candidates and publishing the final lists of candidates contesting presidential (and other) elections. According to Section 55 of the 1992 Act, as amended, governing Presidential elections, candidates were to submit their nomination papers to ELECAM within five days following the convening of the electorate (that is, the announcement of the election date). The election date for this election was announced on 4 September 2011, following much public speculation on whether or not the election would be held in the first place. Some political parties complained that their candidates needed more time to prepare their submissions.

Under Section 54 (2), candidature documents must include certified copies of birth certificates not more than three months old, national identity cards, non-conviction certificates, tax clearance certificates, a residence certificate showing that prospective candidates had resided in the country for upwards of five years, and a certificate attesting to the payment of the required deposit (CFA 5,000,000). As noted earlier, of the fifty-two presidential aspirants, only twenty-three were approved by ELECAM.

2.2.3.2. Issues and Recommendations

Before the establishment of ELECAM, elections were organized, managed, and supervised by the MINAT and NEO. The establishment of ELECAM was, therefore, a significant first step in the democratization process in Cameroon. However, our assessment, based on information gathered from some stakeholders, was that not everyone had the same level of confidence in ELECAM, despite its statutory mandate to discharge its functions impartially and independently. We found out that the suspicion and low confidence levels emanated from the fact that the initial appointments comprised former members of the ruling party. ELECAM was also constrained in its performance by the prevailing legal framework, which it inherited from previous elections: for instance, in our discussions with some members of the Electoral Board, we were informed that certain procedural aspects of the elections, such as the use of multiple ballot papers which we found to be cumbersome, costly and potentially inimical to the transparent conduct of the polls, could not be addressed by ELECAM as it was established by law. ELECAM must do more to demonstrate its neutrality and inspire the electorate's confidence in future elections. In this connection, it would be helpful if the following steps were taken in earnest to enhance the institutional autonomy of ELECAM.

2.2.3.3. Review and Reform of Electoral Laws

There is a considerable number of laws governing elections in Cameroon. For this election, MINAT published a compilation of five excerpts that are directly relevant to presidential elections. This provided some clarity and ease of access to the legal framework. We hope that, ahead of future elections, a complete and comprehensive review of the various electoral laws will be undertaken with a view to commencing a consultative process of electoral reform that captures some of the recommendations in this report, addresses conflicting and unclear provisions, and produces an improved compilation of Cameroon's electoral laws.

We note that the establishment of ELECAM itself, through Law No 2006/011 of 29 December 2006, presents a strong foundation for electoral reform that can be built upon.

2.2.3.4. Autonomy, Independence, and Impartiality of ELECAM

ELECAM should be the sole person managing the electoral process. This should include hearing disputes with the right of appeal to the Constitutional Council, announcing the results, and accreditation of observers. This would address the institutional overlaps in responsibilities that the team found impinged on ELECAM's autonomy. The team recommends progressively transferring the remaining vestiges of electoral functions from MINAT and other institutions to ELECAM.

2.2.3.5. Filling the Gaps in the Electoral Framework

This research echoes the recommendations of the 2004 Commonwealth Observer Group in urging the establishment of the Senate and the Constitutional Council, which have constitutional roles to play where there is a vacancy in the office of the presidency and during the hearing of electoral disputes, respectively; additionally, we urge the review of whether the Constitutional Council should have original jurisdiction to hear election petitions or whether its jurisdiction should be appellate by way of review.

2.2.3.6. The Issue of an Inaccurate Voter List

There should be a new voter registration list completed in time for the next elections in the country. The list of registered voters ought to be available online and in hard copy, readily and easily available in readable print. The master list of all voters provincewide and nationwide should be readily available to voters at will. It should be made clear that once a registered voter's name is on the list, the voter does not require any further documentation other than the official identification to vote in the election.

2.2.3.7. Constrained Election Timetable

A timetable should be designed that allows sufficient time for pre-election activities such as voter registration, candidate nomination, inspection of the voter register, and campaigning. For example, candidates must be given enough time to prepare and present their documents.

2.2.3.8. Nomination of Independent Candidates for the Post of President

The 1992 law (as amended), which governs the conditions for presidential elections, stipulates that any candidate vying for independent status must produce 300 legalized signatures from the electoral college (voters) who should be members of the National Assembly, Consular Chambers, Councilors, and First-Class Chiefs (special high-profile voters) from all the provinces, making 30 per Province. This law currently makes the conditions for running as an independent candidate onerous. It should be amended to allow the signatures of ordinary voters nationwide to support prospective independent candidates to run for office, thereby ensuring a more inclusive process.

2.3. Literature Gap

Literature generally addresses the electoral law and the limitations of EMBs in Cameroon in delivering free, fair, and transparent elections, leaving a gap concerning the role of EMBs in ensuring voter turnout in the face of consistent apathy. The literature review also shows that, in a broader sense, most studies have focused on the independence of the bodies and should have considered the broader picture of how this influences the levels of public trust in the IEBC.

This research, therefore, contributes to filling this gap in more than one way. Future research will be able to draw on this work for literature that compares voter turnout under NEO and ELECAM, as well as the operational and practical measures taken by both EMBs to address voter apathy.

2.4. Theoretical Framework

In the execution of this study, three theoretical models have been utilized as tools for analyses.

2.4.1. Rational Choice Theory

The theoretical background for an economic explanation of voting behavior was submitted by Anthony Downs' (1957) work on "An Economic Theory of Democracy."

This theory is commonly referred to as rational choice theory. The Rational Choice Theory is essentially an attempt to explain electoral behavior, taking as its starting point the work done within the political economy by Kenneth Arrow (1951, 1986) that relates economic parameters - resources, goods, and technology with a political outcome or choice. The premise is simple: if the assumptions of rational choice can explain the market, then they can explain the political functioning. It establishes a direct analogy between consumers, voters, enterprises, and political parties. If companies seek to maximize profits and consumers act to maximize the utility, we can theorize that voters seek to maximize the utility of their vote as the parties act to maximize the benefits of their political proposals.

> *Our central thesis is that parties in democratic politics are analogous to entrepreneurs in a profit-seeking economy. To attain their private ends, they formulate whatever policies they believe will gain the most votes, just as entrepreneurs produce whatever products they think will gain the most profits for the same reason. To examine the implications of this thesis, we have assumed that citizens behave rationally in politics. This premise is a second central hypothesis. (Downs, 1957: 295-296)*

The operation of the model is based on three fundamental premises:

- All decisions — those that voters and political parties make — are rational, that is, guided by self-interest and enforced by the principle of maximization of action's utility;
- The democratic political system implies a level of consistency that supports predictions about the consequences of decisions made by voters and political parties, that is, their agents — voters, parties, and government — are responsible and trustworthy, which makes it possible to make predictions about the consequences that result from different choices and
- The democratic system assumes — despite the consistency stated in the previous point — a level of uncertainty sufficiently important to allow other options.

The concept of rationality is crucial in understanding the theory of rational choice, and it is essential to clarify that, according to Downs' economic theory, rationality is the assumption that voters and political parties act directly according to their interests. From this perspective, the term rationality is applied because the means are appropriate to the goals.

This follows the definition of rational as efficient, i.e., maximizing output for a given input or minimizing input for a given output. Thus, whenever economists refer to a 'rational man,' they are not designating a man whose thought processes consist exclusively of logical propositions, but a man without prejudices, or a man whose emotions are inoperative. In everyday usage, all of these can be considered rational men. But the economic definition refers solely to a man who moves toward his goals in a way which, to the best of his knowledge, uses the least possible input of scarce resources per unit of valued output. (Downs, 1957: 5)

According to this understanding of rationality, elections serve to choose a government, and consequently, rational behavior in an election is oriented towards this objective and not to any other.

The axiom of self-interest applies equally to the activities of political parties. According to rational choice theory, political parties seek to win elections, not by any altruistic motive relating to using a political program, but to gain prestige for themselves and the gains inherent to being in power. Since political electoral victories concretize a party's prestige, the main objective of parties is to win elections. The rational objective materializes if they can get more votes than any other party. Namely, the activities of political parties are guided by the principle of utility maximization of action:

> *"Upon this reasoning rests the fundamental hypothesis of our model: parties formulate policies to win elections, rather than win elections to formulate policies." (Downs 1957: 28)*

The rational choice theory considers that what matters to voters is not ideology but concrete actions that governments take. However, voters need to learn about all government decisions in detail, and it takes effort to understand and thoroughly evaluate their consequences. Thus, the ideologies of parties allow them to focus their analysis on only a few variables and generalize from this sample for all other proposals of that party:

> *"With this shortcut, a voter can save himself the cost of being informed upon a wider range of issues." (Downs, 1957: 98)*

Although what matters to voters is not the parties' intentions or political discourse but their ideology and concrete actions, the rational choice theory argues that comparing ideologies is only used if the voter already has concrete indicators of actions carried out effectively. If the voter has no previous data on the parties' concrete actions and can only distinguish them by their ideology, then this means, in practice, that they are equal regarding the voter's interests.

Strategically, the model posits that an irrational belief about the effectiveness of such action supports the decision to vote in an election. As the elections are aimed at choosing the government and not the expression of preferences, the voter will evaluate the chances of that party winning the election:

> *"Each citizen uses their forecast to determine whether the party they prefer is part of the relevant range of choice. If they believe it is not, rationally command them to vote for another party." (Downs, 1957: 48)*

This decision, made through strategic voting, depends on assessing the chances of the favorite party winning and the risk of the elections being won by a party considered undesirable. It will depend mainly on the importance of the subject and the need to keep a particular party out of government.

For example, let us assume there are three parties: Right, Centre, and Left. Voter X prefers Right to Centre and Centre to Left, but he believes Right has the least chance of winning. If he dramatically prefers Right to Centre and is almost indifferent between Centre and Left, he is less likely to switch his vote from Right to Centre than if he slightly prefers Right to Centre but abhors Left. (Downs, 1957: 49)

According to the rational choice model, the likelihood of citizens voting is higher if their expectations regarding the critical importance of their vote and the expected benefits from voting are more significant than the costs. Faced with the choice between several candidates, the voter must determine the difference in their interests, resulting in the victory (or loss) of candidate A, B, or C. If this analysis does not expect significant differences associated with the victory or defeat of any candidates, the potential benefit of voting is zero, and the probability of not participating in the elections is higher. Likewise, if the voters realize their vote will not have decisive importance for the election result, the likelihood of not voting increases.

Blais (two thousand) critically analyzes this theory based on the finding that "unfortunately for the theory, many people do vote. A clear majority vote in the most essential elections, where the number of voters is enormous, and the probability of casting a decisive vote is minuscule" (p. 2).

Research conducted by Blais allowed him to conclude that the rational choice model has a meager explanatory power of voting behavior. The results of his study show that about half of voters vote without calculating costs and benefits, but are driven by a duty to vote. Even among those whose sense of duty is not so strong, the variables related to the benefits and costs of voting do not have the influence that the rational choice model predicts. Blais (two thousand) concludes that even the price does not significantly influence voting behavior. Given the initial estimates of the model, he found that voters are more likely to vote if they feel that their vote can make a difference, but overestimate its importance. What seems to work is not the perception that one vote can make a difference, but that the result can be very close:

> *Some people may reason that they decide not to vote because that decision will imply that others with similar political attitudes will also abstain. That is, each citizen may regard their single vote as a diagnostic of millions of votes, substantially inflating the subjective probability of one's vote making a difference. (Blais, 2000: 139)*

This same criticism had been made previously by Uhlan (1989), who concluded that the rational theory has difficulty in explaining individual participation in collective action, which, in the case of voting behavior, was tantamount to finding that "Unfortunately for the theory, people do vote" (p. three hundred). Green and Shapiro (1994) took this and other arguments of a methodological nature in what is one of the most important criticisms of rational choice theory. The approach of these authors focuses on methodological issues, which criticize the post hoc development of the theory: "Many of the methodological failings of applied rational choice scholarship are traceable to a style that places great evidence on the development of post hoc accounts of known facts" (Green & Shapiro, 1994: 34), the absence of empirical tests: "Those who seek to derive testable propositions from rational choice models frequently find, moreover, that these theories are constructed in ways that insulate them against untoward encounters with evidence" (p. 38) and the selection, use, and interpretation of selected data: "The biased fashion in which evidence is selected. (...) subtler ways in which evidence is projected from theory rather than gathered independently. (...) the strategic retreat from domains where the theory performs poorly" (p. 42). Voter turnout, which the author analyzes in detail in his book, is used to illustrate the methodological weaknesses that are linked to rational choice theory:

> *For our purposes, the case of voter turnout is interesting not because it is a failure but because it illustrates the characteristic ways that rational choice theorists have reacted to discrepancies between theory and observation. In their resolute determination to declare some variant of rational choice theory victorious over evidence (or to declare peace with honor through artful domain restriction), rational choice theorists have trotted out an astonishing variety of conjectures about the costs and benefits of voting in the process generating an enormous literature, possibly more significant in terms of academic citations and sheer bibliographic length than any other rational choice literature in American politics. (Green & Shapiro, 1994: 47-48)*

This underlying requirement that voters have accurate and detailed information about their interests and parties' proposals is the main weakness of this model. The proponents of this approach try to overcome this weakness using the concept of heuristics and cognitive shortcuts to explain how voters will be able to make decisions based on little information (Lupia, McCubbins, & Popkin, 2000; Popkin, 1994; Simon HA, 1955; Sniderman, Brody, & Tetlock, 1991). It is argued that voters, unable to cope with the complexity and information overload, used indicators such as the positions taken by certain media, public figures, organizations or entities, and heuristics to reason about the interest of the electoral proposals. We are not talking about information on political issues and electoral proposals, but about voters' trust in sources of heuristic reasoning.

Due to a lack of information on the problems and electoral proposals, voters believe a candidate's position is favorable or unfavorable to their interests according to the trust they place in a medium of mass communication, in an organization, an entity, or a personality. That is, voters decide based on trust, not based on information. Despite its limitations, this model is suitable for research as it attempts to provide logical explanations for voter behavior, such as the choice to vote for party X or Y or abstain altogether. However, its shortcomings necessitate considering other paradigms.

2.4.2. Sociological Model of Voting Behavior

The theoretical assumptions of the sociological model of voting behavior are defined in three essential works: The People's Choice (Lazarsfeld,

Berelson, & Gaudet, 1944), Voting (Berelson, Lazarsfeld, & McPhee, 1954) and Personal Influence (Katz & Lazarsfeld, 1955). The research conducted by Lazarsfeld et al. (1944) at Ohio State (Erie County) using a questionnaire as a technique of investigation for the first time in the study of a US presidential election — one which opposed Franklin Roosevelt to Wendell Willkie in 1940 — cuts away from the type methodological approach that hitherto characterized the study of voting behavior (Barnes & Kaase, 1979). Paul Lazarsfeld, whose previous interests had focused on the study of the psychological mechanisms involved in the processes of choice and the effects of publicity, advertising, and mass media on consumer behavior, had two main objectives in this research:

- To study the impact of exposure to the media, that is, to know how voters arrive at their decisions and the role of the media in this process;
- To test a new methodology of successive interviews with a panel of subjects and a control group (Rossi, 1964).

The study, whose report was published under the title 'The People's Choice' (Lazarsfeld, Berelson, & Gaudet, 1944), begins by characterizing the supporters of the two main political parties in the US using a panel of 600 subjects who were interviewed seven times over the seven months of campaign, and then identifying the voters who changed their position during the campaign period, dividing them into three groups: those who decided their vote before beginning the campaign, those whose decision was taken during the party convention, and those who chose their vote only at an advanced stage of the campaign.

The central hypothesis of Lazarsfeld et al. (1944) was that the act of voting is an individual act, affected mainly by the personality of the voter and their exposure to the media. The results, however, contradict the central thesis, suggesting that the effect of the media on electoral decisions was minimal and that the decisive influence was the social groups to which they belonged. In the final two chapters of his book — "The Political Homogeneity of Social Groups" and "The Nature of Personal Influence" — the focus is precisely on the theoretical elaboration of these conclusions, which are presented as revealed by news research:

> *"The study highlighted the significance of this area of political behavior but further investigation is necessary to establish it more firmly." (Lazarsfeld et al., 1968: 69)*

The main finding of Lazarsfeld et al. (1944) was that most voters voted according to their original political predisposition. Only fifty-four changed their position throughout the six hundred subjects included. The association between electoral behavior and the social groups they belonged to was so strong that it was possible to explain the electoral choices using only the three factors that defined the Index of Political Predisposition used in research: socio-economic status, religion, and area of residence.

There is a familiar adage in American folklore that a person is only what he thinks he is. This adage reflects the typically American notion of unlimited opportunity, the tendency toward self-improvement, and so on. Now, we find that the reverse of the adage is true:

> *A person thinks politically as he is socially. Social characteristics determine political preference. (Lazarsfeld et al. 1968: 69)*

The effect of conversion and modification of the voting option identified in the study is primarily distributed among voters whom investigators previously classified as independent, i.e., those who had initial predispositions opposed to candidates — cross-pressures — which, according to the authors, were primarily social in nature and linked to divergent policy preferences associated with one or more social groups to which the subjects belonged.

However, contrary to initial expectations, these voters are persuaded to vote for a candidate, not as the result of an analysis of the proposals submitted by each candidate or the issues under discussion in the campaign, but following pressure from community members. As the authors write:

> *In short, the party changers — relatively, the people whose votes remained determined during the last stages of the campaign, the people who could swing an election in those previous days — were available to the person who saw them last before Election Day. The notion that people who switch parties during the campaign are mainly the reasoned, thoughtful, conscientious people convinced by election issues is just plain wrong. They were mainly just the opposite. (Lazarsfeld et al. 1968: 69)*

The study identifies three possible effects regarding the role of electoral campaigns and associated communication processes: activation of the indifferent, strengthening the link to the political party, and conversion of the undecided. It was found that the campaign's most significant impact is focused on voters who are already predisposed to vote for the candidate backed by this party, thereby strengthening and activating their prior predisposition. Only 8% of voters changed their initial position following the election campaign:

> *"In sum, then, this is what the campaign does: reinforcement (potential) 53%; activation 14%; reconversion 3%; partial conversion 6%; conversion 8%; no effect 16%." (Lazarsfeld et al., 1968: 103)*

However, these results do not mean that the authors conclude that electoral campaigns are useless. Its effect is not living up to initial expectations since the role is more to solidify the cohesiveness of party supporters around their electoral proposals than to convince voters of other parties to change their position. This result appears to be linked to a phenomenon of selective attention of voters on the election campaign, which was reflected in the fact that those who had more interest in politics and had already set their option to vote were also those who paid more attention to the campaign on radio and in newspapers:

> *"In other words, the group which the campaign manager is presumably most eager to reach — the as-yet undecided — is the very group which is less likely to read or listen to their propaganda." (Lazarsfeld et al., 1968: 124)*

However, it was also found that the role of the election campaign is crucial, as the influence of the social groups to which the individual belongs is significant for the results. This is because it identifies a mediation process — involving members of those groups who are committed to opinion leaders — between the communication conveyed by mass media and voters. This process is called the two-step flow of communication:

> *Opinion leaders play a unique role in the network of personal relationships. In Chapter V, we noted that they engaged in political discussion much more than the rest of the respondents. However, they reported that the formal media were more effective as sources of influence than personal relationships. This suggests that ideas often flow from radio and print to the opinion leaders and from them to the less active sections of the population. (Lazarsfeld et al., 1968: 151)*

These results contradict the initial hypothesis that voting is an individual act. The relationship between social groups to which subjects belong, their political choice, and the decisive role of personal contacts in the definition of electoral choices indicate that the decisions of voters are processes of group cohesion rather than individual acts:

> *"In a way, the content of this chapter can be summarized by saying that people vote, not only with their social group but also for it." (Lazarsfeld et al., 1968, p. 148)*

This first study, conducted in Erie County (Ohio), was criticized because it was unsupported by previous theoretical options, translating into explanations constructed later to give intelligibility to the findings (Rossi, 1964). One example of these explanations is the subsequent use of a two-step flow of communication in this work that appears as a hypothesis developed to explain the role of opinion leaders in mediating the communication flow between the media and voters. Lazarsfeld et al. (1944) only refer to it for the first time in the last chapter of the book "The People's Choice", titled "The Nature of Personal Influence", by giving it only three short paragraphs. Katz and Lazarsfeld subsequently developed the concept in "Personal Influence: The Part Played by People in the Flow of Mass Communications" (1955), considered one of the most influential works in research of mass communication, where the authors reaffirmed and developed the idea that the subjects' responses to media messages are mediated through interpersonal relationships and their groups to which subjects belong and that some individuals act as opinion leaders, building and rebuilding the meaning of the messages of media in their social circles.

The sociological model, however, has limitations in explaining the variations in voting that occur due to specific economic factors unique to each election. Social factors may explain the long-term stability of voting behavior but do not explain the variations that occur in the behavior of voters in different elections. It needs to explain why individuals who belong to certain social groups vote according to what one would expect of individuals from various social groups. Although there are attempts to overcome these difficulties within the sociological approach, for example, investigations arguing that the study of voting behavior should not be done from the voter's perspective but valuing contextual factors as the political programs of parties, the role of media, the countries' economic structure and the context in which the relationship between voters and parties becomes stronger (Curtice, 2002; van der Eijk, 2002; van der Eijk, Franklin & Oppenhuis, 1996; Glasgow & Alvarez, 2005 Johnson, Shively, & Stein, 2002; Wright, 1977). These limitations have led to the development of the Michigan psychosocial model, which attempts to overcome them by incorporating the concept of partisanship. This concept aims to connect the influence of sociological and historical long-term factors identified in the sociological model with the social and political short-term factors that characterize each election.

2.4.3. Duverger's Theory

Maurice Duverger's arguments, known as Duverger's Law or Duverger's Theory, are equally relevant to this study. Since its first publication in 1951, Duverger's Political Parties has influenced the entire branch of political science devoted to studying the political consequences of electoral laws.

Duverger, in his basic idea, posits that the plurality rule leads to bipartisanship and proportional representation leads to multipartyism. Duverger's comparative survey of party systems investigated the sources of dualism or the concentration of political party activity in two main parties. National factors explain a great deal, concluded Duverger, but two-party systems are invariably associated with a particular type of institutional arrangement: the single-member district, plurality electoral system.

> *"Dualist countries use the simple-majority vote, and simple-majority vote countries are dualist." (Duverger, 1959: 217)*

Elevating this claim to nomological status, Duverger set out his 'law' in a passage that has been cited countless times in the decades that followed:

> *The simple-majority single-ballot system favors the two-party system. (Duverger, 1959: 217)*

Inferentially, electoral organizations in Cameroon have transitioned from a multiparty system under Ahmadou Ahidjo to a single-party system under Paul Biya, and then back to a multiparty system. Despite these changes, Duverger's law applies strongly. Firstly, Cameroon has continuously operated a plurality electoral system, with simple majority votes and single-member districts (in most instances). This invariably means the system is bound to have two main parties. It has always been the Cameroon People's Democratic Movement (CPDM) and a leading opposition party in recent times. At other times, the opposition parties attempted to join forces and present a joint base to contest against the ruling CPDM party. The main opposition parties have, however, changed over the years, with the Social Democratic Front (SDF), the National Union for Democracy and Progress (NUDP), and the Cameroon Renaissance Movement (CRM) all taking turns at some point as the other main party.

In support of the suitability of these arguments to this study, the figurative table below shows that between 1956 and 2011, the electoral space has always had two main parties in contention in Cameroon.

23 December 1956 French Cameroon Territorial Assembly		
Election* Registered Voters	17,52,902	
Total Votes (Voter Turnout)	725,000 (41.4%)	
Party		Number of Seats (70)
Cameroonian Union (UC)		30
Cameroonian Party of Democrats (PDC)		20
Independent Peasants (PI)		9
Cameroonian National Action Movement (MANC)		8
Others		3

The Territorial Assembly Was Renamed the Legislative Assembly in 1957

Registered Voters	2,05,576	
Total Votes (Voter Turnout)	Not Available (N/A)	
Invalid/Blank Votes	Not Available	
Total Valid Votes	1,37,219	
Party/[Coalition]		**Number of Votes**
Kamerun National Democratic Party (KNDP)		73,305
Kamerun National Congress-Kamerun People's Party [KNC-KPP]		51,384
Kamerun National Congress (KNC)		
Kamerun People's Party (KPP)		
One Kamerun (OK)		2,021
Independents		10,509

24 January 1959 British Southern Cameroons House of Assembly Election

Main Points: Presidential System of Government, Federal Constitution, One Federal Chamber			
Registered Voters	17,71,969		
Total Votes (Voter Turnout)	13,38,178	-75.50%	
Invalid/Blank Votes	9,605		
Total Valid Votes	13,28,573		
Results			Number of Votes
"Yes" Votes			7,97,498
"No" Votes			5,31,075

21 February 1960 Constitutional Referendum

**The referendum was conducted in areas formerly known as French Cameroon, which became the independent Republic of Cameroon on 1 January 1960.*

Registered Voters	19,40,438		
Total Votes (Voter Turnout)	1,349,739 (69.6%)		
Invalid/Blank Votes	Not Available		
Total Valid Votes	13,49,539		
Party/[Coalition]			**Number of Votes**
Cameroonian Union (UC)			6,06,000
Popular Front for Unity and Peace (FPUP)			1,45,752
Cameroonian Party of Democrats (PDC)			1,39,780
Union of the Peoples of Cameroon (UPC)			1,51,379
Progressives Group of Cameroon [GPC]			60,686
Others			2,33,789
Independents			11,853

10 April 1960 National Assembly Election

**The Election Was Conducted in Areas Formerly Known as French Cameroon. French Cameroon Became The Independent Republic Of Cameroon On 1 January 1960.*

Note: On May 5, 1960, the National Assembly elected Ahmadou Ahidjo, President of the Republic. He received eighty-nine of the ninety-nine total votes cast in the election.

Registered Voters	**Not Available**		
Total Votes (Voter Turnout)	Not Available (N/A)		
Invalid/Blank Votes	Not Available		
Total Valid Votes	2,55,433		
Party			**Number of Votes**
Kamerun National Democratic Party (KNDP)			1,40,347
Cameroon People's National Convention (CPNC)			68,458
One Kamerun (OK)			17,733
Others			1,401
Independents			27,494

30 December 1961 West Cameroon House of Assembly Election

**The election was conducted in areas formerly known as British Southern Cameroons. In a plebiscite held on 11-12 February 1961, voters in the Southern Cameroons chose to unite with the Republic of Cameroon, which took place on 1 October 1961.*

Registered Voters	Not Available			
Total Votes (Voter Turnout)	Not Available (N/A)			
Party				**Number of Votes**
East Cameroon				
Cameroonian Union (UC)				18,63,614
Cameroonian Party of Democrats (PDC)				1,29,571
West Cameroon				
Kamerun National Democratic Party (KNDP)				1,92,081
Cameroon People's National Convention (CPNC)				60,485

Registered Voters	Not Available			
Total Votes (Voter Turnout)	Not Available (N/A)			
Party				**Number of Votes**
East Cameroon				
Cameroonian Union (UC)				18,63,614
Cameroonian Party of Democrats (PDC)				1,29,571
West Cameroon				
Kamerun National Democratic Party (KNDP)				1,92,081
Cameroon People's National Convention (CPNC)				60,485

24 April 1964 Federal National Assembly Election

Registered Voters	**28,45,515**			
Total Votes (Voter Turnout)	2,702,098 (95.1%)			
Invalid/Blank Votes	1,401			
Total Valid Votes	27,00,697			
Candidate (Party)			**Number of Votes**	
Ahmadou Ahidjo (UC)/John Ngu Foncha (KNDP)*			27,00,697	

23 March 1965 Presidential Election

**A Joint Ticket with Ahmadou Ahidjo as the Presidential Candidate and John Ngu Foncha was chosen as the vice-presidential candidate. They received 100.00% of the valid votes cast and 99.95% of the votes in the election.*

**Some sources list the election date as 20 March 1965.*

2.5. Single Party Elections

Sole Legal Party: Cameroonian National Union (UNC) 1966-1985; Cameroon People's Democratic Movement (RDPC) 1985-1990.

28 March 1970 Presidential Election

(Ahmadou Ahidjo Re-elected Unopposed) Registered

Total Votes (Voter Turnout)	3,479,186 (99.4%)	
Invalid/Blank Votes	244	
Total Valid Votes	3,478,942	(99.99%)
Ahmadou Ahidjo	3,478,942	(100.00%)

7 June 1970 Federal National Assembly Election (50 Seats)

Registered Voters	3,049,073	
Total Votes (Voter Turnout)	2,928,884 (96.1%)	
Invalid/Blank Votes	52,295	
Total Valid Votes	2,876,589	(98.21%)
UNC	2,876,589	(100.00%)

20 May 1972 Constitutional Referendum

Main Points: Abolish the two-state federation, the creation of a Unitary System of Government, and increased presidential powers.

Registered Voters	**3, 236,280**		
Total Votes (Voter Turnout)	3, 179,634 (98.2%)		
Invalid/Blank Votes	1,612 Total Valid Votes		3, 178,022
'Yes' Votes	3, 177,846	(99.99%)	
'No' Votes	176 (0.01%)		

18 May 1973 National Assembly Election (120 Seats)

Registered Voters	**3,318,390**	
Total Votes (Voter Turnout)	3,262,064 (98.3%)	
Invalid/Blank Votes	578	
Total Valid Votes	3,261,486	(99.98%)
UNC	3,261,486	(100.00%)

5 April 1975 Presidential Election

(Ahmadou Ahidjo Re-elected Unopposed) Registered

Voters 3,502,640	
Total Votes (Voter Turnout)	3,483,328 (99.4%)
Invalid/Blank Votes	163

Total Valid Votes	3,483,165 (100.00%)
Ahmadou Ahidjo	3,483,165 (100.00%)

29 May 1983 National Assembly Election (120 Seats)

Registered Voters	3,657,995
Total Votes (Voter Turnout)	3,628,579 (99.2%)
Invalid/Blank Votes	110
Total Valid Votes	3,628,469 (100.00%)
UNC	3,628,469 (100.00%)

Election Results Table

	Election		Registered Voters		Total Votes (Voter	Invalid/Blank	Total Valid Votes
					Turnout)	Votes	
	Apr-80		33,61,630		3,329,235 (99.0%)	90	33,29,145
	Presidential						-100.00%
	Election						Ahmadou Ahidjo:
	(Ahmadou Ahidjo						33,29,145
re-elected				-100.00%			
unopposed)							
29-May-83	36,57,995	3,628,579 (99.2%)	110	36,28,469			
National				-100.00%			
Assembly				UNC: 3,628,469			
Election (120				-100.00%			
Seats)							
14-Jan-84	39,68,673	3,878,745 (97.7%)	607	38,78,138			
Presidential				-99.98%			
Election (Paul				Paul Biya:			
Biya)				38,78,138			
				-100.00%			
24-Jan-88	36,34,568	3,364,090 (92.6%)	42,218	33,21,872			
Presidential				-98.75%			
Election (Paul				Paul Biya:			
Biya)				33,21,872			
				-100.00%			
24-Jan-88	36,34,568	3,282,884 (90.3%)	1,03,026	31,79,858			
National				-98.75%			
Assembly				RDPC: 3,179,858			
Election (180				-100.00%			
Seats)							
01-Mar-92	40,19,562	2,435,443 (60.6%)	2,38,200	21,97,243			
National				*Two opposition			
Assembly				parties, the Social			
Election*				Democratic Front			
				(SDF) and			
				Cameroon			
				Democratic Union			
				(UDC), boycotted			
				the poll.			
11-Oct-92	41,95,687	3,015,448 (71.9%)	50,012	29,65,436			
Presidential							
Election [Results							
by Province]							
17-May-97	38,44,330	2,906,186 (75.6%)					
National							
Assembly							
Election							

Cameroon Election Results Summary

Election Date	Registered Voters	Total Votes (Voter Turnout)	Invalid/Blank Votes	Total Valid Votes	Additional Information
17-May 1997 National Assembly Election	38,44,330	29,06,186 -75.60%	N/A	N/A	The Supreme Court canceled the election results in seven constituencies due to severe irregularities. On 3 August 1997, further polls were conducted to fill the vacancies. The RDPC won all the seats, thus increasing its representation in the national assembly to 116
12-Oct 1997 Presidential Election	42,20,136	Not Available -81.40%	Not Available	34,22,055	The election was boycotted by three main opposition parties - the Social Democratic Front (SDF), National Union for Democracy and Progress (UNDP), and Cameroon Democratic Union (UDC). A more minor party, the Union of African Populations (UPA), also joined the boycott.

Figure 2.3 Elections Results in Cameroon Indicating Party Strengths: 1956 – 2011
Source: African Elections Database

Duverger's explanation of the number of parties understands free elections as markets in which candidates and voters alter their behavior as they try to get as close as possible to their preferred outcome. Duverger, in contrast, saw party organization as a product of 'social forces,' notably the composition of the electorate. The 'cadre' party was the product of limited suffrage, while universal suffrage would lead to the 'mass-based membership' party. Given that the latter never developed, it is argued that Duverger's logic of the number of parties also applies to their organization.

It is noted how periodic free elections create markets where individuals pursue three fundamental political drives: ambition, choice, and benefits; every political organization must respond to these three drives.

As a corollary, Duverger also stipulated a second proposition that proportional representation (PR) electoral systems were a driving force behind the multiparty systems in many such countries he examined. Although he did not claim the proposition about PR as a 'law,' Duverger stated that PR favors multipartyism, as does the majority system with a second-round runoff format (Duverger, 1959: 239). This pair of propositions came to form the focus for the development of an entire subfield on the political consequences of electoral laws, aimed at linking the form of electoral institutions to variations in the size and concentrations of party systems. The former proposition, linking two-party to single-member district plurality electoral systems, became known as Duverger's law, mainly because Duverger himself had termed this relationship a law. The second proposition, stating that there is a tendency towards multipartyism under proportional systems, came to be known as Duverger's hypothesis. Together, this pair of statements bearing Duverger's name became the focus of an entire subfield of political science, with its journals, conferences, and dedicated sections in professional associations producing an enormous body of scholarly literature.

The declaration of the 'law' that a simple plurality electoral system resulted in the two-party system by Duverger also provoked numerous challengers who aimed to disprove Duverger's propositions. Many observers quickly pointed out that Duverger was hardly the first to have discovered the association in Duverger's Law. Grumm (1958) recalled that Key (1952) had advanced an almost identical argument, asserting that:

> *In a single-member district, only two parties can contend for electoral victory with any hope of success; a third party is doomed to perpetual defeat...That prospect tends to drive their members to one or more of the two parties. The single-member district thus molds parties into a bipartisan pattern (Key, 1952: 224–225).*

Even though scholarly acceptance of Duverger's law and hypotheses was widespread by the time he formulated them (Riker, 1982), it is nonetheless Duverger with whom electoral systems scholars associate them.

Chapter 3 | A Scientific Approach to Election Management Knowledge

3.1. Introduction

The research methodology provides an understanding of the framework for this study. This endeavor concentrates on descriptive content analysis of primary and secondary information to examine the relationships between election management bodies and voter apathy in Cameroon.

This chapter discusses the research methodology to answer the primary and secondary research questions.

The study entails a comparative analysis conducted through the structured, focused comparison approach. This is a qualitative method used to study a group of cases. It involves more than one case at a time to derive comparable data across the cases, which can then be generalized to constitute one case. It entails the development of general research questions that reflect the research objectives, which are administered uniformly to each case. This helps standardize data collection and facilitate systematic comparisons and analyses of the findings. It focuses on addressing specific aspects of the cases (Alexander and Andrew, 2005:77).

3.2. Research Design

This study used a structured, focused, comparative descriptive research design. In this design, the researcher describes variables and examines differences in variables in two or more groups that occur naturally in a setting. This research design is ideally suited for this study and would be further supplemented by collecting primary quantitative data. As such, it would enable the researcher to explain the present and even predict the future by arriving at conclusions about the causes, trends, and effects of past phenomena.

Moreover, this research design describes and explains events as they are, as they were, and will be. The research design, as employed, would entail the researcher extensively gathering secondary data on the historical evolution of elections and electoral systems in Cameroon and subsequently testing covariations with voter behavior.

3.3. Area of Study

The research area was Cameroon. More specifically, the research identified critical sites, including the headquarters of Elections Cameroon in Yaoundé, the various regional offices, and the Ministry of Territorial Administration. Moreover, the research was carried out in the university communities of Buea to obtain a sufficiently rich and objective sample.

3.4. Target Population

The population used for this study was a purposefully selected group of respondents from the identified stakeholders listed below, who were residents within the research site. The stakeholders identified for the study included:

- EMB bureaucrats and professionals in elections management
- Politicians and administrators of political parties
- University lecturers and researchers in elections
- Students of voting age
- Civil society organizations concerned with elections

3.5. Sampling Techniques and Sample Size

This study employed a purposive sampling technique to select its sample. The purposive sampling technique refers to the researcher's decision on who to include in the sample. With its high propensity to generate focused information, this sampling technique selects applicable cases only, thus saving time and resources. In this light, the target population was a purposive sample drawn from political parties, election officials in Cameroon, MINAT scribes, politicians, and academics.

The study's sample size was determined, taking into account unbiasedness and fair representation of the entire population. An equal population was selected from EMB experts, political parties, voters, and potential voters. One hundred respondents were targeted from each segment, totaling a sample population of three hundred respondents.

S/N	Segment	Sample Size	Composition of Respondents
1	EMB experts	100	Men, Women, Youth
2	Political parties and vote holders	100	Men, Women, Youth
3	Potential voters	100	Men, Women, Youth
4	Total	300	

Table 3.1 : Sample Size
Source: Field Work, 2022

3.6. Data Collection Methods

This study extensively utilized both primary and secondary data sources. Primary data were obtained from field observation, questionnaires, and interviews with experts, scholars, politicians, political party leaders, and scribes.

Secondary data were obtained from written, published, and unpublished works, journals, periodicals and magazines, indexes, television, and the World Wide Web. Libraries were consulted enormously to this end.

3.7. Research Instruments

3.7.1. Questionnaires

The questionnaire was the primary instrument used in this study. The questionnaire, titled the Voter Apathy and Voter Turnout Scale (VAVTS), consisted of two sections. Section A concerned the personal information and characteristics of the respondents, while Section B contained ten items on voter turnout and apathy in elections (Appendix 1).

3.7.2. Key Informant Interviews (KII)

Interviews were equally used to supplement the questionnaires. The researcher administered the research instrument with the support of other students as field staff. Experts with knowledge of EMBs and voter apathy (turnout) in Cameroon were targeted and interviewed with guided open-ended questions to gain deeper insights into the subject of study.

Segments	Interviewees
Former NEO, MINAT, and Current ELECAM top staff	10
Political party scribes and vote holders	10
Civil society organization leaders	5
Total	25

Table 3.2 : Distribution of Interviewees
Source: Field Work, 2022

3.8. Data Collection

This entailed visiting the field to administer the questionnaires and interview guides, the primary data collection instruments.

Rendezvous with interviewees were pre-set, and the data collection tools were administered. Data collection was conducted between July 2022 and October 2022.

The researcher used research assistants to collect data efficiently. Respondents were approached both at their places of work and at home for convenience. Face-to-face interviews still proved challenging to manage despite the relative ease of anti-COVID-19 measures. The table below shows the number of questionnaires sent out and the response rate.

Segment	Number	Number	Response Rate (%)
	Administered	Returned	
EMB experts	100	100	100
Political Parties and vote holders	100	88	88
Potential voters	100	92	92
Total	300	280	93.333%

Table 3.3 : Distribution of Questionnaire Administered and Response Rate
Source: Field Work, 2022

3.9. Quantitative and Qualitative Data

The research extensively used both quantitative and qualitative data. Quantitative data were obtained from questionnaires supplemented by some interviews, and qualitative data were obtained from direct field observations and in-depth secondary data analyses.

3.10. Code Guide Development and Coding

Code guide development involves assigning numerical values to words and generating a codebook from the data. The code book is a numerical representation of the work, designed to facilitate the coding of questionnaires. It also compresses the words, enabling software to have no difficulties in analyzing them.

During the coding, figures and numerals were written beside each question in the questionnaire and its responses, whether closed-ended or open-ended. Samples of the questionnaires were used to develop the code guide, after which all the administered ones were coded.

3.11. Data Entering and Cleaning

Cueing in the raw data together with the words and numerals for accessible analyses is the actual process of data entry. After the data was cued into the computer software, it was cleaned. At this stage, the goal was to remove any unwanted scientific errors from the data, which significantly reduced the error margin during entry.

3.12. Methods of Data Analysis

To generate relevant information from the study, appropriate statistical techniques help present the data using the most straightforward methods for understanding. The following analytical techniques were applied across the work:

- Percentages
- Frequencies
- Charts and graphs

The research strategies enunciated in earlier paragraphs produced both qualitative and quantitative data. The data collected were presented in simple tables, graphs, pie charts, and bar charts.

Data analysis was done predominantly in content form (qualitative). A consideration of data type and data layout preceded the data analysis. Once the data was entered and checked for errors, the researcher started data analysis using an exploratory data analysis approach. This included trends over time, proportions, and distributions.

3.13. Validity and Reliability

Experts in the subject area verified and cross-verified the face validity and content validity of the research instruments. The various suggestions were used to modify the instruments. The Alpha (α) reliability measure for research data was 0.92 for the questionnaire.

3.14. Ethical Considerations

The research adhered to the principle of informed consent from all its critical informants as an essential guide in research ethics throughout the study, from data collection and analysis to the presentation of the research findings. Similarly, the study exercised due diligence and maintained the confidentiality of participants' records and identities, as required.

Additionally, the study sought authority to use relevant official documents. The research was guided by existing legislation on research in the study countries. This study also adhered to academic honesty and objectivity by acknowledging the authors/sources of all materials and references cited throughout the study. This was done to the best of the researcher's knowledge.

Chapter 4 | Empirical Support of Elections Umpires in Cameroon

This chapter presents the study's findings and the analysis, interpretations, and discussions that emanate from them. It also presents the respondents' information background and the analysis of findings based on the study's objectives. The researcher employed both descriptive and inferential statistical methods to analyse the study's qualitative and quantitative data findings.

This section focuses heavily on how EMBs in Cameroon have functioned in terms of autonomy and operations, which have affected voter turnout in one way or another. The study's findings are explained in sub-sections of this section, and the summaries are presented in the appropriate figurative forms.

300 questionnaires were administered in the research area, and 280 were returned, giving a rate of just over 93%. Regarding qualitative data, 25 key informants were interviewed across Cameroon. Trickling down from the foregoing, this chapter presents the findings of this research as follows:

4.1. Demographic Characteristics of Key Respondents

- Presentation and analysis of the data from the issues raised
- Hypothesis testing
- Interview analysis
- Discussion of findings

Items	Frequency	Percentage (%)
Female	135	45
Male	165	55
Total	300	100

Table 4.1. Distribution of Respondents by Gender
Source: Fieldwork, 2022

The above table shows the gender distribution of the respondents for this study. The findings reveal that of the 300 respondents, 135 were female, and the other 165 were male. This indicates that more male respondents were more comfortable responding to questions on EMBs and voter turnout, further suggesting that males are more interested in election issues than females.

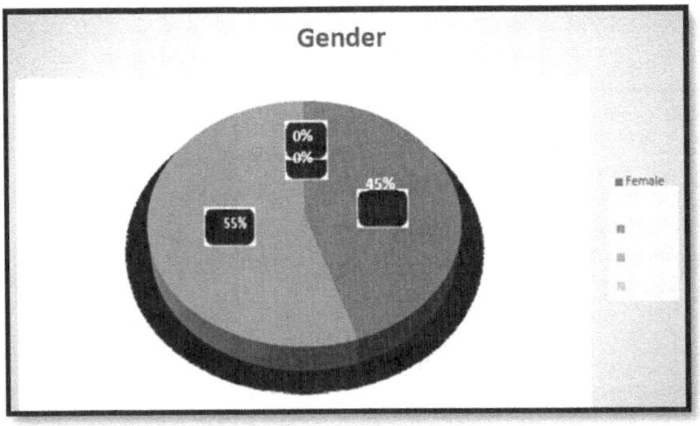

Figure 4.1: Distribution of Respondents by Gender
Source: Field Work, 2022

Figure 4.1 presents the demographic data of respondents to the questionnaire of this study by gender. The figure depicts that 45% of respondents were female and 55% were male. This indicates that more males than females responded to the questionnaire.

Age	15-19	20-35	36-49	50-60	Total
Frequency	15	113	130	42	300
Percentage	5%	37.7%	43.3%	14%	100%

Table 4.2 : Distribution of Respondents by Age
Source: Field Work, 2022

Table 4.2 above illustrates the age distribution of the respondents targeted by this study. The findings indicate that the majority of respondents (130) fell within the 36-49 age bracket, accounting for 43.3% of the total. This was followed by the respondents of the age group bracket of 20-35, with 37.7% representing 113 respondents of the total respondents.

The 50-60 age bracket had 42 respondents, accounting for 14%, while the least represented age group was the 15-19 age bracket, with only 15 respondents, accounting for 5%. Of course, the least represented age group can be explained as partially being the voting age and needing more knowledge of elections. The most populous age group represents those who are still active, of voting age, and have sufficient experience. Therefore, this age group has lived through the three EMBs in Cameroon and can voice a comparative opinion. Overall, this distribution suggests that the youthful population is highly interested in elections and that the population of Cameroon, in any given location, is predominantly youthful.

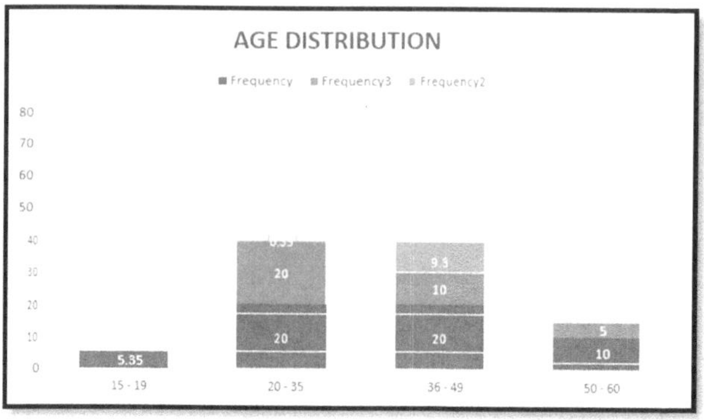

Figure 4.2: Distribution of Respondents by Age
Source: Field Survey, 2022

Figure 4.2 above illustrates the age distribution of the respondents. This illustration supports the table it precedes, showing that the intermediate population responded more than any other age bracket to the questionnaire.

Level of Education	Frequency	Percentage
Ordinary Level (OL)	8	2.6%
Advanced Level (A'L)	60	21.5%
Bachelor's Degree	117	41.8%
Master's Degree	95	33.92%
Total	280	100%

Table 4.3: Distribution of Respondents by Level of Education
Source: Field Survey, 2022

The table above depicts the respondents' level of education. The findings reveal that most respondents had a bachelor's degree or above. 41.8% of the respondents (117) had a bachelor's degree, while 33.92% (95) were holders of a master's degree. 60 respondents (21.5%) were holders of the Advanced level certificate, while only 8 (2.5%) were holders of the

Ordinary level certificate. There is a clear indication that awareness and interest in elections increase with increased education.

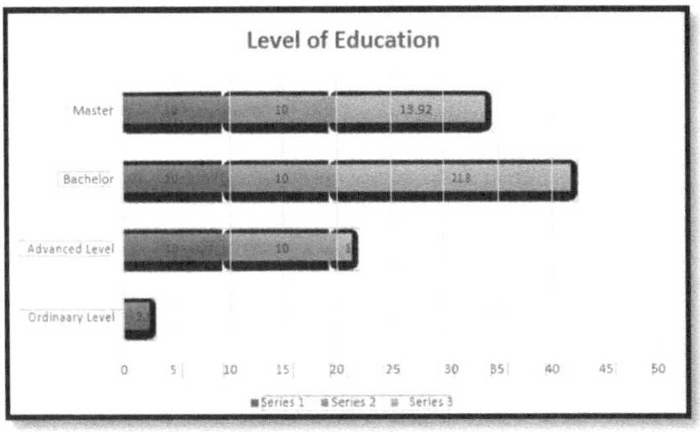

Figure 4.3: Distribution of Respondents by Level of Education
Source: Field Survey, 2022

Figure 4.3 above illustrates the educational levels of the respondents. This chart demonstrates that the respondents to this research are at least holders of the Ordinary Level certificate and must hold a Bachelor's degree, indicating that they understand the questions they are being asked and can provide answers.

Items	Single	Married	Total
Frequency	115	165	280
Percentage	41.07%	58.92%	100

Table 4.4: Marital Status of Respondents
Source: Field Survey, 2022

The findings from the above table indicate that most of the respondents (165), representing 58.92% of the total respondents, were married as opposed to the 115 (41.07%) who were unmarried. This suggests that although there is a larger number of married respondents, given the not-so-significant difference, both married and single Cameroonians are concerned about elections and voter turnout.

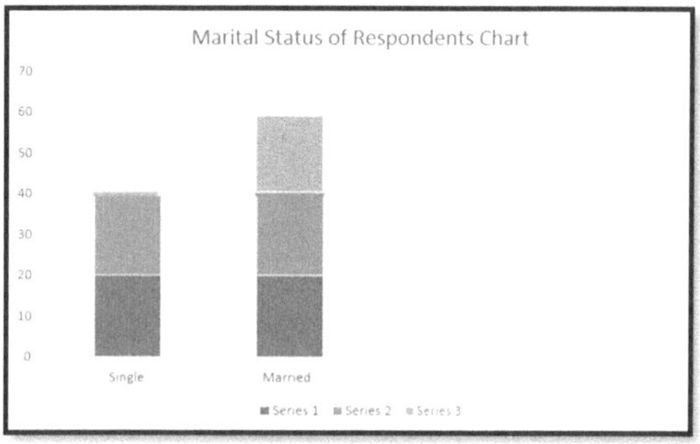

Figure 4.4: Marital Status of Respondents
Source: Field Survey, 2022

Figure 4.4 above illustrates the marital status of the respondents to this study. The findings reveal that the questionnaires were administered to more married than single people.

Items	Not Employed	Employed	Total
Frequency	98	182	280
Percentage	35	65	100

Table 4.5: Employment Status of Respondents
Source: Field Survey, 2022

The above frequency distribution table indicates the employment status of the study's respondents. Most respondents (182), with a total of 65%, were employed, as opposed to the 35% (98) who indicated they were not employed.

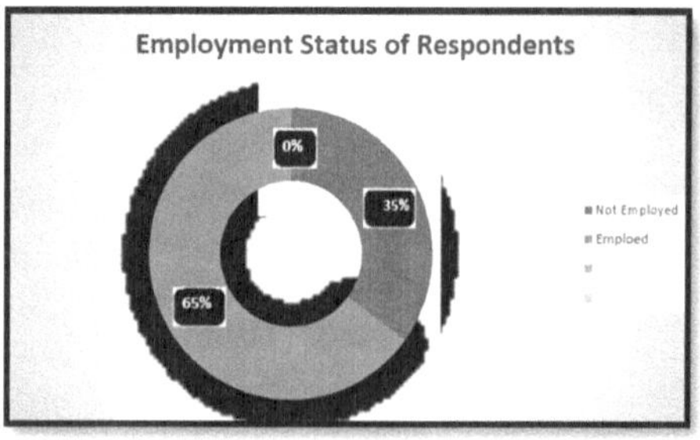

Figure 4.5: Employment Status of Respondents
Source: Field Survey, 2022

Figure 4.5 above presents the employment status of the respondents to this study and reveals that the majority (65%) indicated that they were employed, as opposed to those (35%) who were unemployed.

Items	Student	House wife	House husband	NGO Worker	Civil Servant	Entrepreneur	Total
Frequency	25	42	5	50	52	106	280
Percentage	8.92%	15%	1.78%	17.85%	18.57%	37.8%	100

Table 4.6: Distribution of Respondents by Profession
Source: Field Work, 2022

The above table presents the distribution of respondents by their respective professions. The table indicates that most of the respondents (37.8%) were entrepreneurs. Interestingly, many respondents held professions that overlapped. The majority of respondents were students who identified themselves as entrepreneurs. Then, some students were stay-at-home spouses, entrepreneurs who were civil servants, and NGO workers who were entrepreneurs.

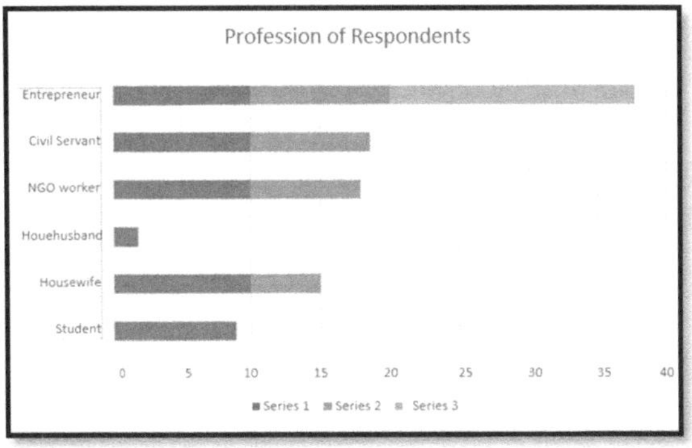

Figure 4.6: Distribution of Respondents by Profession
Source: Field Survey, 2022

As explained in table 4.6 above, figure 4.6 maintains the respondents' profession distribution. The figure reveals that the majority of respondents identified themselves as entrepreneurs.

4.2. Presentation and Analysis of Data from the Issues Raised in the Questionnaire

4.2.1. Analysis of the Public Awareness of the Electoral Roster in Cameroon

Items	Frequency	Percentage
Yes, aware of elections	132	47%
No, unaware of elections	112	40%
Uncertain	36	13%
Total	280	100

Table 4.7 : Awareness of the Electoral Roster in Cameroon
Source: Field Survey, 2022

Table 4.7 illustrates the extent of public awareness (or lack of) about the running of elections in the country. The majority (47%) attested to knowing the running of elections before they are run, while 40% indicated that they usually do not have knowledge of elections in time, and 13% (36 of the 280) indicated they were unsure. This suggests that electoral communication is occurring, but still needs to be improved to reduce the number of people who are unaware or unsure.

4.2.2. Analysis of the Public Awareness of the Requirements to Participate in Elections in Cameroon

	Frequency	Percentage
Yes, I am aware of the requirements	118	42%
No, I was unaware of the requirements	162	58%
Total	280	100

Table 4.8: Awareness of Elections Requirements in Cameroon
Source: Field Survey, 2022

Regarding awareness of the requirements to partake in elections (both as voters or candidates), the majority (58%) indicated needing to be made aware, as opposed to 42% having ample knowledge of the requirements. This again points to a need for more electoral education.

4.2.3. Analysis of Public Trust and Confidence in the EMBs in Cameroon

Items	Frequency	Percentage
Yes, EMBs are just and fair	106	38%
No, EMBs are unjust and not fair	174	62%
Total	280	100%

Table 4.9: Public Opinion of the Level of Honesty and Fairness in EMB Dealings
Source: Field Survey, 2022

The findings, as indicated in the table above, reveal that the majority of respondents (62%) thought that EMBs in Cameroon are usually not fair and just in their dealings. This is as opposed to 38% who have a contrary opinion.

4.2.4. Analysis of the Public Rating of ELECAM's Performance

Items	Frequency	Percentage
Excellent	80	28.57%
Good	145	51.8%
Average	32	11.42%
Poor	20	7.14%
Very Poor	3	1.07%
Total	280	100

Table 4.10: Public Opinion of ELECAM Performance So Far

Concerning the public rating of ELECAM's performance so far, respondents to the questionnaire of this study indicated, as the table above illustrates, that the EMB performance is mostly Good (51.8%). Second on the scale were those who rated ELECAM excellent with 28.57%, followed by Average with 11.42%, Poor with 7.14%, and Very Poor with only 1.07%. This suggests that, overall, despite the challenges and shortcomings, most respondents believe that ELECAM is doing a good job of analyzing public awareness of the causes of voter apathy in Cameroon.

4.2.5. Analysis of the Public Awareness of the Causes of Voter Apathy in Cameroon

Items	Frequency	Percentage
Votes will not count	62	22%
Insecurity	106	38%
Lack of confidence in political leaders	34	12%
No confidence in EMBs	56	20%
Cumbersome voting procedure	8	3%
Changing election dates (roster)	6	2%
Electoral violence	0	-
No time	8	3%
Total	280	100

Table 4.11: Awareness of the Causes of Voter Apathy in Cameroon
Source: Field Survey, 2022

The table above illustrates respondents' opinions regarding the causes of voter apathy in Cameroon. The majority of respondents believe that low voter turnout results from a sense of insecurity. In recent years, the country has faced security threats from several sectors. The North-West and South-West regions have been shaken by an armed insurgency, while the Northern regions have been under threat from Boko Haram for almost a decade now.

The East is also under constant threats to peace and security emanating from the troubled Central African Republic. These threats to peace and security have led to low voter turnout, with 38% of respondents holding this opinion.

22% of respondents believe voting is a waste of time, as votes will not count because the winners and losers are already known even before the elections. Another 20% believe that there is low voter turnout because Cameroonians do not trust EMBs. This is closely followed by 12% who think the lack of confidence in political leaders is the cause of voter apathy. 3% of voters believe that the electoral procedure is too cumbersome and that they have no time, while finally, 2% opine that changes in dates and the electoral roster are the causes of voter apathy.

There are many causes, as the respondents are mostly evenly divided regarding the causes of voter apathy in Cameroon.

4.2.6. Analysis of the Level of Electoral Communication by EMBs in Cameroon

Items	Frequency	Percentage
Very satisfactory	55	19.6%
Satisfactory	106	37.8%
Neutral	3	1.07%
Unsatisfactory	56	20%
Very unsatisfactory	60	21.4%
Total	280	100

Table 4.12: Electoral Communication by EMBs in Cameroon
Source: Field Survey, 2022

The table above illustrates the respondents' opinions when probed on the level of electoral communication by EMBs. The emphasis here was to measure how effectively EMBs have communicated before and after elections in Cameroon. Most respondents (37.8%) maintained that the communication was satisfactory, as opposed to 21.4% and 20% for very unsatisfactory and unsatisfactory, respectively. 19.6% of respondents rated electoral communication very acceptable, while 1.07% disagreed.

The very divided opinions indicate that EMBs in Cameroon still have work to do regarding electoral communication. However, the number of opinions saying satisfactory communication indicates ELECAM, in particular, is doing a lot to communicate before and after elections.

4.2.7. Analysis of Respondents' Views on the Need for Democratic Electoral Reforms

Items	Frequency	Percentage
Elections are very satisfactory, and no reforms are needed	25	9%
Elections are satisfactory	62	22%
No opinion	0	0
Elections are unsatisfactory, and reforms are needed	193	68%
Total	280	100%

Table 4.13: The Need for Democratic Electoral Reforms in Cameroon
Source: Field Survey, 2022

The table above illustrates that 68% of respondents believe that elections are not democratic enough and that electoral reforms are necessary. This was followed by 22% who believe elections are democratic enough and 9% who indicated that elections are very satisfactory, meaning reforms are unnecessary.

This suggests that most respondents believe electoral reforms are necessary to ensure proper democracy prevails.

4.2.8. Analysis of Respondents' Views on ELECAM's Independence

Items	Frequency	Percentage
Yes, ELECAM can be independent of government	80	28.6%
No, ELECAM cannot be independent of government	200	71.4%
Total	280	100%

Table 4.14: The Need For EMBs to Be Independent of Government
Source: Field Survey, 2022

Table 4.14 illustrates respondents' views when asked if they felt the government has the political will and capability to sustainably secure democracy by staying off ELECAM. The majority (71.4%) of respondents said no, expressing their uncertainty about ELECAM ever being independent and autonomous, while 28.6% of respondents answered yes. It indicates that respondents realize how much the government is resolved to control and have a say in EMB's operations and existence.

4.2.9. Analysis of Respondents' Views on Whether or Not the Opposition Stands a Chance of Seizing Power through the Ballot Box

Items	Frequency	Percentage
Yes, they have every chance of winning	80	28.6%
No, they cannot win the ruling party through the ballot box	200	71.4%
Total	280	100%

Table 4.15: The Chances of Opposition Parties to Genuinely Win Elections
Source: Field Survey, 2022

The table above shows respondents' views when asked if they felt that opposition parties had a real chance to win elections. 61.4% said no, as opposed to 38.6% that said yes. This suggests that most respondents believe the electoral system currently does not permit opposition parties to effectively challenge the ruling party. A fair, just, transparent, and independent system may imply that the playing field is level for all parties to compete for power and have an equal chance.

4.2.10. Analysis of Respondents' Views on Internet Voting to Increase Turnout

Items	Frequency	Percentage
Yes, internet voting will increase turnout	220	78.6%
No, internet voting will not work	60	21.4%
Total	280	100%

Table 4.16: The Institution of Internet Voting to Increase Turnout
Source: Field Survey, 2022

The table above shows that 78.6% of respondents, as opposed to 21.4%, think internet voting, if instituted in Cameroon, will increase voter turnout and make elections more credible. Although internet voting presents challenges and costs, it is a way of making elections more participatory, and respondents generally shared this opinion. Especially given the constraints of insecurity and the health pandemic, internet voting can significantly increase voter turnout if well managed.

4.2.11. Analysis of Respondents' Views on the Use of DREs as a Means of Increasing Turnout

Items	Frequency	Percentage
Yes, DREs, if used, will increase turnout	123	43.9%
No, DREs will not work	75	26.8%
I have no idea about DREs	82	29.3%
Total	280	100%

Table 4.17: The DREs to Increase Turnout
Source: Field Survey, 2022

As illustrated by the table above, 43.9% of respondents thought using DREs would be a game-changer and increase turnout and election credibility, while 26.8% were of the contrary opinion, and 29.3% had no idea what DREs were or if they would work. This indicates a weak level of electoral culture, a testament to the insufficient electoral knowledge among many respondents, who have yet to acquire it. On the other hand, this issue suggests that most respondents believe DREs can increase voter turnout if effectively utilized and should be considered by EMBs in Cameroon.

4.3. Hypotheses Testing

This study was guided by the following hypotheses, which we seek to test at this juncture:

- Hi: EMBs' inability to inspire trust and work independently stems from the legal framework that created them.
- Ho: The inability of EMBs to inspire trust and to work independently does not stem from the nature of the legal framework putting them in place.
- Hi: Government heavy-handedness, lack of genuine autonomy, voter apathy, and corruption have plagued both NEO and ELECAM.
- Ho: Government heavy-handedness, lack of genuine autonomy, voter apathy, and corruption are not challenges that have plagued both NEO and ELECAM.
- Hi: The timing of elections, electoral communication, party politics, the nature of the electoral law, and registration procedures are some of the main factors that affect voter turnout in Cameroon.
- Ho: The timing of elections, electoral communication, party politics, the nature of the electoral law, and registration procedures are not some of the main factors that affect voter turnout in Cameroon.
- Hi: To increase voter turnout, the framework, procedures, and operations have been starkly shifted from NEO to ELECAM.
- Ho: No stark framework, procedures, and operations have shifted from NEO to ELECAM to increase voter turnout.

4.3.1. Test of Hypothesis One

Issues on the Frequindepenciesdence of EMBs and the trust they inspire	Perception of Respondents					
	SA	A	N	SD	D	Total
The Independent Electoral Commission is fair, honest and just in their dealings?	10 3.57%	16 5.71%	4 1.2%	113 40.35%	137 48.92%	280 100%
The nature of elections is democratic enough and need no reforms	3 1.07%	55 19.64%	50 17.85%	92 32.85%	80 28.57%	280 100%
The government has the political will and capability to sustainably secure democracy by staying off ELECAM?	30 10.71%	61 21.78%	5 1.78%	120 42.85%	64 22.85%	280 100%
Total	43	132	59	325	281	840
Percentage	5.11%	15.71%	7.02%	38.69%	33.45%	100%

Table 4.18: Observed Frequencies
Source: Field Survey, 2022

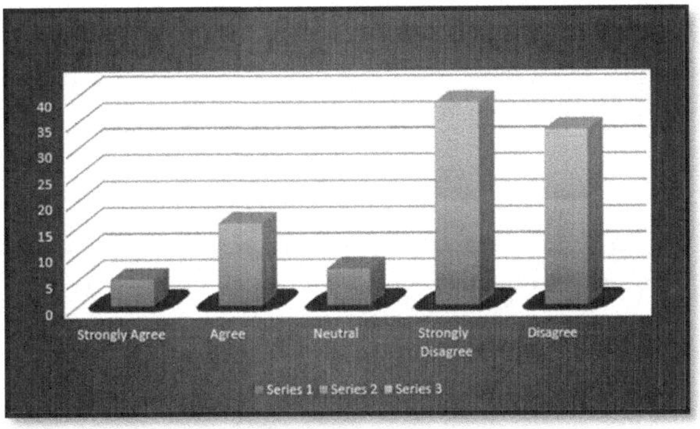

Figure 4.7: Distribution of Respondents According to H1
Source: Field Survey, 2022

No	Categories	Fo	Fe	Fo-Fe	$(Fo-Fe)^2$	(-)
1	R1C1	10	14.3	-4.3	18.49	1.29
2	R1C2	16	44	-28	784	17.82
3	R1C3	4	19.7	-15.7	246.49	12.51
4	R1C4	113	108.3	4.7	22.09	0.20
5	R1C5	137	93.7	43.3	1874.89	20.01
6	R2C1	3	14.3	-11.3	127.69	8.93
7	R2C2	55	44	11	121	2.75
8	R2C3	50	19.7	30.3	918.09	46.60
9	R2C4	92	108.3	-16.3	265.69	2.45
10	R2C5	80	93.7	-13.7	187.69	2.00
11	R3C1	30	14.3	15.7	246.49	17.24
12	R3C2	61	44	17	289	6.57
13	R3C3	5	19.7	-14.7	216.09	10.97
14	R3C4	120	108.3	11.7	136.89	1.26
15	R3C5	64	93.7	-29.7	882.09	9.41
	Total					**160.03**

Table 4.19: Distribution Showing Calculation of Chi-Square Using Fo and Fe

Source: Field Survey, 2022

$X^2 = \underline{(O-E)^2}$ E

Therefore Chi-Square = 160.23

But Degree of Freedom = (nc-1) (nr-1)

= (5-1) (3-1)

= 4 x 2

DF = 8

At a Significance Level of 0.05,

Table or Critical Value = 46.60

- Hi: The inability of EMBs to inspire trust and to work independently stems from the nature of the legal framework putting them in place.
- Ho: The inability of EMBs to inspire trust and to work independently does not stem from the nature of the legal framework putting them in place.

From the preceding, the test of hypothesis one reveals that the chi-square (χ^2) value of 160.03 is far greater than the table value of 46.60 at a significance level of 0.05. The alternative hypothesis, which states that the inability of EMBs to inspire trust and work independently stems from the very nature of the legal framework putting them in place, is accepted. On the other hand, the null hypothesis, which states that the inability of EMBs to inspire trust and work independently is not a result of the legal framework putting them in place, is rejected.

The results presented above align with the questionnaire responses, which also indicated that most respondents disagreed or strongly disagreed with the tentative answer to the issue raised.

4.3.2. Test of Hypothesis Two

Issues of Government heavy-handedness, lack of genuine autonomy, voter apathy, and corruption are challenges that have plagued both NEO and ELECAM alike	Perception of Respondents					
	SA	A	N	SD	D	Total
1. Voter apathy (low voter turnout) is less pronounced under ELECAM than NEO/MINATD	137 48.92%	59 21.07%	4 1.42%	30 10.71%	50 17.85%	280 100%
2. ELECAM faces the same operational challenges and structural problems like NEO/MINATD	116 41.42%	80 28.57%	0 0%	4 1.42%	80 28.57%	280 100%
3. Government heavy-handedness, lack of genuine autonomy, voter Apathy and corruption are the main challenges that have plagued both NEO and ELECAM alike	130 46.42%	57 20.35%	5 1.78%	50 17.85%	38 13.57%	280 100%
Total	383	196	9	84	168	840
Percentage	45.59%	23.33%	1.07%	10%	20%	100%

Table 4.20: Observed Frequencies
Source: Field Survey, 2022

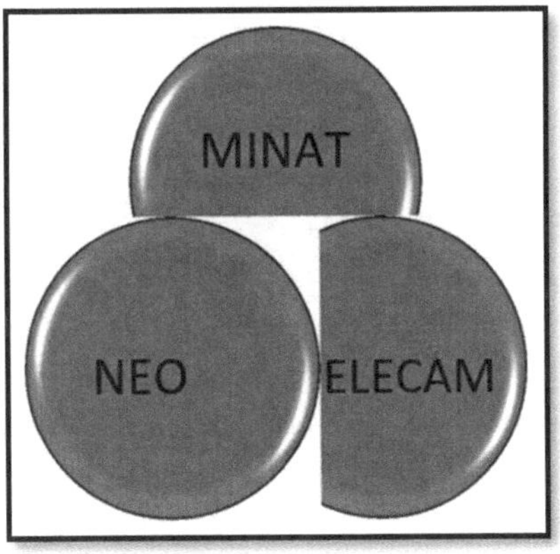

Figure 4.8: Illustration of an Intersection Showing Overlapping Challenges Facing All EMBs in Cameroon
Source: Field Survey, 2022

No	Categories	Fo	Fe	Fo-Fe	$(Fo-Fe)^2$	(-)
1	R1C1	137	127.67	9.33	87.0489	0.68
2	R1C2	59	65.33	-6.33	40.0689	0.61
3	R1C3	4	3	1	1	0.33
4	R1C4	30	28	2	4	0.14
5	R1C5	50	56	-6	36	0.64
6	R2C1	116	127.67	-11.67	136.1889	1.07
7	R2C2	80	65.33	14.67	215.2089	3.29
8	R2C3	0	3	-3	9	3.00
9	R2C4	4	28	-24	576	20.57
10	R2C5	80	56	24	576	10.29
11	R3C1	130	127.67	2.33	5.4289	0.04
12	R3C2	57	65.33	-8.33	69.3889	1.06
13	R3C3	5	3	2	4	1.33
14	R3C4	50	28	22	484	17.29
15	R3C5	38	56	-18	324	5.79
	Total					**66.14**

Table 4.21: Distribution Showing the Calculation of Chi-Square Using Fo and Fe
Source: Field Survey, 2022

$X^2 = (O-E)^2 E$

Therefore, Chi-Square = 66.14

But Degree of Freedom = (nc-1) (nr-1)

= (5-1) (3-1)

= 4 x 2

DF = 8

At a Significance Level of 0.05,

Table or Critical Value = 3.00

- Hi: Government heavy-handedness, lack of genuine autonomy, voter apathy, and corruption have plagued both NEO and ELECAM.
- Ho: Government heavy-handedness, lack of genuine autonomy, voter apathy, and corruption are not challenges that have plagued both NEO and ELECAM.

From the above statistical analysis, the test of hypothesis two indicates that the chi-square (x^2) value results of 66.14 are more significant than the table value of 3.00 at a significance level of 0.05. The alternative hypothesis is, therefore, deemed significant and accepted, while the null hypothesis is rejected.

4.3.3. Test of Hypothesis Three

Issues on the timing of elections, electoral Frequencies communication, party politics, the nature of the electoral law, and registration procedures are some of the main factors that affect voter turnout in Cameroon	Perception of Respondents					
	SA	A	N	SD	D	Total
1. There is high awareness of the holding of elections each time there are elections in Cameroon?	135 48.21%	92 32.86%	1 0.36%	20 7.14%	32 11.43%	280 100%
2.ELECAM/NEO have been commendable in communicating Before and after Elections?	76 27.14%	162 57.86%	0 0%	20 7.14%	22 7.85%	280 100%
3. The nature of electoral landscape is democratic enough and needs no reforms?	29 10.36%	30 10.71%	3 1.07%	80 28.57%	138 49.28%	280 100%
4. The political parties in The opposition has a chance Against the ruling party through elections?	40 14.28%	80 28.57%	0 0%	102 36.42%	58 20.71%	280 100%
Total	280	364	4	222	250	1120

Table 4.22: Observed Frequencies
Source: Field Survey, 2022

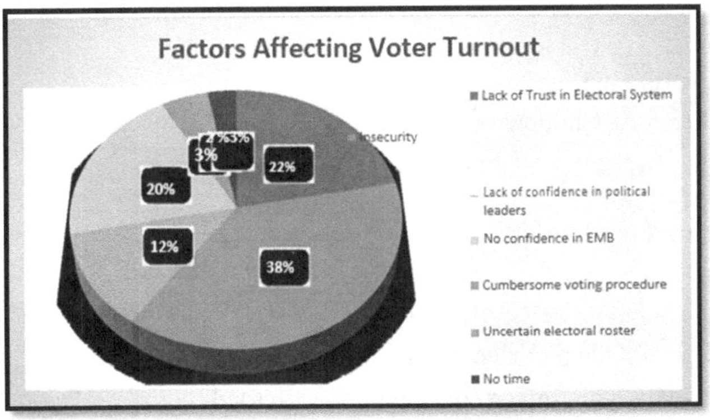

Figure 4.9: Illustration of Factors That Affect Voter Turnout in Cameroon

No	Categories	Fo	Fe	Fo-Fe	$(Fo-Fe)^2$	(-)
1	R1C1	135	70	65	4225	60.36
2	R1C2	92	91	1	1	0.01
3	R1C3	1	1	0	0	0.00
4	R1C4	20	55.5	-35.5	1260.25	22.71
5	R1C5	32	62.5	-30.5	930.25	14.88
6	R2C1	76	70	6	36	0.51
7	R2C2	162	91	71	5041	55.40
8	R2C3	0	1	-1	1	1.00
9	R2C4	20	55.5	-35.5	1260.25	22.71
10	R2C5	22	62.5	-40.5	1640.25	26.24
11	R3C1	29	70	-41	1681	24.01
12	R3C2	30	91	-61	3721	40.89
13	R3C3	3	1	2	4	4.00
14	R3C4	80	55.5	24.5	600.25	10.82
15	R3C5	138	62.5	75.5	5700.25	91.20
16	R4C1	40	70	-30	900	12.86
17	R4C2	80	91	-11	121	1.33
18	R4C3	0	1	-1	1	1.00
19	R4C4	102	55.5	46.5	2162.25	38.96
20	R4C5	58	62.5	-4.5	20.25	0.32
	Total					**429.21**

Table 4.23: Distribution Showing the Calculation of Chi-Square Using Fo And Fe
Source: Field Survey, 2022

$X^2 = (O\text{-}E)^2E$
Therefore, Chi-Square = 429.21
But Degree of Freedom = (nc-1) (nr-1)
= (5-1) (4-1)
= 4 x 3
DF = 12
At a Significance Level of 0.05,
Table or Critical Value = 40.89

- Hi: The timing of elections, electoral communication, party politics, the nature of the electoral law, and registration procedures are some of the main factors that affect voter turnout in Cameroon.
- Ho: The timing of elections, electoral communication, party politics, the nature of the electoral law, and registration procedures are not some of the main factors that affect voter turnout in Cameroon.

From the above statistical analysis, the test of hypothesis three indicates that the chi-square (x^2) value of 429.21 is greater than the table value of 40.89 at a significance level of 0.05. Therefore, the alternative hypothesis is deemed significant and accepted, while the null hypothesis is rejected.

Furthermore, this outcome aligns with the questionnaire results, as most respondents (32.5%) agreed that the variables raised by this hypothesis affect voter turnout and can cause voter apathy.

4.3.4. Test of Hypothesis Four

Issues on whether FrequenciesS/Nthere has been a stark shift in framework, procedures and operations from NEO to ELECAM in order to increase voter turnout		Perception of Respondents					
		SA	A	N	SD	D	Total
1	You are aware of the requirements ____ to partake in elections.	98 35%	86 30.71%	2 0.71%	30 10.71%	64 22.85%	280 100%
2	ELECAM's performance has been excellent so far.	55 19.64%	132 47.14	0 0%	28 10.02%	65 23.2%	280 100%
3	Internet voting in your country can be installed as a means of increasing voter turnout?	140 50.02%	61 21.78%	5 1.78%	20 7.14%	54 19.28%	280 100%
4	Direct Recording Electronic voting Machines (DREs) in voting in your country will be good as a means of increasing voter turnout?	57 20.36%	80 28.56%	40 14.29	33 11.76%	70 25%	280 100%
	Total	350	359	47	111	253	1120
	Percentage	31.25%	32.05%	4.19%	9.91%	22.59%	100%

Table 4.24: Observed Frequencies

Source: Field Survey, 2022

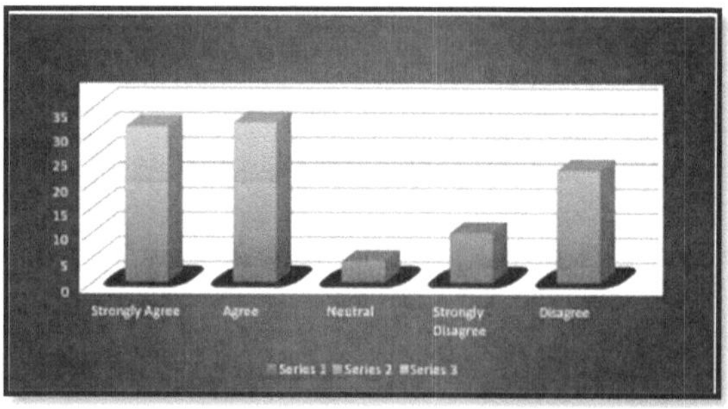

Figure 4.10 : Distribution of Respondents According to H5

Source: Field Survey, 2022

No	Categories	Fo	Fe	Fo-Fe	(Fo-Fe)^2	(-)
1	R1C1	98	87.5	10.5	110.25	1.26
2	R1C2	86	89.75	-3.75	14.0625	0.16
3	R1C3	2	11.5	-9.5	90.25	7.85
4	R1C4	30	27.75	2.25	5.0625	0.18
5	R1C5	64	63.25	0.75	0.5625	0.01
6	R2C1	55	87.5	-32.5	1056.25	12.07
7	R2C2	32	89.75	-57.75	3335.0625	37.16
8	R2C3	0	11.5	-11.5	132.25	11.50
9	R2C4	28	27.75	0.25	0.0625	0.00
10	R2C5	65	63.25	1.75	3.0625	0.05
11	R3C1	140	87.5	52.5	2756.25	31.50
12	R3C2	61	89.75	-28.75	826.5625	9.21
13	R3C3	5	11.5	-6.5	42.25	3.67
14	R3C4	20	27.75	-7.75	60.0625	2.16
15	R3C5	54	63.25	-9.25	85.5625	1.35
16	R4C1	57	87.5	-30.5	930.25	10.63
17	R4C2	80	89.75	-9.75	95.0625	1.06
18	R4C3	40	11.5	28.5	812.25	70.63
19	R4C4	33	27.75	5.25	27.5625	0.99
20	R4C5	70	63.25	6.75	45.5625	0.72
	Total					**202.17**

Table 4.25: Distribution Showing the Calculation of Chi-Square Using Fo and Fe

Source: Field Survey, 2022

$X^2 = (O-E)^2 E$

Therefore, Chi-Square = 202.17

But Degree of Freedom = (nc-1) (nr-1)

= (5-1) (4-1)

= 4 x 3

DF = 12

At a Significance Level of 0.05,

Table or Critical Value = 9.21

- Hi: To increase voter turnout, the framework, procedures, and operations have been starkly shifted from NEO to ELECAM.
- Ho: No stark framework, procedures, and operations have shifted from NEO to ELECAM to increase voter turnout.

From the above statistical analysis, the hypothesis four test indicates that the chi-square (x^2) value results at 202.17 are more significant than the table value of 9.21 at a significance level of 0.05. The alternative hypothesis is, therefore, deemed significant and accepted, while the null hypothesis is rejected.

Although respondents did not overwhelmingly indicate that they are aware of ELECAM changing the frameworks and procedures to boost voter turnout, a significant number agreed.

4.4. Interview Presentation Analysis (15 Interviews)

The interviews were structured according to the four research objectives to complement the questionnaires. Of the 280 respondents who participated in the study, 15 key informant interviews were conducted with top officials of ELECAM, who mainly had worked for both MINAT and NEO in the past (8), some political party scribes (4), and some civil society leaders (3), bringing the total to 15 interviewees.

4.4.1. Qualitative Analysis of Interviews Relating to the Legal Frameworks Governing EMBs and How They Have Affected NEO/MINAT and ELECAM

The legal frameworks managing EMBs are the lifeline on which these institutions exist. They set prerogatives and define the institutions' roles and duties. The legal texts further depict their functioning (managerial, financial, operational) and set their limits. Therefore, an EMB can be understood as destined to be flawed before it goes operational and manages any elections. As revealed by 80% of the respondents who worked for MINAT, NEO, and ELECAM, the legal framework in place was such that government oversight was ensured. This implied a need for greater managerial and, especially, financial autonomy. "Being an appointed official makes one's every move to be in alignment with the powers that be. Appointments come with benefits, and not toeing the line would result in losing one's position and the benefits that come along" (KI 3, 2022).

Civil Society and opposition political leaders also heavily criticized the legal framework for being too rigorous. To them, it allows the government to appoint current and former civil servants to EMBs. More significantly, individuals with strong ties to the ruling party are appointed and commonly perpetuate the ruling party's wishes while in office.

4.4.2. Qualitative Analysis of the Intrinsic Challenges That Have Affected EMBs in Cameroon (NEO and ELECAM)

The interviews revealed that NEO, MINAT, and ELECAM have dealt mainly with the same intrinsic challenges over the years.

92% of interviewees who had served in previous dispensations and are now at ELECAM indicated that funds are a significant challenge. The institutions have no actual means of generating their funds, and a constitutional provision allocates funds to them to function and achieve their targets. Due to their lack of financial independence, all have relied on government funding, which comes more quickly than they would prefer and, most importantly, strips them of their freedom —a characteristic crucial in defining an EMB.

The interviews also allowed the research to unravel training and development challenges. It was revealed that there has been a cruel lack of training and professional development within the EMBs. This was especially so when new election management and practice technologies were involved.

Again, the interviews allowed the study to explore the infrastructural challenges that significantly impacted NEO and MINAT. These institutions had no premises, resorting to sharing premises with some ministerial departments. This meant their security and privacy were not guaranteed.

This challenge only applies to ELECAM, which boasts its premises across the national territory today.

These challenges came across as significant challenges for the EMBs.

4.4.3. Qualitative Analysis to Assess the Main Causes of Voter Apathy in Cameroon

The leading causes of voter apathy were largely unraveled using the questionnaires. The interviews were similar. However, while ELECAM officials would not blame themselves or their institutions, civil society leaders and political parties went all out to blame the electoral laws and the lack of independence of the EMBs, which have killed the trust and confidence of potential voters.

ELECAM officials and former staff of the previous EMB dispensations indicated that low voter turnout in the past was due to poor communication and the lack of funds to elaborate a broader reaction scheme. These days, factors such as insecurity and inconsistencies within political parties that choose to stay out of certain elections can better account for low voter turnout.

4.4.4. Qualitative Analysis of Interviews to Evaluate the Legal, Institutional, and Operational Measures Made by EMBs in Cameroon (NEO and ELECAM) to Increase Voter Turnout

The interviews of ELECAM top officials permitted this study to discover the various efforts made to increase voter turnout. These efforts are those which were not created by previous EMBs and are as follows:

ELECAM has decentralized registration on electoral registers, with registration booths scattered throughout the major towns in Cameroon.

ELECAM has also ensured that registrations are completed at several periods each year, even when elections are not in view. This enables less congestion for registration when elections are near.

Additionally, recent efforts have been made to alleviate the constraints at the registration booths, simplify the procedures, and make them more user-friendly.

There is an increasing chance of internet voting with ELECAM to overcome the challenge of insecurity during voting days.

The interviewees claimed that these efforts are aimed at increasing voter turnout and curbing voter apathy.

4.5. Discussion of Findings

Credible elections are today considered the cornerstone of an inclusive and sustainable democracy. The credibility of elections in many struggling democracies, such as Cameroon, has been compromised by flaws characterized by fraud and numerous irregularities that render the electoral process a farce, making the people's will meaningless and contributing to worrying voter apathy. This state of affairs has been attributed to the lack of a credible election management body to manage the electoral process in an unbiased, transparent, and independent manner. EMBs play a pivotal role in the electoral process and must adhere to specific minimum standards to ensure the ballot outcome is acceptable to all stakeholders. These minimum standards, comprising internationally accepted norms and practices, have been succinctly elucidated in this work. Using these standards, it has been amply demonstrated that the management of elections in Cameroon during the NEO/MINADT era was marred by numerous flaws and irregularities, as the electoral management institutions failed to meet the requisite international standards. It has been demonstrated that these institutions lacked the necessary legal safeguards for their independence, impartiality, and effectiveness, which ultimately led to unpopular elections marked by voter apathy.

The flawed nature of elections in Cameroon has stalled the drive for democratization and reinstated autocratic rule, masquerading as democracy. The electoral process has been subverted. Elections lost significance because more credible institutions needed to manage them in Cameroon. They became a mere ceremony through which the ruling elite validated their legitimacy without affecting the people's will.

The attempts of the government to remedy these problems through the creation of ELECAM are half-hearted and highly dubious because ELECAM still retains most of its predecessors' major structural and institutional weaknesses and fails to adhere, on many counts, to the minimum standards set out. A careful examination of the significant facets of ELECAM's legislative and institutional framework has demonstrated that the government, especially the Presidency of the Republic, still wields enormous and arbitrary powers over ELECAM and has multiple avenues of manipulating the institution to serve its whims and caprices. ELECAM was designed as an independent electoral institution; however, compared to similar bodies worldwide, especially the IEC of South Africa, one discovers that it lacks all the safeguards against interference and impartiality. It is, therefore, highly doubtful that ELECAM can turn the tide of flawed elections and ensure transparent and credible ballot and popular polls despite its commendable strides to increase voter registration and turnout.

Chapter 5 | On the Relevance of Election Management Bodies

This chapter deals with general election management, particularly in Cameroon during the MINADT/NEO to ELECAM eras. It sets out to analyze and discuss the findings from the key informant interviews with stakeholders, on the one hand, and to qualitatively demonstrate that EMBs in Cameroon are set up with flaws that result in voter apathy on the other hand. The chapter examines the institutional framework within which elections are managed and highlights the significant irregularities that lead to voter apathy. The chapter further assesses ELECAM and discusses voter turnout and apathy in relation to the case under investigation.

Before exploring EMBs in Cameroon, it is essential to outline the concept and global standards associated with them.

5.1. The Concept of Election Management and Election Management Bodies

The election management body (EMB) is the authority charged with administering the electoral process. Due to the complexity and extraordinary skills necessary for electoral management, a specific institution is usually required to manage the electoral activities. Such bodies have a variety of forms and sizes, with several titles, including Electoral Commission, Electoral Council, Electoral Unit, Department of Elections, Electoral Board, and so on.

Elections, or voting in general, are often among the most significant activities organized in a democratic country. They are a complex administrative operation implemented in a politically charged atmosphere.

Traditionally, the management of multiparty democratic elections has not been a newsworthy topic and has been kept under a low profile compared to other political activities. The accomplishment of many electoral processes largely went unnoticed, except for those directly affected, like the losing political parties, when they set their complaints against the election conduct and results. However, this situation changed within the last quarter of a century. The administrative details of democratic elections began to be perceived and reported as a central issue to measure: the rights of individuals to vote and participate in governance, the sustainability and transparency of the democratic process, transitions from authoritarianism, reconciliation, conflict resolution, and so on. Political parties, the media, and international and domestic election observers (Dundas, 1993) have scrutinized electoral management more closely.

During the same period, there have also been unprecedented electoral reforms around the world, driven by the perception in political elites that changing political and social environments required a rethink and improvement of electoral management, by the critical attention of the academic institutes, media, election observers, and by the emergence of global and regional organizations promoting democracy. At that time, the lack of credibility and diminished public confidence in election results, and thus in electoral management, was an outcome of the lack of experience and the knowledge gap in technical and administrative instruments to manage elections; this factor was overtaken by many electoral institutions in many democracies as an important motivation to achieve electoral management reforms.

Although many democratic states have been focusing on electoral system reform to enhance representation, reforms in the instruments for organizing and managing electoral processes have been equally important. These include the establishment of autonomous electoral management bodies with wide-ranging authorities and responsibilities, as well as improving the efficiency of electoral management bodies to deliver better-quality electoral services, while enhancing the freedom and fairness of electoral processes (Goodwin-Gill, 1998).

As a term, the election management body has been coined to refer to the body responsible for electoral management, regardless of the broader institutional framework applied. EMB is an organization or institute with the principal purpose of managing all or some of the core elements essential for conducting elections and directing democracy activities such as referendums, recall votes and citizens' initiatives. These core elements include:

- Determining who has the right and is eligible to participate in voting or not

- Accepting and validating the nominations of election candidates from individuals and political parties
- Preparing and opening the polling centers (which includes all the procedural and logistical efforts and preparations)
- Dealing with electoral complaints and disputes
- Declaring the results of elections or the voting process in general, and some EMBs may be responsible for electoral boundary delimitation (IFES, 2007: 59).

If various bodies manage these core elements, all bodies with a share of these responsibilities can be considered EMBs. However, an EMB may also be a stand-alone institution or a distinct administrative department within a larger institution, which may also have non-perministrative duties.

In addition to these core elements, EMBs may undertake other tasks that support and assist in the final conduct of elections and voting processes, such as voter registration, voter education, media monitoring, and arranging electoral observation.

However, any governmental or non-governmental institute that does not have the direct responsibility to deal with any electoral responsibilities other than some specific elements like electoral dispute resolution, election media monitoring, and voter education (such as electoral courts, media monitoring commissions, and civic education commissions) is not considered to be an EMB because it is not managing any of the essential elements of elections as identified above (Dundas, 1993).

Election management or election administration, as it is commonly called, is an administrative undertaking of considerable size and complexity involving a series of operations, actors and institutions, and intricate monitoring activities (Baxter, 1994: 1).

According to Trebilcock & Chitalkar (2009:97), Election administration is the broad institutional framework for voting and electoral competition. It involves rulemaking, i.e., designing the basic rules of the electoral process; rule application, i.e., applying those rules to organize the electoral process; and rule implementation, i.e., resolving disputes arising within the electoral process.

Election management is the mechanics of how elections are run, ranging from preparation for the election and the methods by which people cast their ballots to how the winners are declared. It involves a whole range of activities, including running elections on election day as well as all pre and post-election activities such as maintaining voter registration lists, drawing electoral boundaries, selecting polling sites, procuring equipment, recruiting and training poll officials, canvassing the vote and implementing the electoral law (IDEA, 1997:7). Election management is complex and requires specialist skills to manage the electoral process effectively. This makes the establishment of specialized institutions responsible for election management very necessary. Many such institutions exist worldwide in various forms, shapes, and sizes. They are called the 'Election Commission,' 'Department of Elections,' 'Electoral Council,' 'Electoral Unit,' or 'Electoral Board.'

The term 'electoral management body' is a generic term coined to refer to the bodies responsible for managing elections, despite differences in form, size, and title. Simply put, an electoral management body is the formal unit accountable for organizing and conducting elections (Mozaffar, 2002). According to the ACE Electoral Knowledge Network, an EMB is an organization that was founded for and is legally responsible for managing one or more of the essential elements for the conduct of elections and direct democracy instruments such as referendums, citizen initiatives, and recall votes if those are part of the legal framework (Ace Electoral Knowledge Network, 2010).

The essential elements referred to above include determining who is eligible to vote, receiving and validating the nominations of electoral participants, conducting balloting, counting votes, and totaling votes from various polling stations. Depending on the legal framework, most EMBs' mandates also include the authority to conduct voter registration, boundary delimitation, voter education, electoral dispute resolution, oversight of campaign financing, and procurement of electoral materials (ibid).

5.2. Types of Electoral Management Bodies

Different organizational approaches exist to designing and conducting elections, but all electoral managers face many common themes and issues. Electoral bodies primarily reflect electoral systems, political and geographical boundaries, and demographic factors of the state. In some classic democracies, the electorate accepts governmental officials on both national and local levels to manage election management due to their neutrality. Ordinary courts have authority over electoral disputes, as they have a tradition of fairness and enjoy the voters' confidence.

Elsewhere, in emerging democracies, the trend is to establish independent EMBs as an essential step in building and sustaining a tradition of impartiality, thereby building the confidence of voters and political parties in the electoral process. However, the lack of a universally recognized standard for independence means that the term 'independent EMB' refers to autonomy and impartiality.

Based on various standards, the types of election management bodies can be classified; however, three essential criteria generally exist to categorize EMBs. These criteria are:

- The independence of functions (independent, governmental, and mixed EMBs)
- The geographical jurisdiction (centralized and decentralized EMBs)
- The duration of jurisdiction (permanent and temporary EMBs)

In addition to these three main criteria, there is a limited type of EMB called "International EMBs," which exclusively deals with transitional election management processes (Lopez Pintor, 2000: 21-30).

Studies on EMB types around the globe have come up with three broad categories into which any EMB can be classified, depending on aspects such as institutional arrangements, composition, formal accountability, funding, and the terms of office of members of the EMB. These categories are the non-autonomous EMB (located within the formal government bureaucracy), the semi-autonomous EMB (situated within the formal government bureaucracy but under the supervision of an autonomous body established for that purpose), and the autonomous EMB, commonly referred to as an Independent Electoral Mission (Trebilcock & Chitalkar, 2009).

The non-autonomous EMB is said to follow a governmental approach because regular civil servants mostly conduct elections, and the electoral process is entirely in the hands of the government. This EMB type is prevalent in Western European countries where the democratic culture is well-developed. This EMB type is exemplified by France, where election management at the national level is entirely in the hands of the Ministry of the Interior.

The semi-autonomous or mixed model is an EMB type in which elections are managed by the executive branch through a ministry with some level of oversight provided by an independent component of the EMB, taking, for example, what obtains in Senegal, where the MINADT manages elections under the supervision of the Commission Electoral Nationale Autonome (CENA).

The autonomous EMB, or what is commonly called the Independent Electoral Commission, is the most prevalent among EMB types in the world today. A survey by R. Lopez-Pintor reveals that 53% of EMBs worldwide follow the autonomous model (2000, 19-30). First introduced in India and Costa Rica, this EMB is wholly dissociated from the government and has full responsibility for the entire election process. Elections are managed by an EMB, which is institutionally independent and autonomous from the executive branch of government, as is the case with the EMBs of South Africa, Ghana, and Kenya.

This model has some distinctive advantages. The EMB has an electoral corporate identity. It manages its budget, thereby enjoying financial autonomy and accountability. Therefore, it is in control of its funding and electoral implementation. The EMB is not accountable to a government ministry or department, but may be responsible to the legislature, the judiciary, or the head of state. The EMB possesses a high level of technical efficiency due to its permanent professional personnel.

The EMB is also less likely to be subject to restrictions on who can be involved in electoral management, as it may be able to draw from outside talent. Its concentration in electoral business may result in better planning and more cohesive institutionalization of election tasks.

In Cameroon, all the institutions are highly subservient to the executive, and the President of the Republic wields extraordinary and sometimes arbitrary powers that he can use to manipulate the institutions. Since the advent of political pluralism in Cameroon, the government has constantly demonstrated its zeal for influencing elections, and public confidence in the government's ability to organize credible elections has been shallow. It is, therefore, of utmost importance, in the present dispensation, to establish an EMB with all the guarantees of independence and credibility. A fully autonomous EMB is most suited to inspire confidence in a distrustful, polarized, and previously disenfranchised electorate.

Below is a table that illustrates the distinctive characteristics of the main EMB types in the world. The table is further buttressed by a categorization done by other scholars:

Aspects of The model And component EMB (s)	**Independent model** Independent EMB(s)	**Governmental model** Governmental EMB(s)	Mixed Model **Independent component** Component Independent EMB	**Governmental component** Component Governmental EMB
Institutional arrangement	Is institutionally independent of the executive branch of the Government	Is located within or under the direction of a Department of State and of / or Local Government	Is institutionally independent of the executive branch of the Government	Is situated in or under the direction of a Department of State and of / or Local Government
Implementation	Excessive full responsibility for implementation	Implementation is subject to the executive branch of government's direction	Has autonomy to monitor or supervise and, in some cases, set policy for implementation	Implementation is subject to the executive branch of government direction and monitoring or supervision, in some cases policy setting by independent components
Formal accountability	Does not report to the executive branch of government but, in very few exceptions, is formally accountable to the legislative, judiciary or Head of State	Fully responsible to the executive branch of government	Does not report to the executive branch of government and is officially accountable to the legislature, the judiciary, and the Head of State	Fully responsible to the executive branch of government
Powers	Has powers to develop the electoral regulatory framework independently under the law	Powers are limited to implementation.	Has powers to develop the electoral regulatory framework independently under the law. Monitors or supervises those who implement elections	Powers are limited to implementation
Composition	It is composed of members who are outside the executive branch	A minister or publicservant leads it. With very few	It is composed of members who are outside the executive branch	A minister or public servant leads it. Has no

	While in the EMB office.	Exceptions include no 'members,' only a secretariat.	while in the EMB office	'members,' only a secretariat.
Term of office	Offers security of tenure, but not necessarily fixed term of office.	Usually, there are no members; therefore, N/A secretariat staff are civil servants whose tenure needs to be secured.	Offers security of tenure but not necessarily fixed term of office.	The term of office needs to be secured.
Budget	Has or manages its budget independently of day-to-day governmental control	A budget is a component of a governmental ministry's or local authority's budget.	Has a separately allocated budget	A budget is a component of a governmental ministry's or local authority's budget.

Table 5.1: Characteristics of the Three Broad Models of Electoral Management and their Component EMBs
**A few countries, such as Hungary, use the Independent or Mixed Model of Electoral Management and do not have Independent EMBs with regulatory powers.*
Source: Adopted from the ACE Electoral Knowledge Network available on http://aceproject.org/ace-en/topics/ei/eif/eif01 (accessed 30/08/22)

5.2.1. Independent, Governmental, and Mixed Election Management Bodies

The Independence of election management bodies refers to the institutional autonomy of EMBs from the executive branch of the state, where the EMB has direct responsibility and authority to manage the elections, and it manages its budget; independent EMBs are composed of members who are outside the executive while in the EMB office. In other words, an independent EMB is not accountable to any governmental ministry or department. At the same time, it may be responsible to the legislative branch, the judicial authority, or the head of state. Independent EMBs may also enjoy some autonomy regarding financial and performance accountability unless that conflicts with other authorities, such as the legislatures or judiciary, when they have constitutional jurisdiction over all the state's institutions regarding economic and performance accountability (Wall & Ellis, 2006).

Some independent EMBs are divided into two sub-institutes or bodies due to the distribution of duties and responsibilities, both of which are self-governing and autonomous from the executive branch, and can thus be considered independent EMBs. Somehow, the mechanism of the two election management sub-bodies applies the same idea of the relationship between the legislative and executive branches of the state.

One of these sub-bodies is likely to have the task and authority for legislation and decisions about the electoral process. In contrast, the other one is responsible for conducting and implementing electoral operations (ibid). Such provisions may insulate the implementation of EMB from interference by the EMB policy in staffing and operational matters. Examples of this 'double-independent' framework under the Independent Model include Jamaica, Romania, Suriname and Vanuatu.

The Governmental EMBs refer to the situation where elections are implemented and managed by institutions belonging to the executive branch, typically through a ministry (mainly the Interior Ministry) and local governments. The members and officials of governmental EMBs are considered governmental officials, and their budget is always included within the whole budget of a ministry or local government. Thus, the functions and financial issues of governmental EMBs are subject to accountability by the executive branch through the usual mechanism of governmental accountability (Wall and Ellis, 2006: 56).

In mixed election management bodies, two or more EMBs work collectively to organize and manage the elections. Under mixed EMBs, there are usually dual or multiple structures, and the division between these structures is based on the functions and responsibilities assigned to each one.

Policy making, legislating, and supervising are likely to be assigned to independent EMBs, which are autonomous from the executive branch of the state (the same as in the independent EMBs). In contrast, the duties of conducting and managing elections are assigned to one or more bodies within the state's executive branch, such as a ministry, department, or local government (as precisely as in the governmental type of EMBs). Under the mixed model, elections are organized by the component governmental EMB, with some oversight provided by the independent EMB. The mixed model is used in France, Japan, Spain, and many former French colonies, especially in West Africa, such as Mali, Senegal, and Togo (ibid).

There is a diversity of models within the mixed type of EMBs due to the complexity of the relationship between different components in this type. Limits of power, harmony in functions, and identification of responsibilities are the most influential factors in classifying different models of mixed EMBs. However, the classification of particular models using the mixed EMBs can be more precise. The relationship between the component EMBs in a mixed model is sometimes clearly defined in legislation or interpreted by stakeholders, and friction can happen (Lopez Pintor, 2000: 55).

5.2.2. Permanent and Temporary Election Management Bodies

Classifying the election management bodies as permanent and temporary is based on the duration of jurisdiction for the electoral bodies. This jurisdiction is related somehow to various functions and responsibilities required to conduct multiple phases of the electoral process; for example, these phases include the drafting of electoral procedures, voter registration, registration of political parties and candidates, recruitment and training of electoral staff, monitoring the electoral campaigns, polling and counting operations, electoral disputes resolution, auditing of results, results declaration and archiving. All the previous technical phases and others can be grouped within one term, the electoral cycle.

The required workload throughout the electoral cycle is the main factor in determining whether a permanent or temporary EMB is appropriate. The financial issue is another factor; the expenses of maintaining a permanent EMB must be compared with the costs required to establish a temporary EMB for each electoral or voting process.

Permanent EMB is justifiable in countries where the electoral cycle is too short, elections and other related activities (such as regular partial elections and continuous voter registration) frequently occur within short periods, and continuing promotional-related work (such as constant voter education and electoral law reforms) is needed (Wall and Ellis, 2006:56).

Temporary EMBs exist only during the electoral period; thus, maintaining the institutional archive relating to elections is a significant factor to be considered in the temporary bodies. Temporary EMBs may follow independent, governmental, or mixed models. In some governmental EMBs, the jurisdiction must be temporary within the required time for implementing elections, as civil employees who manage elections have other long-term responsibilities beyond those of managing elections. They are redeployed to the EMB only during electoral periods and for short periods between elections to address some electoral issues, such as updating the voter's list and voter education activities.

5.2.3. Centralized or Decentralized Election Management Bodies

Concentration and devolution of power are the main factors identifying the geographical jurisdiction of the EMBs, which is usually defined in the electoral law. These factors depend very much on the form of the government and the shape of the political system in the state. The electoral legal framework may distinguish between functions and authorities assigned to national EMBs and those assigned to subnational, regional, or local EMBs.

This vertical division of authorities and functions between different branch levels of the one EMB must guarantee the optimal value of functional harmony between the national EMB and provincial, regional, and local EMBs.

Centralized EMBs refer to national EMBs, which are individuals and the only institute with complete jurisdiction over all the parts of the state to organize and manage elections and related activities. There is a possibility of assigning some unessential electoral activities to one or more institutes, but that does not put these institutes in the same category as EMBs. In some electoral democracies, the electoral legal framework may define separate EMBs at national, regional, and local levels, with different authorities and responsibilities at each level. However, hierarchical accountability is highly required in the relationship between the national 'central' EMB and the subordinate offices at the provincial and local levels (Wall & Ellis, 2006).

Highly decentralized EMBs are more likely to exist in governmental and mixed bodies that may rely on local authorities to implement all or part of electoral activities. These EMBs usually consist of a national EMB for observation and policy-making issues and local EMBs for managing elections. Assigning authorities and responsibilities to different local EMBs always needs appropriate oversight to maintain the equality between different electoral constituencies in the quality of services and the transparency and fairness of elections. The most highly decentralized EMB cases can be found in federal countries, where different EMBs at national and each federal district or state levels may operate different electoral legal frameworks, possibly applying even different electoral systems, like in the United States of America, Australia, Canada, India, Nigeria, Switzerland, and the Russian Federation (Wall & Ellis, 2006).

In decentralized models, the relationship between different EMBs and the distribution of authorities and responsibilities depend principally on the provision of law. These relationships and distributions of power between different EMBs may take several shapes and forms. However, the variety of approaches and forms may include the following (Lopez Pintor, 2000:69):

- National EMBs are responsible exclusively for managing national elections, coexisting with and cooperating with sub-national EMBs responsible only for managing provincial and local elections.
- The national EMB is responsible only for policy making, supervising, declaring results, and resolving disputes regarding elections and any other voting activities, while managing all kinds of elections (national, regional, and local) is the responsibility of different, separated sub-national EMBs.

5.2.4. International Election Management Bodies

The term 'International EMB' refers to institutions set up to deal temporarily with some transitional elections within particular circumstances following a conflict or crisis. Primarily, international EMBs are a result of global, regional, and national efforts to manage disputes and post-conflict environments, and they are typically sponsored and established by international or regional organizations, such as the United Nations (UN), and comprise or include international experts as members. Countries where transitional international EMBs have been set up include Cambodia (1993), South Africa (1994), Bosnia and Herzegovina (1996), East Timor (2000), and Afghanistan (2004) (Kumar, 1998; Hasovic, 2003).

Some international EMBs may have the form of national institutions with provisions for the appointment of global members. The aim of engaging international experts in transitional elections is to leverage their technical knowledge and comparative electoral experience, particularly in situations of deep-rooted conflict where consensus-building through mediation and dialogue is necessary. Moreover, the presence of international experts may promote stakeholder confidence in supporting the electoral process (Okello, 2006:25-27).

5.3. Standards of Election Management

Normative benchmarks for electoral management can be derived from international and regional human rights instruments, as well as internationally recognized best practices. Although the Universal Declaration of Human Rights and the ICCPR provide vital normative benchmarks on elections, how elections should be managed is not the subject of any specific provision in these international instruments (Articles 21 & 25 of the Universal Declaration and ICCPR, respectively). In a general comment to Article 25 of the ICCPR on the Right to Participate in Public Affairs, the Human Rights Committee has set out essential standards on election management and the minimum requirements to which EMBs should adhere. The General Comment provides for establishing an independent electoral authority to supervise the electoral process and ensure that it is conducted fairly, impartially, and by established laws compatible with the Covenant.

At the African regional level, many standards have been elaborated that significantly affect election management and EMBs. According to the African Charter on Democracy, Elections, and Governance, state parties to the Charter reaffirm their commitment to regularly holding free, fair, and transparent elections and undertake to establish and strengthen independent and impartial national poll bodies responsible for managing elections (African Charter on Democracy, Elections and Governance, 2007).

Perhaps the most critical and unambiguous standards of election management are set out in the 2002 Durban Declaration on the Principles Governing Democratic Elections in Africa. It provides that 'democratic elections should be conducted by impartial, all-inclusive, competent, accountable institutions staffed by well-trained personnel and equipped with adequate logistics' (Declaration on the Principles Governing Democratic Elections in Africa, 2002).

In a resolution adopted in 1996, the African Commission on Human and Peoples' Rights urged state parties to preserve the credibility of the electoral process, particularly election management, and to provide EMBs with sufficient resources to organize free and convincing elections.

In addition to the above, many international non-governmental organizations working on issues of governance and democracy have come up with various codes of conduct, principles, and best practices for election management and EMBs, which essentially elucidate the standards set out in the above instruments. Prominent among such codes, principles, and practices are those elaborated by the International Institute for Democracy and Electoral Assistance (IDEA) (IDEA 'Code of Conduct for the Ethical and Professional Administration of Elections', 1997), the Electoral Institute of Southern Africa (EISA) and the ACE Electoral Knowledge Network (ACE, 2010). The standards of election management have been summarized by Godwin Gill in an Inter-Parliamentary Union publication (1998) as follows:

> *Elections should be organized and administered by independent, impartial, and trained officials within a national election commission or other competent institution. Election administrators should be free from government or party interference and be provided with sufficient funds to fulfill their responsibilities. The principles of openness, accountability, transparency, and disclosure apply equally to the electoral administration, political parties, and candidates.*

5.4. Minimum International Benchmarks for EMBs

Today, there is an international consensus on specific minimum requirements that electoral institutions must meet to be considered credible and capable of inspiring confidence in the electorate.

Below, we discuss some of the most essential requirements to show how they impact the credibility and efficiency of EMBs and, hence, the outcome and acceptability of election results.

5.4.1. Independence

This is one of the most essential criteria often employed to gauge the credibility and level of confidence that an electoral institution inspires in the electorate. An EMB must be independent of all parties or stakeholders interested in the outcome of elections, especially the government and political parties. In Africa, where most governments have a track record of manipulating election results, any EMB, to inspire confidence in the electorate, must be seen as incredibly independent of the government (Okello, 2006).

The independence of an electoral institution from the influence of stakeholders in the electoral process, especially from the executive, is the hallmark of its credibility and efficiency. EMBs must have both formal (institutional) independence and substantive (practical) independence (Mozaffer, 2002:90). Formal autonomy is based on the law creating the EMB. It deals with such aspects as the appointment of members of election commissions, their terms and conditions of office, funding of the EMB, and the legal creation of the EMB itself. Substantive independence, conversely, refers to the practical or actual application of the autonomy conferred on the EMB by legislative texts. An EMB must be seen as 'exercising' or 'living' its independence, not merely possessing it. EMBs perceived as biased often have difficulties because they persuade stakeholders to accept the election outcome. Formal and substantive independence must coexist for an EMB to be considered credible.

Many different ways of safeguarding the independence of EMBs have been advanced in the various codes of conduct and best practices elaborated by international actors and authors in the field of elections. First, provisions regarding the mode of appointment, removal, and terms of service of members of the EMB must be established in legislation and insulated from government control. It is generally accepted that entrenching the creation of an EMB in the constitution is one of the best ways of safeguarding its independence (AAPAM, 1993). Constitutional entrenchment of an EMB is very important because the Constitution is the supreme law of the land and cannot be altered through ordinary legislative procedures. In situations where the executive can manipulate the constitution at will (as is the case in Cameroon), providing provisions relating to the EMB that can only be amended by a qualified majority or referendum would expedite. This serves as a mechanism for limiting sudden change by executive action or ordinary legislative processes and ensuring the EMB's permanency. In Costa Rica and Venezuela, for example, the constitution establishes the EMB as the fourth branch of Government after the executive, the legislature, and the judiciary. The EMBs of South Africa and Botswana are also constitutionally entrenched.

The operational autonomy of the EMB must be equally safeguarded for its independence. This means that in exercising its functions, the EMB must not be under the control, influence, or direction of any armed government, political party, or organized group, and this must be clarified in the law creating the EMB.

5.4.2. Mandate and Powers of the EMB

The mandate conferred on an EMB is an essential determinant of its credibility and efficiency. An EMB vested with a broad mandate covering a range of activities central to free and fair elections is more likely to effectively organize democratic elections (Trebilcock & Chitalkar, 2009:204). A broad mandate that encompasses activities such as resolving election disputes, allocating campaign funds, drawing electoral district boundaries, and establishing standards for acceptable electoral practices is imperative for the effectiveness of an EMB. Many of these activities are very contentious because of the high political stakes that go with them. Allocating responsibility over such activities to an independent and impartial body rather than the government is indispensable for ensuring fairness and credibility in the electoral process (ibid).

Election Commissions in Africa that have proved their worth in organizing credible elections, such as the Independent Electoral Commissions of South Africa and Ghana, generally have comprehensive mandates, and their success has been partly attributed to the extensive powers of these bodies (CODESRIA, 2010).

An EMB must also have sufficient powers to execute its mandate. One such power crucial for the efficiency and independence of the EMB is the power to hire and fire its staff according to its needs. This way, the staff employed by the EMB will, in all likelihood, owe their allegiance to the EMB and enhance its independence as opposed to a situation where the EMB staff is seconded from the government bureaucracy. An EMB should be allowed to request human resources from the public service, but this should be done discreetly to ensure the institutional independence of the EMB. The EMB must equally be able to determine its agenda and activities and how to execute its mandate within its legal framework.

5.4.3. Composition of the EMB

The composition of an EMB is another facet of its institutional framework that significantly affects its independence and credibility. The quality of people, including how they are appointed and dismissed, their backgrounds, political affiliations, and integrity, plays a significant role in shaping public perceptions about the credibility of electoral institutions in general. The mode of appointment of members of an EMB is a confidence-building measure and contributes immensely to its image in the eyes of stakeholders and the public (Okello, 2006:11).

According to the African Union Commission and the Association of Electoral Authorities in Africa, 'the selection and appointment procedures for commissioners should be determined by parliament and should be transparent, inclusive, and sensitive to gender equality and the representation of diverse groups' (EISA, 2013:12). The manner of selecting members of an EMB is very fundamental to its independence and image. It is generally accepted that the selection and appointment of commissioners should not be the exclusive preserve of one branch of government, especially the executive and should involve the legislature and judiciary equally to assure inclusiveness.

Practice differs widely in the appointment of commissioners in various electoral institutions worldwide. While some EMBs are composed exclusively of party representatives, others are made up exclusively of judges, and others are drawn from diverse backgrounds and experiences.

The appointment of party nominees is seen as suited for political systems where there is a high degree of political polarization and low levels of confidence in the impartiality and independence of the civil service. This can help build consensus and improve broad-based participation and mobilization of the electorate (Lopez-Pintor, 2000:64).

However, the risk of politicizing the EMB is equally high where such a method of appointment is employed.

The appointment of judges as commissioners has also been argued as the ideal method of ensuring impartiality, as judges are believed to be impartial and respected. However, the conflict of interest that might arise if an electoral institution's decision is appealed in the courts has been cited as the major weakness of this selection mode (ibid).

The appointment of independent personalities with requisite professional experience in election management is generally accepted as the best way of assuring the impartiality, independence, and professionalism of an EMB. These individuals can be drawn from diverse backgrounds, such as academia, civil society, the media, business, and other sectors, provided they are not involved in active politics. They should not be seen to have any conflict of interest in discharging their duties.

Commissioners' appointment and dismissal procedures are closely related to the composition of an EMB. The appointment and dismissal procedures should be laid down, and the process should be undertaken in an impartial, accountable, and transparent manner. The procedures should also consider the need to ensure the permanency and institutional continuity of the EMB (ESIA, 2013:12). The legal framework should equally specify the terms and conditions of service, such as salaries, allowances, and immunities. It is also necessary for the commissioners' service conditions to be regularly reviewed by an independent body created specifically for that purpose. Review by an independent body is essential to reduce the influence of the executive in the process that can undermine the independence of the institution (Okello, 2006:12). The term of office must be reasonable, not too short to create uncertainty, and not too long to entrench commissioners in their offices. The legal framework must also provide immunity from legal action for official action undertaken in good faith by members of the EMB.

Stringent procedures must govern the removal of commissioners from office. Such removal should be undertaken by a particular body comprising representatives from the three branches of government to guard against the risk of arbitrariness in the process and insulate commissioners from abusive removal.

5.4.4. Funding

To properly administer elections is costly and requires enormous financial, material, and human resources. Therefore, the legal framework for setting up an EMB should make provisions for the structure's timely, adequate, and independent financing. An EMB must be financially autonomous from the government because its independence can be adversely affected if it is entirely dependent on the government for its funding, which can starve it of funds for political gain. Although it is practically difficult for an EMB to function in a completely independent manner from the government regarding its financial resources, it is expedient that such a link does not create a dependency relationship that can compromise the independence and effectiveness of the EMB (Trebilcock & Chitalkar, 2009: 204).

To mitigate the risk of financial dependency of an EMB on the government, it is generally accepted that the budget of the EMB be voted directly by parliament (EISIA, 2013:12). In situations where there is fear that parliament may be under the influence of the executive, it would be prudent for the approval of the EMB's budget to require a supra-majority decision. The EMBs of India, Canada, South Africa, and Botswana are financed through a consolidated fund under the direct control of parliament and not the executive. It is also imperative that the EMBs have an average running budget and an election budget in an election year.

5.4.5. Accountability of the EMB

EMBs are public bodies funded with taxpayers' money, and like all public bodies, they must give an account of their activities and how public funds entrusted to them have been used. Accountability of EMBs is necessary to ensure that they carry out their functions effectively and that public funds allocated to them are put to the use for which they are intended. Therefore, although an EMB is supposed to be independent of any form of control, it must, however, remain accountable for the use of its resources and the execution of its mandate (Padmanabhan, 2002:77). Accountability may take the form of submission and publication of activity reports and the auditing of the financial accounts of the EMB.

The most critical concern regarding the accountability of an EMB is the organ of government or personality to which it should be accountable. Who an EMB is responsible to is crucial in maintaining its independence, integrity, and public confidence in its impartiality. It is generally accepted as a matter of best practice that EMBs submit their activity reports to parliament for scrutiny and should equally make their reports available to the public as a matter of transparency. To maintain financial probity, it is generally accepted that the financial accounts of the EMB should be audited by an independent entity, such as the Auditor General, in countries where this exists.

The preceding discussion has explored the various standards of election management, the different types of EMBs, and the essential minimum elements that EMBs must possess to be considered credible. These standards have been drawn from international instruments and multiple codes of conduct endorsed by many electoral bodies worldwide. The discussion has generally been prescriptive, considering the peculiar political context and circumstances of the Cameroonian political system.

Though there is no perfect EMB in the world, the crucial test is always whether an EMB is sufficiently founded on independence, non-partisanship, professionalism, and adequacy of resources to enable it to discharge its duties and, most importantly, how voters perceive it. Therefore, the beginning of this chapter sets the framework within which election management in Cameroon will be analyzed in subsequent paragraphs, both during the NEO era and within the context of ELECAM.

Multiparty elections were first held in March 1992 in Cameroon after adopting a new electoral code in December 1991. This followed a lengthy episode of a one-party regime and non-competitive elections instituted in the mid-1960s. The transition to democracy in Cameroon began in the early 1990s when President Biya reluctantly allowed the creation of political parties following increasing demonstrations for democratic change. Disputes were lodged by 32 political parties in these elections. These elections were notably run by the then Ministry of Territorial Administration. It is fair to point out that it was not independent and did not inhibit trust in voters and political hopefuls.

In the wake of the 1992 elections, the ruling CPDM, Biya's party, won 88 of the National Assembly's 180 seats. The Union Nationale pour la Démocratie et le Progrès (UNDP) won 68 seats, followed by the Mouvement pour la Défense de la République (MDP) with 18 seats, and the Union des Populations Camerounaises (UPC) with 6. After that, the CPDM joined forces with the MDR to gain the majority in the National Assembly. On October 11, 1992, presidential elections were conducted, and with 39.9% of the vote, Biya was re-elected. The Social Democratic Front (SDF) and UNDP each received 35.9% and 19.2% of the vote.

These elections needed to be more popular. To counter the risks of a total opposition boycott, the government made 500 million CFA francs available to each participating party. Only 35 of the 69 registered parties participated in the elections, with a low voter turnout of about 30%. Since opposition parties claimed several anomalies, the consensus was that these elections were not free and fair. On the other hand, because of the close outcome of the elections, some commentators concluded that the elections were generally free and fair (Derrick, 1992:2).

The most contentious issue surrounding all these elections before 2002 was the role that the different electoral laws (particularly Law No. 91-020 of December 1991 as modified by Law No. 97-13 of March 1997) conferred on the Ministry of Territorial Administration. This strategic Ministry is usually headed by one of the closest collaborators of the president and a member of the ruling party, and acted, until the 2002 elections, as an EMB with wide-ranging powers in organizing and supervising elections. It controlled and directed operations at national, provincial, divisional, and sub-divisional levels. As a result, the conduct and supervision of elections were inseparable from the highly politicized system of territorial administration, whose administrators were appointed by the president of the Republic and held office at his command. Each election was usually preceded by transfers, promotions, and the reallocation of officials at MINAT all over the country, raising suspicions of a deliberate design to place individuals capable of carrying out the political instructions issued to them in strategic positions and critical constituencies (National Democratic Institute for International Affairs, 1993:34).

As it existed, the Electoral Law created a series of commissions charged with responsibility for various aspects of the electoral process. These can be summarized as follows:

- A commission for the revision of the electoral registers, which existed at the council, sub-divisional, or district levels, and its membership comprised a chairperson appointed by the Senior Divisional Officer (SDO), the mayor or a municipal representative, and a representative of each political party contesting in an election in the constituency.

- A commission charged with supervising the establishment and distribution of registration cards, with a composition identical to that of the commission for revising the electoral registers.
- A local polling commission at the level of polling stations, whose chairperson was appointed by the SDO and was composed of representatives from the different political parties.
- A divisional supervisory commission at the level of each division is composed of the President of the High Court, three administration representatives appointed by the SDO, one independent person appointed by the SDO, and a representative of each political party.
- The National Commission for the Final Counting of Votes, whose membership comprised a Supreme Court judge appointed by the President of the Supreme Court as Chairperson, two other judicial officers also appointed by the President of the Supreme Court, ten representatives of the administration appointed by the Minister of Territorial Administration and ten representatives appointed by the political parties taking part in the elections.
- The Constitution provided for the proclamation of the results by the Constitutional Council after verification of the polling operations based on the reports and documents forwarded by the National Commission for the Final Counting of Votes (art 48 of Law No 96-6 of 18 January 1996 to amend the Constitution of 2 June 1972).

As the Constitutional Council had yet to be created, its powers were being exercised by the Supreme Court, which the Head of State appointed on the advice of the Higher Judicial Council.

Because of the critical role played by MINAT and the government in determining the composition and actual running of these different commissions, there was a vast scope for abuse. For example, 11 of the 13 members of the National Commission for the Final Counting of Votes (NCFV), appointed by the government and charged with overseeing, counting, and tabulating the votes during the hotly contested 1992 presidential elections, were drawn from the president's ethnic group in the Centre and South provinces. It, therefore, lacked an ethnic, regional, or political balance that could inspire confidence in its transparency, both among voters and other political parties, except for the ruling party.

In December 2000, responding to pressure from opposition demands for democratic change, parliament adopted a bill establishing the Observatoire National des Elections (ONEL) or National Elections Observatory (NEO), an election watchdog body responsible for controlling and supervising all stages of the electoral process in Cameroon. The opposition resisted this and argued that the proposed EMB would not be sufficiently independent and impartial, given that President Biya would single-handedly appoint its members. Indeed, they felt that the commission would partially favor the government.

5.5. National Elections Observatory (NEO)

On December 19th, 2000, President Biya promulgated Law No 2000/016, a bill introduced on November 30th, 2000, in parliament, creating the National Elections Observatory (NEO) and thus finally yielding to considerable international and national pressure to create an independent EMB. NEO immediately swung into action, supervising the 2002 municipal and legislative elections.

5.5.1. A general Overview of NEO

The Cameroonian NEO appears to have been inspired by a similar body created in Senegal that had successfully organized and supervised the elections that enabled the incumbent president, Abdou Diouf, to be beaten by his long-time rival, Abdoulaye Wade. However, the Cameroonian version of the Senegalese law differs from the latter in many material respects.

The NEO Law describes NEO as 'an independent body supervising and controlling elections and referendums' (Law No 2000/016 of 19 December 2000). Section 2 of the Law states that its mission is to 'contribute to the observance of the electoral law to ensure regular, impartial, objective, transparent and fair elections, and to guarantee voters and candidates the free exercise of their rights.' The NEO comprised 11 members appointed by presidential decree for a mandate that ends as soon as the electoral process ends. They were to be chosen from among 'independent personalities of Cameroonian nationality with a reputation for moral rectitude, intellectual honesty, neutrality and impartiality' and who, in the discharge of their duties, should not 'request or receive instructions or orders from any public or private authority' (ibid). A chairperson and vice-chairperson from among the NEO members were also to be appointed by presidential decree.

Section 5 of the Law contained a long list of persons who could not be appointed as members of the NEO. They included:

- Members of government and persons of similar status;
- Judicial and legal officers in active service;
- Secretaries-general of ministries and persons of similar status;
- Directors in the central administration and persons of similar status;
- Governors, senior divisional officers, and their assistants;
- Sub-divisional officers and their assistants;
- District heads in active service or on retirement for less than three years;
- Traditional rulers

The only permanent feature of the NEO was its permanent secretariat, which was to be headed by a secretary-general appointed by presidential decree on the advice of the NEO Chairperson. The NEO had the prerogatives to set up corresponding structures in the different regions, divisions, and councils, the composition and functioning of which were to be determined by decree. During elections and referendums, the NEO could establish corresponding structures in provinces, divisions, and councils that served as its branches (Decree No. 2001-306 of 8 October 2001). These structures were to be 'dissolved' as soon as the election concerned was over. The NEO duties enumerated in section 6 of the Law were extensive and included some responsibilities usually associated with EMBs. The NEO's duties were limited to 'supervising and controlling' the specified activities. It could perform these duties on its initiative or at the request of the competing political parties, candidates, or voters. It also had the power to draw up its internal rules and regulations.

As regards the cost of running the NEO, section 20 of the Law states that the 'state should place at the disposal of NEO all the human and material resources necessary for the accomplishment of its mission' and that its running expenses and those of its branches were to be borne by the state and be included in the state budget. Section 7 provided that members of the NEO will be granted 'allowances and traveling expenses under conditions determined by decree.' All other matters not dealt with by the Law were subject to section 21, which provided that a decree shall lay down the modalities for implementing the law. The 2001 implementation decree allowed the Chairperson of the NEO to request from any minister that employees of that ministry be placed at the disposal of the NEO for the duration of an election.

5.5.2. An Appraisal of the National Elections Observatory (NEO)

Managing the 30 June 2002 municipal and legislative elections provided the NEO with its first significant test. The elections were due for January 2002 but were postponed to 23 June 2002 due to concerns that needed more time and resources for NEO to resolve. Some of these concerns were alleviated when the British government provided £ 73,000, which the British Council and Electoral Reform International Services (ERIS) utilized in a capacity-building program project that combined training for election observers with the implementation of a voter education program. However, on polling day, 23 June 2002, after polling had started, a presidential decree was issued, postponing the elections for another week because of a lack of preparation on the part of MINAT. After the results of the elections had been announced, there were renewed calls from the opposition and some international organizations to establish an EMB that was independent of the government.

The NEO started its life from a severe disadvantage because, apart from the ruling party, most other parties were openly hostile to it, considering it a body set up by the government to cover up electoral fraud. These misgivings were primarily due to the controversy surrounding the handling of the NEO bill. The bill was introduced at the eleventh hour on 30 November 2000, and the government rejected the opposition parties' proposed amendments. In protest, these parties boycotted the final session of 6 December 2000, during which the bill was finally approved. The opposition parties argued that the NEO Law was unconstitutional. Still, due to the abstract, preventive, and restricted character of the system for control of the constitutionality of laws introduced by the amended 1972 Constitution, they could only bring this issue before the Supreme Court. However, after its creation, the NEO went to considerable lengths to organize meetings with the opposition parties' representatives to build trust and confidence and allay their fears.

The doubts about its independence from the government and the ruling party were at the heart of the NEO's problems. The NEO Law describes it in section 1 as an 'independent body.' In the context of EMBs, this was usually taken to mean that it was not subject to the control of the government of the day or any political party or other body and that it could act independently, impartially, reasonably, and professionally towards all parties. However, the reality was that several provisions in the NEO Law render the possibility of it not acting independently. For example, section 3 gave the President of the Republic the sole right to appoint the members of the NEO and its chief officials, the Chairperson and Vice-chairperson. Although President Biya, by appointing the 11 members of NEO on 10 October 2001, ensured that all the ten provinces in the country were represented, most of those appointed were known supporters or members of the ruling party. The Chairperson himself was a prominent member of the CPDM and held numerous ministerial positions for many years.

It may be true that the NEO or similar bodies can only be partially independent because somebody must always appoint the members. However, it can be argued that there was a need to allay all suspicion by providing for such appointments only after consultations with the opposition parties, or at least those represented in parliament.

Under the NEO Law, the functions of the NEO are essentially limited to 'supervising and controlling' elections. In contrast, the actual organization of the polls remained with the much-criticized MINAT. Given the time constraints under which it was operating and with only 2116 personnel throughout the country, it was difficult for NEO to operate independently. As opined above, while Decree No 2001-306 of 8 October 2001 allowed the NEO to set up structures in provinces, divisions, and councils and borrow civil servants, it strangely required it to 'dissolve' all these structures immediately after the elections. As a practical matter, working with MINAT was inevitable, and it offered many organizational advantages. The NEO could utilize the services of MINAT's experienced staff and its decentralized electoral management structures, as well as the voter information and other vital data it has accumulated over the years.

However, several disadvantages must be considered more seriously to warrant an earnest consideration regarding the desirability of maintaining these links. Firstly, many of the numerous irregularities that had marked post-1990 multiparty elections in the country were often attributed to MINAT and its top officials. Leaving MINAT responsible for organizing elections, which is the most crucial aspect of the electoral process, removes any resemblance of a process that can be impartial and fair. All that said, it cannot be said that the NEO was structured so that it was sufficiently insulated from individuals, parties, or institutions interested in the outcome of the elections that it was required to supervise and control.

Secondly, the fact that the NEO was a temporary body required to 'dissolve' the decentralized structures it needed to set up after every election meant that there was the risk of an inconsistent approach to electoral management, loss of election 'archives,' and little opportunity for the adoption of a professional approach to its tasks. This only reinforced its dependence on MINAT.

From its inception, the lack of trust from various stakeholders, as well as its somewhat preordained dependence on MINAT, has negatively impacted NEO in terms of voter turnout. In essence, the 2002 elections were the first supervised; a total of 4,389,572 Cameroonians were registered on the electoral registers, representing a dismal 36.89% of the total population of voting age. In the final analysis, only 65.66% of the registered voters turned up to vote. This figure represented a decrease of over 10% from the statistics of the previous parliamentary elections in 1997, organized by MINAT.

5.6. Elections Cameroon (ELECAM) from a Comparative Perspective

The recurrent allegations of fraud, massive rigging, and severe irregularities that accompanied each election organized in Cameroon during the NEO/MINADT era, coupled with intense pressure from opposition parties, civil society, and the international community for electoral management reforms, were what led to the establishment of Elections Cameroon in December 2006 (Law No 2006/011 of 29 December 2006 to set up and lay down the organization and functioning of Elections Cameroon). ELECAM was established as the sole institution that will henceforth be responsible for managing the entire electoral process in Cameroon. Its members were appointed on December 30th, 2009. Still, the body was only officially functional in January 2010, following the signing and transfer of all electoral materials and records from the MINADT to ELECAM.

This part of the research analyzes, in detail, various facets of ELECAM's institutional and legislative framework to determine whether it is sufficiently set up to spur trust in voters and is insulated from government control and manipulation to enable it to turn the tide of unpopular elections in Cameroon. The analysis of ELECAM's mandate is effected using a comparative approach. Each facet of its institutional and legislative framework is first compared to the defunct NEO to determine whether there has been an improvement or the status quo has been maintained.

Similarly, the standards of EMBs set out earlier in the chapter serve as a yardstick for comparison to gauge the degree to which ELECAM conforms to international standards that underlie the functioning of EMBs. Finally, ELECAM can be compared to the Independent Electoral Commission of South Africa (IEC), the Commission Electoral Nationale Autonome of Senegal (CENA), and other electoral institutions that have proven their worth in election management elsewhere. Such a comparative approach will help expose any shortcomings of ELECAM and serve as a starting point for recommending reform.

5.6.1. Institutional Framework

Elections Cameroon is an independent model EMB with an independent board known as the Electoral Board (EB) and an executive department known as the General Directorate of Elections (GDE) (Section 5, Law No 2006/011 of 29 December 2006). The Electoral Board is the legislative and supervisory organ of ELECAM and is the institution's main policy-making body. On the other hand, the executive unit, the General Directorate of Elections, is responsible for implementing the decisions of the Electoral Board and overseeing the election process.

According to the law establishing ELECAM (the ELECAM law), 'the EB shall ensure compliance with the electoral law of all stakeholders to guarantee impartial, free, fair, transparent and credible polls' (Section 6 of the ELECAM law). The EB comprises twelve members appointed by presidential decree for a four-year renewable term, from among independent personalities of Cameroonian nationality who are reputed for their stature, moral uprightness, intellectual honesty, patriotism, neutrality, and impartiality. The unit is headed by a chairperson and a vice-chairperson (Section 8 (1-4) of the EELCAM law). The DGE, on the other hand, is responsible for the organization and management of the poll and is headed by a Director General assisted by a deputy, both appointed by decree of the president for a period of five years renewable (Sec 18-20 of the ELECAM law). The DGE wields much power over election management, and the Director General seems to be the most crucial officer in ELECAM.

ELECAM is a centralized structure with its head office in Yaoundé. It has branches at regional, divisional, and council levels, the organization and functioning of which are laid down by the EB. The Director General of ELECAM appoints all branch officers upon the approval of the EB. Elections Cameroon is a permanent institution that operates during both election and non-election periods. In this respect, it conforms to the international norms that require EMBs to be permanent structures within the institutional dispensation of states.

The institutional framework of ELECAM is markedly different and significantly more developed than that of the defunct NEO. First, as a permanent institution, ELECAM stands a better chance of developing a professional approach to elections than NEO, conserving institutional memory (archives), and developing a consistent approach to election management.

The two-pronged structural set up of ELECAM is also vastly different from that of the NEO. It can be an added impetus to the body's efficiency because managerial and supervisory functions are separated, leading to each organ developing expertise in its area of concern. However, some commentators have criticized it as being too bureaucratic and a potential breeding ground for conflicts of interest between the EB and the DGE. The excessive powers vested in the Director General of ELECAM can lead to authoritarian management of the institution, as has been the case with most Parapublic institutions in Cameroon that have a similar institutional set up (Kijem, 2005:97).

5.6.2. Legislative Framework

ELECAM needs a more robust legal framework. The principal instrument that governs the legal foundations of ELECAM is Law no 2006/011 of 19 December 2006. This law establishes ELECAM and provides for its composition, mandate, powers, administrative structure, funding, and the terms and conditions of office of the members of ELECAM. This law is supplemented by an enabling presidential decree that caters to the effective putting in place of ELECAM and the decrees appointing members of ELECAM, the Chairperson and Vice-chairperson, and the decree appointing the Director General and his deputy. ELECAM, just like the defunct NEO, does not have any constitutional foundation. The law creating the institution can be amended by parliament following the standard procedure for the amendment of laws.

According to the international standards on election management set out above, an EMB ideally needs to be established in the constitution and its provisions entrenched to prevent arbitrary change by the government.

A simple legislative enactment poses a grave danger not only to ELECAM's independence and efficiency but also to its very survival, given the prevailing political situation in Cameroon. The executive head in

Cameroon has wide-ranging legislative powers and can propose amendments to any law (articles 8(7), 27 & 28 of the 2008 revised Constitution of the Republic of Cameroon). Given that the present government has a large majority in a highly subservient parliament, any proposed amendment (even that which seeks to curtail the independent functioning of ELECAM) can easily sail through parliament.

The legal foundation of ELECAM is akin to that of the Commission Electorale Nationale Autonome of Senegal, which is not enshrined in the Constitution of Senegal but is simply a legislative enactment that can be amended at any time by parliament through ordinary legislative processes. This contrasts sharply with the legislative framework of the South African IEC, as outlined in the 1996 Constitution of the Republic of South Africa, one of the institutions that supports constitutional democracy. The Constitution sets out general guidelines for the IEC and provides for its functions, composition, and independence. The South African Constitution has very stringent amendment procedures, which have the positive effect of insulating the IEC from any arbitrary interference with its freedom and larger institutional framework by the executive. The Electoral Commission of Ghana (EC) (Chapter VII, sec 43-56 of the 1992 Constitution of Ghana), just like the Electoral and Boundaries Commission of Kenya (parts 88 & 89 of the 2010 Constitution of the Republic of Kenya), equally owes its legal foundation to its constitution. This is an essential safeguard against any government's arbitrary interference with the legal framework of the electoral institution.

5.6.3. Mandate and Powers of ELECAM

As mentioned earlier, the mandate and powers attributed to an electoral institution are critical to its effectiveness and independence. ELECAM has been conferred with a relatively broad mandate of organizing, managing, and supervising all electoral and referendum operations in Cameroon (Section 1(2) & 4(1) of the ELECAM law). To execute this mandate, the Electoral Board and the General Directorate of Elections have been vested with varying powers and duties to oversee the smooth conduct of the polls.

Accordingly, the EB, the legislative and supervisory organ of ELECAM, is charged with ensuring compliance with the electoral law of all stakeholders to guarantee free, fair, impartial, regular, transparent, and credible polls (Section 6(1) of the ELECAM law). For this purpose, it is vested with various oversight functions over the conduct of the elections by the GDE. These include scrutinizing and publishing the lists of multiple candidates contesting any election within its competence, publishing election trends, controlling the preparation of election materials and documents within the deadlines fixed by law, examining disputes regarding pre-election and elections operations and ordering corrections as appropriate, determining the organization and functioning of branches and a host of other oversight tasks (secs 6 & 7 of the ELECAM law).

The DGE, the executive organ of ELECAM, has wide-ranging powers regarding managing the electoral process. It is responsible for organizing and managing the poll under the supervision of the EB. It is, therefore, responsible for managing the 'essential elements' of the electoral process. Some of these essential elements include the following (sec 22 of the ELECAM law):

- Drawing up, managing, updating, and keeping the national elections register as well as election documents and materials,
- Procuring and distributing election materials and documents,
- Drawing up and publishing voters' lists and issuing and distributing voter cards,
- Organizing and supervising the training of electoral personnel,
- Organizing polling stations and appointing officers to the said polling stations,
- Coordinating all bodies responsible for election operations,
- Coordinating the work of observers appointed by the appropriate national authorities,
- Forwarding election reports to the EB for the publication of electoral trends and
- Implementing the ELECAM budget and elections budget.

Compared to the NEO, ELECAM has registered a significant improvement in broadening its mandate. Unlike the restrictive mandate of the NEO that was limited to supervising and controlling the management of the electoral process by the MINADT, ELECAM has a more significant and preponderant role in the electoral process, and the MINADT has primarily been relegated to the margins, though not wholly pushed out of the electoral theatre. ELECAM's mandate also contrasts sharply with that of the CENA of Senegal, which only has powers of oversight and regulation over the electoral process in Senegal, just like the defunct NEO. The actual organization and management of elections in Senegal is still the exclusive preserve of the Ministry of Territorial Administration and

Decentralization, and the CENA serves as a watchdog institution, albeit with considerable regulatory powers (Articles 2, 3 & 8 of the Law No. 2005-007 of the law establishing the CENA).

However, when one examines the mandates of other credible electoral institutions in democracies worldwide, one notices that they have broader mandates than ELECAM and execute tasks with high political stakes.

In this wise, reference can be made to the South African IEC, which, in addition to the essential elements included in ELECAM's mandate, is additionally vested with powers of promoting conditions conducive to free and fair elections (Section 5(c) of the Electoral Commission Act 55 of 1996), declaring the result of various polls within seven days after such elections (Section 5(1) (n) of the Electoral Commission Act) and registering political parties (Section 15 of the Electoral Commission Act). Also included in the mandate of the IEC is the power to manage the Represented Political Party Fund, allocate these funds to various represented political parties, and ensure that the parties are accountable for using such funds (Public Funding of Represented Political Parties Act 103 of 1997).

The Electoral Commission Act of Ghana goes further by conferring on the EC the power to demarcate electoral boundaries for national and local government elections and to undertake the preparation of identity cards (articles 2(b) & (d) of the Electoral Commission Act 451 of 1993; see also 45 (a) of the 1992 Constitution of Ghana). The 2010 Constitution of Kenya also vests extensive powers of boundary demarcation on the Independent Electoral and Boundaries Commission of Kenya. It makes it responsible for regulating the amount of money that may be spent by or on behalf of a candidate regarding any election. In Costa Rica, the Supreme Electoral Tribunal (SET) is responsible for convoking elections, conducting official counts of votes, and declaring results. Still, it is also mandated to interpret all constitutional and legal provisions on electoral matters. In addition, before enacting any law concerning electoral issues, the Legislative Assembly must consult the SET.

The demarcation of electoral boundaries, funding of political parties, campaign financing, and registration of political parties have traditionally been contentious issues in Cameroon's electoral history. All these aspects of the electoral process are known to have been used by the government to influence the outcome of the polls to its advantage. These remain a potential weapon of electoral malpractice in the hands of the government since they are not included in ELECAM's mandate, which, given its status as an independent institution, would have been better suited to handle these issues.

5.6.4. Composition and Mode of Appointment of Members of ELECAM

According to the law establishing ELECAM, members of the EB shall be designated from the midst of independent personalities of Cameroonian nationality reputed for their stature, moral uprightness, intellectual honesty, neutrality, and impartiality. The EB comprises twelve members appointed for a four-year renewable term of office (Section 8(2) of the ELECAM law). The various categories of persons barred from holding office as members of the EB include members of government and persons ranking as such; members of the Constitutional Council; magistrates in active service; persons with a running mandate in national, regional or local bodies; various categories of administrators; members of political parties or support group of a political party and a host of others (Section 13 of the ELECAM law). The Law does not provide for the Director General of ELECAM and his deputy, the most influential members of the institution, to adhere to the above conditions of moral uprightness, intellectual honesty, neutrality, and impartiality, and the incompatibilities listed in section 6. This means that a person with a tainted personality who is highly partisan and does not meet the above criteria may be appointed Director General of ELECAM.

The Chairperson and Vice-chairperson, as well as all the other members of the EB and the Director General and his deputy, are appointed by the President of the Republic after consultation with political parties represented in parliament, as well as civil society organizations (sections 8(1) (3) & 20 of the ELECAM law). Such consultations are, however, non-binding to the president, which implies that the appointment of ELECAM members and its key officials is technically the exclusive preserve of the President of the Republic. This appointment is arbitrary, restrictive, devoid of transparency, and involves no input from other government organs. This mode of appointment undermines ELECAM's credibility and only serves to reinforce negative public perceptions about its independence and impartiality. This is in stark disregard of the international standards set out above, which require that the selection and appointment of members of an EMB be transparent and inclusive and should involve all the organs of government.

In this regard, ELECAM has followed in the footsteps of the NEO, whose members were equally appointed exclusively by the president, with disastrous consequences for its credibility (Art 3 of the NEO law). The CENA of Senegal, which, like ELECAM, has twelve members, also follows this mode of appointment. The law creating the CENA states that members of the CENA shall be chosen from amongst personalities of Senegalese nationality known for their integrity, honesty, neutrality, and impartiality after consultation with the institutions and various actors in civil society (Article 4 of Law No 2005-007 of the law establishing the CENA). Civil society in Senegal is stronger and more active than in Cameroon, and has been able to wield considerable influence over the selection of members of the CENA.

5.6.5. Removal of ELECAM Members from Office

The ELECAM law provides for two situations through which the functions of a member of the Electoral Board of ELECAM can be terminated. These are physical incapacity duly ascertained by ELECAM; serious misconduct duly ascertained by ELECAM, notably breach of oath and penalty imposed for a felony (life or fixed-term imprisonment coupled with banishment and civic disqualification) (Section 11 of the ELECAM law). An ELECAM member's mandate can also end through non-renewal of the mandate, resignation duly established by ELECAM, or temporary incapacity ascertained by ELECAM (Sections 9 & 10 of the ELECAM law).

This method of terminating the mandate of an ELECAM member is undesirable because the process is open to manipulation, non-transparent, and restrictive. The termination of a member's mandate, especially in cases of serious misconduct, only needs to be ascertained by ELECAM members without any external review. This is an affront to the principles of natural justice because ELECAM effectively becomes a judge in its cause in this instance. Similarly, the president has multiple ways of removing ELECAM members from office, either by forcing resignation or having most ELECAM members declare the individual to be physically incapacitated or in breach of oath. Additionally, the fact that members of ELECAM may serve indefinitely, provided that the president renews their mandate every four years, is a cause for concern, as this can serve as an incentive for them to maintain a pro-government agenda to retain their positions. Another worrying issue is that the Constitutional Court can establish that ELECAM is incompetent, and the president is empowered to take necessary corrective measures (Section 41 of the ELECAM law).

These are structural weaknesses that effectively operate to diminish any semblance of independence that ELECAM may possess.

The defunct NEO did not have such removal procedures since the mandate of its members ended immediately after the conduct of the polls (Article 3 (2) of the NEO law). In Senegal, the mandate of a member of the CENA cannot be terminated except on the member's demand or because of physical or mental incapacity duly ascertained by a medical doctor designated for that purpose by the National Order of Medical Practitioners (Article 6 of the Lois No 2005-007 establishing the CENA). This is far better than the situation in Cameroon because the ascertainment of incapacity is done by an external body that is also independent.

In South Africa, the procedure for removing commissioners from office is stringent, transparent, and inclusive, helping to insulate the IEC from outside interference. According to the Electoral Commission Act, the president may only remove a commissioner from office for misconduct, incapacity, or incompetence. Removal from office on the above grounds can only be effected after a finding by a committee of the National Assembly upon the recommendation of the Electoral Court. Most of the national assemblies must then adopt a resolution calling for that commissioner's removal from office (Section 7(2) of the Electoral Commission Act).

5.6.6. The Funding and Accountability of ELECAM

The Director General is charged with preparing the draft budget of ELECAM. Such a budget must be approved by the EB, which then submits the same to the government for consideration. After much consideration, the government submits the budget to parliament for adoption as part of the finance law (Sections 27–30 of the ELECAM law). Therefore, ELECAM cannot elaborate its budget independently, and the government has the final say on what to submit to parliament as ELECAM's budget. This is a sorry state of affairs since the government can, at any given time, decide to starve the institution of funds.

This would inevitably render the body ineffective because election management requires substantial financial resources. This is the same situation that occurred with the defunct NEO. NEO officials repeatedly claimed they could not effectively carry out their restrictive mandate because they needed more financial means. This is the same fate that is likely to befall ELECAM.

Regarding accountability for the funds entrusted to it, the minister in charge of finance is responsible for appointing a treasury accounting officer and a public accountant to ELECAM to ensure financial probity (Sections 31 & 32 of the ELECAM law). ELECAM must also submit its administrative and management accounts to the finance minister and the Audit Bench of the Supreme Court. Regarding its day-to-day management, ELECAM must submit copies of minutes and progress reports to the Minister of Territorial Administration and Decentralization (Section 40 (2) of the ELECAM law). Again, this needs to be more consistent with international standards, which require an EMB to be accountable for its management and finances to an independent institution, such as parliament or the Auditor General. In this regard, ELECAM has effectively maintained the status quo of what was obtained during the NEO era since NEO was not accountable to an independent institution but to the President of the Republic, a personality with a vested interest in the outcome of the polls.

The CENA in Senegal has a more robust and independent funding mechanism. The CENA elaborates its budget in collaboration with the state's competent technical services, which is then adopted in parliament as an autonomous budget in the finance law. The budget must be available to CENA at the beginning of the fiscal year (Article 19 of Law No. 2005-007 establishing the CENA). As with ELECAM, the finance minister appoints a public accountant to the CENA to ensure probity in managing funds entrusted to it. The CENA is required to submit election and annual reports to the President of the Republic.

In South Africa, the budget of the IEC is approved by Parliament, which then releases funds to it (Section 13 (1) of the Electoral Commission Act). According to section 181(5) of the Constitution, the IEC, one of the six institutions supporting democracy, is accountable to the National Assembly and must report on its activities and the performance of its functions to the Assembly at least once a year. It must also submit an audited statement of income and expenditure annually. The IEC can expend money without authority from any quarter to ensure financial autonomy. The Chief Electoral Officer, as the accounting officer of the IEC, is responsible for the financial accounting of the IEC. To ensure financial probity, the IEC's accounts must be audited by the Auditor-General, whose office is constitutionally independent (Section 13(3) of the Electoral Commission Act).

5.6.7. Terms and Conditions of Service of Members of ELECAM

The ELECAM law provides for the terms and conditions of service of members of the EB and the Director General and Deputy Director General. The Chairperson, Vice-chairperson of ELECAM, the Director General, and his deputy are entitled to monthly remuneration and statutory benefits (Sections 37 (1) & 38 of the ELECAM law). The other members of the EB are only entitled to session allowances during meetings of the EB and a refund of all expenses incurred upon presentation of supporting documents. They are equally entitled to session and mission allowances. All the forms of remuneration mentioned above are exclusively determined by the President of the Republic by decree (Section 37 (3 & 4) of the ELECAM law). Therefore, the terms and conditions of service of ELECAM members are left to the whims and caprices of the President, who can use his discretion to manipulate the institution.

The exclusive powers conferred on the president to determine the remuneration of ELECAM officers, without any form of oversight, is dangerous to the independence and efficiency of the body because the president can use such powers to entice ELECAM members with attractive salaries and get them to toe a pro-government line or set the remuneration in a way that will affect the effectiveness of the members of ELECAM. ELECAM has, in this sense, followed closely in the footsteps of the NEO since the President of the Republic exclusively decided the terms and conditions of service of the members of NEO.

In Senegal, the terms and conditions of service of members of the CENA follow a similar pattern. The law establishing the CENA states simply that members of the CENA shall be entitled to indemnities and mission allowances under conditions fixed by a decree of the president of the Republic (Article 21 of the Law No 2005-007 establishing the CENA). This contrasts significantly with the method of remuneration of members of the Electoral Commission of Ghana, whose chairman and deputies are entitled to the same terms and conditions of work as a judge of the Court of Appeal and High Court, respectively. The remuneration of the other members of the Commission is fixed by parliament (Section 5 of the Electoral Commission Act of Ghana). In South Africa, the President fixes the remuneration of members of the IEC in consultation with the Commission on the Remuneration of Representatives (Section 7(2) of the Electoral Commission Act). The systems in Ghana and South Africa are more inclusive, preventing arbitrariness and any likelihood of manipulation.

5.7. Efforts Made by ELECAM to Increase Voter Turnout

Learning from the shortcomings of its predecessors, Elections Cameroon has implemented several measures that help explain the observed increase in turnout. This general increase in turnout comes from a notable increase in the number of registered voters. However, it is still fair to say that it is less than 60% of Cameroonians of voting age. The following are the efforts that have been made:

5.7.1. The Biometric Voters Registration Machine

This merges fingerprint and photo identification to identify voters during election registration. This method is used to identify and detect duplicate impersonation, thereby reducing fraud during the electoral registration process.

Following the controversial presidential election of October 2011, the Cameroon government reformed the electoral system by dissolving the existing pen-and-paper voter registration system and replacing it with a biometric system (Agbor & Mukum, 2012). The biometric voter registration is in two forms: the stationary finger scanner and the handheld or mobile scanner.

Figure 5.1: Biometric Stationary Finger Scanner Y Interface
Source: Researcher

Figure 5.2: Handheld Biometric Finger Scanner
Source: Researcher

The most important feature of the biometric voter registration machine is the fingerprint. "If you look at the surface of any finger, you will find ridges and furrows which make the fingerprint unique," argue Jain and Prabhakar (2005: 10). According to Moor (2005), the advantages of the finger scanner include the following:

- It is 100% accurate during the voter registration process,
- It is an easy way to identify voters and can be deployed in a range of environments.

This measure appears to have facilitated the registration process for ELECAM, while also increasing trust in voters and candidates by reducing the margin for electoral registration fraud.

5.7.2. Electronic Voting (E-voting)

In 2012, due to pressure from opposition parties, ELECAM introduced the biometric voter registration system. This was the dawn of e-voting in Cameroon, followed by the deployment of 12000 biometric kits nationwide to register voters.

The biometric voter registration scheme aimed to ensure the credibility of election outcomes, improve election transparency, and reduce irregularities in the voting process by matching five fingerprints, photos, and additional identification information (Menang, 2015).

Even though e-voting has been practised for a while in Cameroon, election outcomes have yet to yield satisfactory results. This is an indication that the diffusion rate has been relatively slow. However, most states have abandoned e-voting projects due to fear or risk of potential technical error (EDRI, 2009). A glaring example is the 2000 US presidential election, in which technical malfunctions caused the screens of some electronic voting devices to lock up on election day. A similar case occurred in Ohio during the 2004 election in the United States, where electoral irregularities resulted from an error in the vote-counting system that gave more votes to one candidate than to the others (Global Research, 2009).

5.7.2.1. The Electronic Voting Machine

The electronic voting machine is composed of two connected interfaces: the ballot box and the control unit. As seen in the picture, the ballot box is designed principally for the voter and is connected to the control unit, which is intended for the polling officers.

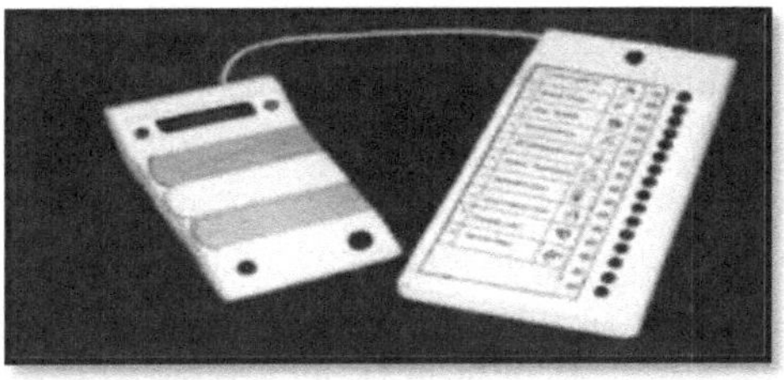

Figure 5.3: The Ballot Box And Control Units Linked Together

- The Ballot Unit: In a traditional voting system, voters cast their votes in paper form in a ballot box, but with the introduction of the electronic voting machine, it is done electronically.
  The features of the electronic ballot box include a list of political candidates and their respective parties, along with corresponding control buttons that allow voters to select their preferred candidate during the voting exercise. Voting is done by simply pushing the button corresponding to your candidate of interest. This tool's user-friendly and straightforward nature allows voters to press one button pointing to their desired candidate, explaining why it is an easy, reliable, and safe way to conduct elections (Ashok & Sariba, 2012).
- The Control Unit: This interface is designed to monitor voting activities by polling officers. It displays the total number of votes cast, marks the end of the election, and declares the results (Ashok & Sariba, 2012). Just a push of one button gets the required information. For example, a push on the result button automatically displays the result, which makes it easy to use.

5.7.2.2. E-Voting Adoption and Its Requirements

Building an e-voting system entails an in-depth understanding of a host of requirements. Technology upgrades in elections are always challenging projects that require careful deliberation and planning (International Institute for Democracy and Electorate Assistant [IDEA], 2011). Adopting electronic voting is the most difficult upgrade, as this technology directly impacts the core of the electoral process, including casting and counting votes. To explain some of the requirements for e-voting adoption (IDEA, 2011), it made it clear that for any e-voting project to be successfully adopted, the following factors must be considered.

5.7.2.2.1. Political Consensus

Adopting an electronic voting system can succeed if there is a political consensus regarding the new system's relative advantages as opposed to the pen-and-paper ballot. However, some political actors may oppose electronic voting due to technical concerns or fear that introducing a new voting system will benefit their opponents. Building trust and confidence in the new system may be difficult or impossible with such opposition. Therefore, all political parties must work on a common platform to introduce a new voting system. (IDEA, 2011: 19)

5.7.2.2.2. Social Context

There are key social actors in any political setting. This includes election experts and non-governmental organizations. These bodies usually have strong opinions and concerns about elections and voting systems. These actors should be included early in the introduction of a new voting system. This should be done by providing them with information regarding the new system and seeking their opinion. Information and communication technology security experts and organizations are often strong opponents of e-voting systems; their views and opposition are essential because they are experts in that domain and should be considered. "It is important to hear and address their concerns by clarifying any misunderstandings, correcting weaknesses, or accepting certain risks as a trade-off for the benefits of introducing the new system. Non-technical concerns must also be seriously considered." (IDEA, 2011:19)

5.7.2.2.3. Operational and Technical Foundations

A supportive socio-political environment is crucial for the successful adoption of e-voting. Even a poorly designed e-voting strategy can be successful if the environment is supportive. However, it becomes an issue when technical problems grow too big over time; they become more visible and further complicate the process.

As issues become increasingly visible, doubts about the electoral process build up, the election administration and the e-voting system lose credibility, and at some point, e-voting may need to be scrapped altogether to restore trust in the electoral process. Building an e-voting system on a solid technical foundation is essential to maintain trust and credibility. (IDEA, 2011)

5.7.2.2.4. Communication Channels

Communication is a crucial process in the adoption of new technological innovations. It is generally agreed that good and reliable communication channels positively affect any technological project, such as e-voting. Poorly designed communication channels will have a negative impact. An adequate flow of information will increase the credibility, trust, and transparency of a new voting system. (IDEA, 2011:24)

5.7.2.2.5. IT Competency (Knowledge of e-voting)

IT competency includes the technological know-how of the country in question. This is not limited to technology, but also focuses on the available resources for individuals who work with technology. The implication is that the organization or group implementing e-voting should be technologically savvy. An organization's ability to implement an innovation dramatically depends on the competence of the staff during the adoption process.

5.7.2.2.6. Top Management Support

Approval from top management should be a top priority for carrying out any IT innovation in an organization or with a group of people. Top management must also allocate available resources to realize the project. This implies that the decision to adopt e-voting must be a top priority of the organization or country concerned.

5.7.2.2.7. Government E-readiness

This refers to the technological infrastructure put in place by the government for an e-voting project. It refers to the government's readiness regarding technological infrastructure to support the adoption and implementation of e-voting. If the government plays a vital role and creates a favorable environment, the full potential for implementation can be realized.

5.7.2.2.8. Compatibility

In this study, compatibility refers to the "degree of consistency of the innovation with existing values, experience and need for potential adopters. An idea which does not align with the values and norms of the social system will not be adopted as fast as a compatible innovation" (Rogers, 2003:15). For an e-voting project to be fully adopted and implemented, the affected population must be able to identify themselves with this novelty about their norms and beliefs. If e-voting could connect with some of Cameroon's social and cultural norms, this would positively affect the adoption rate.

5.7.2.2.9. Complexity

Complexity refers to how easy or difficult the tool is to understand or use. The usability aspects of the tool should be a top priority during implementation and adoption. "Some innovations are easy to understand by members of a social system while others are more complicated" (Rogers, 2003:16). If the e-voting tool is easy to use, then it is likely that its adoption rate will be faster.

5.7.2.2.10. Liability

This refers to the extent to which an innovation may be "experimented" with on a limited basis (Rogers 2003, p.16). In this case, "liability will generate new ideas. The instalment plan can speed up the adoption rate" (Rogers, 2003, p. 16).

If a pilot study were conducted in Cameroon to try e-voting before the implementation, the diffusion rate would be faster. The fact that e-voting has yet to go as expected or hoped indicates that ELECAM lacks some or several of these requirements.

5.8. The Challenges of Elections Management

Since the return to multiparty politics in Cameroon, elections have been characterized by unsuccessful management at all levels – before, during, and after elections – resulting in detrimental and disputed aftermaths (Fombad, 2010: 535). EMBs have faced numerous challenges that have eroded the credibility of elections, leading to voter apathy. A few of these are:

5.8.1. Lack of Respect for the Rule of Law

Democracy is a system bound by rules, and it is derivative. Everybody and institutions should work and be controlled by the law. However, the law has been more frequently breached over the last few decades. The executive and ruling party's supremacy frequently superseded the rule of law. Several observers have contended that this has inspired the lack of genuine political competition, which breeds distrust in the system and results in voter indifference and apathy (Albert, 2005:82; Beckman, 2010:161-162; Bratton & van de Walle, 1997:7; Campbell, 2010:2; Joseph

2008:99-102; Lynch & Crawford 2011:282-285; Lindberg, 2004:62; Okafor, 2008:5; Oyovbaire 2007:15; Sklar et al, 2006:101).

This is reinforced by the fact that power is prized too highly as a channel to wealth. Given the political culture and socialization of the political class or elites, politics tends to conflict (Jega, 2013, 2015).

5.8.2. Inadequate Institutionalization of EMBs

In appraising the ineffectiveness of EMBs in Black Africa, Omotola (2010: 20) argues that insufficient institutionalization has rendered EMBs lacking financial and managerial autonomy. In Nigeria, for example, the Electoral Reform Committee (2008: iii) opined and showed that the need for more independence of the EMBs at both the Federal and State echelons is a fundamental shortcoming of the electoral process. This is generally a result of the inclination of ruling governments to manipulate the EMBs to execute narrow and parochial interests in their effort to hold power by all means and to monopolize the political marketplace. Hence, the ruling regimes have yet to see any need to develop vital, independent electoral administrations. Right from the MINAT era down through the ELECAM era, the government has consistently been suspected of manipulating electoral proceedings (Fombad, 2010; Adejumobi, 2007:14; Ibrahim, 2007b:5; Jega, 2012:8; National Democratic Institute, 2008, 2011; Obianyo, 2008:49; Omotola, 2010). A case in point is the recently conducted 2018 elections, during which the country experienced numerous logistical issues, including inadequate arrangements for delivering sensitive electoral materials to various polling units and collation centers across the country by ELECAM. Despite all the breaches associated with MINAT and NEO, no sanctions have been known to have been meted out on officials responsible.

Equally, finance is used to compromise the autonomy of EMBs in Cameroon. EMBs have been at the mercy of the executive as they rely on the government for funding. The executive determines when, how, and what should be released to the EMBs. When the party in power needs the cooperation of the EMBs, especially as elections approach, it appropriates substantial financial and material resources. Still, as soon as elections are over, the EMBs are de-prioritized (Agbaje & Adejumobi, 2006:32).

5.8.3. Rising Unenthusiastic Opinions or Public View of EMBs

Another challenge that precedes this is the rising unenthusiastic attitude or public perception of EMBs, particularly in politics. The public view or state of mind is one of the fundamental elements that influence the success of an electoral process. Voting is an individual initiative that implies individuals vote or not, depending on their impressions of the electoral process and the EMB. The management periods of MINAT and NEO generated considerable distrust, leading to a decline in confidence in ELECAM's work, despite visible efforts (Crisis Group, 2018). Many Cameroonians are found to no longer have confidence in EMB's capacity to conduct credible elections, given the terrible and unacceptable experiences the country has had with EMBs (ELECAM, 2017:2). This is one of the principal perceptions that EMBs have to address. In general, the strategies that need to be adopted to address this challenge will have a more significant impact on the credibility of the election process and voter turnout.

5.8.3.1. The Disposition of Cameroonian Politics and Political Parties

The roles of political parties in influencing the electoral process must be emphasized. Political parties assure a viable democracy (Lindberg, 2007:215; Walle, 2003). Political parties are expected to sum up and convey options in the public space; prepare or educate voters; transmute and incorporate voters by way of socialization into groups; stand in as a linkage connecting government and the public; designate aspirants for known offices and organize electoral support to aspirants during elections (Alapiki, 2004:91-92; Ojo, 2002:12; Omoruyi, 2001:2-4). According to MINAT (2009:103), political parties serve a fundamental function to offer the voting public an alternative of contenders and programs to choose from and thus, from time to time, assist in determining which parties or partnerships of parties will govern. The EMBs, by rule, synchronize the endeavors of political parties remarkably during the campaigning process. This involves supervising political parties to foster internal democracy, principally during party primaries.

The challenge lies here. According to the Electoral Reform Committee (2008:26) and the National Democratic Institute (NDI) (2011:8), the structure of political parties in Cameroon lacks internal democracy, as most parties' primaries are organized under inexplicable conditions, with many party leaders selecting aspirants or candidates. The case of the Social Democratic Front, which is nearing a divide over the choice between Joshua Osih and J.M. Nitcheu for elections, is a good example. The crisis's primary motivation is the excessive pursuit of power to control resources. As Wapmuk (2016:99) aptly holds, elections are tussles over the right to use the resources managed by the state, which are the most valuable resources in society. Given these lofty prizes, politicians resort to various approaches — whether or not crooked — to reach public office. Indeed, for the political class, the realization of political power is perceived as an assurance of limitless and overwhelming access to the resources of the state usurped for personal use.

5.8.3.2. Training and the Usage of Ad-hoc Staff

Ad-hoc staff have been known to be the main feature of EMBs. MINAT and NEO frequently and constantly made use of staff from ministries. Even the legal frameworks of these EMBs provide civil servants from ministries the ability to sit in when needed. However, these ad-hoc staff need to be given quality training. Usually, they are briefed for a few days on their expected duties, not giving ample room for proper assessment by EMBs before being deployed to their various places of assignment (Fombad, 2012:11; Omotola, 2010:542). The need for additional time to train ad hoc personnel and conduct assessments underscores the fundamental developmental challenges facing the EMBs. It exposes the EMBs to forces whose interests are outside the principles of the institutions. During the 2018 presidential elections, ELECAM engaged about 1 million poll officials who needed proper profiling and handling of these ad-hoc staff, which constituted a considerable challenge to ELECAM because some were affiliated or card-carrying members of competing political parties who unjustifiably influenced the outcome of the election.

5.8.3.3. Security Challenge

This is another obstacle to the conduct of free and fair elections in Cameroon. Elections in Cameroon have been portrayed in recent years as a do-or-die affair where winners win all and losers lose all (Ake, 1996; Jega, 2013:9). This has led to severe security trepidations such as assaults on electoral personnel on duty and destruction of electoral materials by hired thugs, misapplication of security orderlies attached to VIPs/politicians, the act of violence on political opponents and intimidation of voters (Jega, 2013:10). In the 2018 Presidential elections, leading opposition candidate Maurice Kamto was placed under a prolonged house arrest and later jailed in connection with post-elections violence both in Cameroon and out of Cameroon (violence in Cameroonian embassies in Germany and France).

The security question also relates to parts of the country that have been facing peace and security threats for several years. Voter turnout in these areas was observed to be characteristically dismal, as observed in the

North-West and South-West regions battling with a violent insurgency and the Far-North region suffering incursions from Boko Haram and ISWAP. Special measures are needed in such areas to secure election officials and materials, as well as to ensure voters and prevent the voting outcome from being invalidated by external factors. These require adequate time, means, skills, and resources, often needing improvement.

5.8.3.4. Material Poverty of the More Significant Part of Cameroonians

The 2011 National Bureau of Statistics report stated that over 70% of Cameroonians lived on less than $1 daily. The unemployment rate as of 2014 was rated around 24% (WBG, 2014:5). Poverty not only makes the electorate vulnerable, but also destabilizes and perverts the electoral process through undue monetization of politics. (Ake, 1996:10; Bratton, 2008)

According to Bratton, politicians in Cameroon, or their representatives, often present money, food items, and other necessities in exchange for votes. Vote buying is most often prevalent among people with low incomes. Electoral officials are also stained with money and other gratifications (Bratton 2008:4-6). When the poor accept money or bribes for votes, they collude in commoditizing their franchise, thereby reinforcing their subordination and converting the election into suppression (Ake, 1996:11).

5.8.4. Communication and Logistics

Communication and logistics are other challenges that have delayed the conveyance of electoral materials and officials to various polling centers, especially in mountainous, hinterland, and crisis-stricken regions where transportation means are relatively complex (Jinadu, 1997). This has intensified political apathy as voter turnout for elections is low. Many Cameroonians need more confidence in participating in elections (WBG & FES, 2011).

5.9. Gender Issues Arising from Electoral Development

According to the General Population and Housing Census (2005), women comprise nearly 50.5% of the estimated population of 19,406,900 inhabitants. The growth rate of the female population from 2005 to 2015 was 10.1%, compared to 9.9% for males (GPHC, 2010). Women are socio-economic agents of change required in every sector of any economy. Even though the situation has improved in several areas of national life, women's participation continues to be a cause of concern because of persistent gender inequality in crucial areas such as education, health, economy, politics, and employment (African Development Bank Group, 2015).

To eliminate these inequalities, the Cameroonian government has ratified numerous international treaties, conventions, and laws that establish human rights, and, most importantly, the rights of women, which incorporate a gender perspective for sustainable and equal development.

As stated by Alexandra Diwouta T. Christele in her book titled 'The Place of Women in the Political Sphere', women in the South-West of Cameroon region, for example, are still limited in almost all significant areas of human competence where the status of a woman is always a reflection of the label of cultural views of the woman's role in a myopic society being that of childbearing and home management. Due to limited stereotypical cultural precincts, she has little or no opportunity to explore broader aspirations and achieve her dreams, particularly in the socio-economic and political sectors. This has perpetually resulted in female children being given little or no opportunity to further education beyond the secondary level (Alexandra, 2004).

Despite making up 52% of the adult population in Cameroon, women account for less than half of registered voters, according to figures released by the elections management body ELECAM (Voice of Africa, 2017). In Cameroon, women are underrepresented in voter rolls and decision-making circles, from village councils to parliament. About one-third of seats in the National Assembly are held by women, and Cameroon has just 31 female mayors out of the total 360 in the country. According to the Municipal Development Counselling Group (2013), the Fako Division in the South-West Region of Cameroon has had only 154 females out of 877 councilors, barely 18% (MUDEC, 2006). It is still being determined if this problem relates to women's lack of awareness of the laws prescribing their political participation in the country. It necessitates an assessment of the existing political structure at a more critical level. According to studies, the male-dominated political landscape in Cameroon may contribute to the underrepresentation of women in policy-making. Although there has been noteworthy progress towards equitable political representation, men still hold a greater share of political authority, and female leadership needs to be present at the highest level of Cameroon governance (Goheen, 1996).

Excluding women from government is an inefficient use of human resources. This is why the plight of women is not heard in the national sphere, which causes voter apathy, weakens democracy, and hinders national development.

Cameroon's first democratic elections took place in 1996, and many analysts viewed these elections as a significant benchmark in the evolution from one-party rule to a genuine democracy. In the 2007 municipal and council elections, the total number of registered electors stood at 4,940,203, including 1,729,563 women and 3,210,640 men (Elecam, 2007). The total number of electors registered in 2011 stood at 7,525,532, which included 3,853,208 women and 3,537,047 men (Mufua, 2014:11). A notable increase was experienced in the number of registered women that year, when measured up to previous municipal elections of 2002–2007, as the total number of councilors stood at 9,963 (8,303 men and 1,661 women) [13.1%]. In 2002, out of the 337 mayors elected, only 10 were women; however, in 2007, out of 339 mayors, 23 were women, representing a fraction of 4.5% and 5%, respectively (Mufua, 2014:11).

The presence of women in democratic governance has evenly led to considerable gains for women folks in general. For example, during the 2007–2012 mandate, the Tombel Council, headed by a woman, undertook projects such as building schools, health facilities, toilets, and boreholes for water. Thus, statistics point to a slight increase in women's representation in local governance, and Cameroon is yet to reach the desired quota advocated for at the international level (Mufua, 2014:12). In the National arena, the amendment of the 1972 Constitution in 1996 and 2008, respectively, established the principle of equality.

The April 19, 2012, Electoral Code states that each list of candidates must consider the following:

- Various sociological components of the constituency concerned and
- Gender aspects (Sect. 171, (3) (National Assembly, 2012).

The 2012 Electoral Code gives no room for the tactical representation of women in the different elective positions. Gender considerations in the composition of the candidatures list did not assume a compulsory zebra list, which creates room for both sexes to alternate. Moreover, gender consideration does not automatically solve the issue of equal participation of women and men in electoral mandates and functions. Despite this, women have continued to gain access to leadership structures, though at a slow to moderate pace, throughout the past few years. This resulted in a significant step forward in history for the Cameroonian women (Mufua, 2014).

The Electoral Code of Cameroon approved a law in April 2012, which was amended and supplemented by another bill passed in December 2012. As a result, gender issues became a legal prerequisite for compiling all candidate lists for the municipal, legislative, regional, and Senate elections (UN Women Cameroon, 2013).

Year	Voter Registration	Total Votes/ Voter Turnout	Invalid /Blank Votes	Total Valid Votes	% Turnout
1 March 1992 National Assembly Election	4,019,562	2,435,443	238,200	2,197,243	(60.6%)
11 October 1992 Presidential Election	4,195,687	3,015,448	50,012	2,965,436	(71.9%)
17 May 1997 National Assembly Election	3,844,330	2,906,186		938,144	(75.6%)
12 October 1997 Presidential Election	4,220,136	Not Available	Not Available	3,422,055	(81.4%)
30 June 2002 National Assembly Election	Not Available	Not Available			
11 October 2004 Presidential Election	4,657,748	3,830,272	72,051	3,758,221	(82.2%)
22 July 2007 National Assembly Election	5,000,000 (approx.)	Not Available (N/A)			
9 October 2011 Presidential Election	7,251,651	4,951,434	114,185	4,847,249	(68.3%)
9 October 2018 Presidential Election	7,251,651	4,951,434	114,185	4,847,249	(68.3%)

Table 5.2: Elections Management and Voter Apathy Since 1990
Source: Field Survey, 2023

5.10. Elections Management Bodies, Voter Apathy, and the Consolidation of Electoral Democracy in Cameroon

Voter apathy is a significant challenge to the democratic process and is an excellent signal that the election process lacks credibility. The study by Mataka, Blessing, Nkandu, Mwaka, and Ossin URI (2020) reveals a positive correlation between voting and the growth of electoral democracy, as voting promotes citizen participation, a key element in the development of electoral democracy. They further reveal that elections foster political tolerance and promote peaceful power transfer. However, they have considered many factors contributing to voter apathy, including the failure of leadership changes, the inability of victorious candidates to honor campaign promises, electoral violence, religious beliefs, age eligibility requirements, limited voting hours, and inadequate voter education. The study concludes that voter apathy poses a significant threat to any democratic process, and it is exacerbated when the election process lacks credibility.

The study recommends that an automated biometric voter registration system be a continuous process, allowing those who have attained the voting age and relocated to be registered in their new areas. It further recommends changing the voting system to allow compulsory voting for everyone with a national registration card, thereby increasing voter turnout. The study also suggests reforms to the Electoral Commission of Zambia (ECZ) to ensure it is an independent, competent, autonomous, and impartial arbiter that inspires confidence in the electoral process. They finally advocate for education to be strengthened and conducted occasionally to empower voters with the necessary knowledge and skills about elections.

Aside from the common developmental and infrastructural challenges facing many areas in the country, there is a legitimate concern that the current state of roads and general access to many localities may impact voter turnout. Residents in remote areas have complained about the miles they must travel to reach voting centers. Some citizens complained that they had to walk between four (4) and six (6) hours, while others had to use canoes to cross rivers to be able to register during the exercise. It is evident that in such circumstances, the likelihood that some citizens, particularly aged persons, pregnant women, and PhDs, may decide not to cast their vote on election day remains high. The campaign period and election day usually occur during the rainy season, swelling rivers and rendering already muddy roads impassable.

Accessing voting grounds can be physically demanding and a barrier to citizens exercising their right to vote. This situation highlights a form of marginalization and raises concerns about equal access and inclusivity in the electoral process. It also promotes voter trafficking, a growing challenge in which politicians exploit citizens through free transportation to registration centers and voting sites in exchange for money.

The difficulty of accessing voting centers is also demoralizing for security officers, who are already facing the challenging task of maintaining peace and order during the rainy season polls and need more opportunities for backup in the event of an emergency.

The timing of elections in the rainy season is an issue raised by international and domestic observer groups in 2011 and 2018. Still, the date has yet to be adjusted despite these recommendations. Civil society organizations have raised concerns about the election dates, arguing that this can contribute to low voter turnout if the expected heavy rains materialize. Past experiences suggest that heavy rains render the roads impassable for many aspirant voters traveling long distances to access the voting centers. Cameroonians continue demonstrating their determination to participate in the electoral process despite these genuine challenges.

Figure 5.4: An Example of Roads During the Rainy Season
Source: Field Survey, 2023

Madubuegwu, C. (2017) argues that election is an ideal of democracy, and the participation of people in this democratic process underscores the substance of representative governance beyond symbolism. Sadly, emerging and advanced democracies worldwide are challenged by the unpleasant phenomenon of voter apathy today. Observations and studies have shown a decline in voter turnout in recent national and sub-national elections. It revealed a persistent trend of voter apathy sustained by exacerbating conditions with adverse effects on democratic consolidation. The work argues that measures to reverse the trend of voter apathy in Nigeria can be streamlined into two-dimensional perspectives to strengthen the process of democratic consolidation through increased voter enthusiasm.

As a democratizing polity, Cameroon is grappling with myriad socio-political challenges that have, over the years, constrained efforts and processes toward democratic consolidation and national development. Notably among these problems is a crisis in the election process. Today, the election crisis constitutes one of the daunting challenges in the country's multiparty democracy. Hence, it manifests in dysfunctional election management, logistical inadequacies, violence, and apathy. In a specific sense, voter apathy represents an ugly trend in electoral democracy. In recent years, this situation has been a source of serious concern among scholars, electoral practitioners, and election observers, as it has had adverse effects on the country's fractured democratic process.

In a generic sense, voter apathy is a global phenomenon. A cross-sectional analysis of electoral democracies has shown that the percentage of citizens who vote in elections varies significantly across countries (IDEA, 2005, p. 23). In advanced democracies such as the United States, the rate of voter turnout has been fluctuating since 1960, ranging from 62.8 percent in 1960 to 52.8 percent in 1980, 53.3 percent in 1984, and 50.3 percent in 1988. The percentage rose to 55.2 percent in 1992 and fell to 50.3 percent in 2000, and again rose to 55.5 percent in 2004. It, however, recorded an exponential rise in 2008, reaching 60 percent. It was 57.5 percent in 2012 and 58.1 percent in the 2016 presidential elections. (Ethridge and Handelman, 2012, p.99, and Anderson, 2017, p.2). In Europe, there has been persistent voter apathy since the 1990s and incidences of lower voter turnout have been witnessed in North and South American countries and the African continent (IDEA, 2005, p.11). Over the years, this global electoral challenge has stimulated national discourse and scholarly literature on the best modalities to sustain voters' interest in liberal democracy. In Cameroon, the same optimism is shared to evince the scope and relevance of this discourse. The discourse is premised on an explicit analysis of the dynamics and causes of voter apathy, as well as the extent to which it has compromised the process of democratic consolidation in Cameroon.

Democracy is a term that underscores the significance of civil liberty, popular and alternative views, and the rule of law, which are entrenched in governance and the political process. However, the analysis of the theory and practice of democracy is often depleted, with many varied perspectives among scholars and practitioners of management. Being a derivative of two Greek words, "rule of the people", the central theme of the concept, 'democracy', is popular governance or rulership of the people. The notion of the rule of the people was first conceived in Athens and best captured in Pericles' (415–429BC) funeral oration as chronicled by Thucydides (Ikin, 1981, p.60). Ikin's view provides historical insight into the practice of democracy, which was first documented in the 5th-century ancient Athens city-state of Greece, but failed to explain the process of people's rule from what scholars classified as 'direct democracy'. In this sense of gap, Sabine and Thomson (1973) illustrated the direct form of democracy as seen in Athenian Ecclesia or Assembly (the whole people assembly), which holds its sessions to discuss democracy, a concept deeply rooted in the affairs of the 'polis', where every male citizen (who had reached twenty years of age) attended, is a system that empowers people. Beyond its classical form, democracy has a modern meaning, as illuminated by Birch (1995) in Ezirim et al. (2016, p.98). From the American perspective, it has been used to mean somewhat more than a structure to indicate a phenomenon, with the term 'democratic' indicating a "degree of social equality, not a form of government." This idea depicts people-ness or being people-centered, probably resulting in the most popular and ordinary definition of it being the one generally credited to Abraham Lincoln as a "government or rule of the people, by the people and for the people." It conveys the idea that people are responsible for their affairs, both individually and collectively. The American perspective of democracy, as enunciated by Abraham Lincoln, underscored the importance of representative democracy or modern democracy, where the people are the ultimate source of power.

Similarly, Appodari (1974) viewed modern democracy as representative and indirect, where the people govern through their periodically elected representatives. The preceding analysis, however, merely projected the symbolism of democracy (as a people-driven system of governance) without a critical review of its indices and attributes. In this regard, Omemma (2016, p.129) illuminated the indices fundamental in liberal democracy:

- Substantial individual freedom of belief, opinion, discussion, speech, publication, broadcast, assembly, demonstration, petition, and the internet.
- Freedom of ethnic, religious, racial, and other minority groups (historically excluded majorities) to practise their religion and culture and participate in political and social lives.
- The right of all adult citizens to vote and to run for office (if they meet certain minimum age and competency requirements).
- Genuine openness and competition in the electoral arena, enabling any group that adheres to the constitutional contest for office.
- Legal equality of all citizens under the rule of law, in which the laws are clear, publicly known, universal, stable, and non-retroactive.
- An independent Judiciary to naturally and consistently apply the law to protect individual and group rights.
- Due process of law and freedom of individuals from torture, terror, and unjustified detention, exile, or interference in their personal lives by the state or non-state actors.
- An independent legislature, court system, and autonomous agencies do institutional checks on the power of elected officials.
- Genuine pluralism in sources of information and forms of organization, state independence, and thus a vibrant civil society.
- Control over the military and state security apparatus by civilians who are ultimately accountable to the people through elections.

A pertinent question is, therefore, asked, "What does consolidation of democracy entail?" For Odoh and Aro (2016), democratic consolidation has garnered the broad interest of scholars over the years, referring to the institutionalization of democratic culture and the democratization of rule. Thus, when democracy is consolidated, it becomes legitimate in the perception and estimation of citizens. However, Odo and Aro's views failed to clarify the specificities of what is institutionalized about culture and the attributes of what the masses conceived as 'legitimacy'. In an attempt to dissect the significance of legitimate attributes in democratic consolidation, Ikpe (2011) stressed that the consolidation of democracy is the process of achieving broad legitimization, such that all significant political actors of both the elite and masses believe that the democratic regime is better for their society than any other realistic alternative they can imagine. However, Ikpe's perspective is depleted with ambiguity.

Succinctly, Bretton (1981) conceived of democratic consolidation as involving the widespread acceptance of rules to guarantee political participation and social stability (Regular. Volume 5. Number 2. June 2020 Page 46 competition). According to him, elections remain fundamental, not only for installing democratic governments but as a necessary requisite for broader democracy consolidation.

Elections' regularity, openness, and acceptability signal whether basic constitutional foundations are being laid for sustainable rule. This perspective underscored the imperative of 'election' as a veritable process advancing democratic consolidation. Corroborating Bratton's assertion, David (1990) averred that the consolidation of democracy involves the institutionalization of rules that fully guarantee political participation and competition. For him, elections that empower ordinary citizens to choose candidates of their interest guarantee democratic consolidation. However, critics of David's view argue that institutionalized rules that guarantee freedom and participation may be violated when the correct orientation and attitude are lacking. More elaborately,

Payne and Nasser (2003) argued that the consolidation of democracy is a long-term process that continues after countries have transitioned to democracy. It, therefore, involves behavioral, attitudinal, and institutional changes. Behaviorally, a democratic regime is consolidated when there is no significant effort to change the government by force and when most people believe democratic institutions and procedures are the most appropriate for their society. Institutionally, a democratic regime is consolidated when society, including the government, believes that specific laws, methods, and institutions must govern the society. In an implicit sense, the Payne and Nassar conception illuminates certain illusions and realities underlying the challenges of Cameroon's democracy. The absence of intermittent military usurpation of political power in the current democratic dispensation does not essentially imply that the country's democracy has been consolidated. This is because the democratic process is bedeviled with institutional and procedural deviances, as exemplified in the undemocratic tendencies of institutions and political processes that satisfy the inordinate interest of the political elite in violation of democratic norms and public interest.

To this extent, we have laws, procedures, and institutions that are weak and susceptible to the authoritarian tendencies of the political elite.

Curiously, for democracy to be consolidated, certain conditions are expedient:

- A condition must exist that makes it relatively easy for a civil society to develop, protect its interests, inform the public, and challenge the government through acceptable processes.
- Specific arrangements must be made for groups and individuals to compete for political power. This usually means developing and functioning core institutions such as political parties, interest groups, and an electoral system.
- Society must respect and uphold the rule of law; an independent judicial system must exist to determine the law.
- There must be an institutionalized economic society with a significant degree of market autonomy and the right of individuals to own property (Payne and Nassar, 2003, p.238).

Fundamentally, democratic consolidation is characterized by the following indices:

- It is a phenomenon that precedes democratization or democratic transition.
- It reflects the capacity of the government and governance to respond promptly and proficiently to the anxieties and expectations of the masses.
- It reflects an institutionalized and efficient system of checks on governance and state institutions to prevent abuses, infractions, and corruption.
- It reflects the reasonable extent of patriotism, awareness, and enthusiasm among the citizens to identify with the affairs of the state and engage constructively with the persons in government on issues of public importance.
- It reflects the existence of an independent and efficient judicial system in the process of justice administration.
- It reflects a transparent, credible, and free election process at the state level and within political parties and other social institutions where the values of liberty, the rule of law, discipline, and tolerance are upheld.
- It reflects the existence of state institutions that are accountable, effective, and responsive in their conduct and service to the state.

- It reflects the civility and sensitivity of civil society organizations in advocating for issues of public interest.
- It reflects the inclusive and participatory process of state policies in deference to the socio-economic realities and expectations of the state.
- It reflects foreign policy options and diplomatic engagements that protect rights, guarantee safety, and explore the potential of the citizens within the country and across various continents globally.

With the varied perspectives of scholars and assumptions of this discourse, the election is one of the fundamentals of democratic consolidation. Regarding elections, voting, and voter apathy, we note that elections are vital to democratization and democratic consolidation because they are widely recognized as the only legitimate form of transfer and exercise of power in modern states. They have, thus, become the primary theater of political participation, whereby voters actively exercise their democratic rights by electing representatives through periodic, accessible, and fair elections (Ballington, 2001; English, 2005).

In this vein, elections and voting are essential attributes of democracy. The two concepts share certain affinities in process and essence. Technically, there are apparent disparities. Hence, the election may be defined as the choice process agreed upon by a group. It enables them to select one or a few people out of many to occupy one or several authority positions (Nnoli, 2003, p. 220). Similarly, Held (1999) viewed the election as a competition for votes among political parties. In this regard, the election is a process by which people decide between competing candidates and political parties for positions of authority in the state. Significant to these definitional views of election is the "people and choice." The election is, therefore, the mandate of the people to decide on the array of promises and ideologies by the political parties that will better meet the people's expectations (Yorons, 2017, p.251).

To this end, Adejumobi (1998) underscored the importance of the symbolism of elections within the context of popular sovereignty and the expression of the social pact between the states and the people, as elections are seen as the kernel of political accountability and the means of ensuring reciprocity and exchange between the government and the governed. Adejumobi's view establishes the inextricable nexus between election and democracy as a people-driven process. In other words, the election reinforces the democratic process. Election is necessary for democracy, even if it may not be sufficient.

Accordingly, Conteh (2013) remarked that a free and fair election is sovereign and has the right to keep or vote out the government. It also reflects the will of the people and is, therefore, the only legitimate means of democratic leadership. By exercising their vote freely, the people choose and give legitimacy to their leaders, while free and fair elections mirror the extent of freedom in society (Nwankwo, 2018, p.4).

Similarly, Yorons (2017) further established the nexus between elections and democracy apparent under the following:

- Elections are part of democracy. Therefore, if they are misused, the entire democratic process loses its credibility.
- Elections allow the electorate to decide on a more credible candidate or party in the next round of elections if the incumbent does not govern well.

A cursory observation of the election showed that voting is central in the process. KwonNdung et al. (2014) held that voting is widely used in contemporary democratic politics to choose leaders for various electoral positions. Thus, Zahida and Younia (2014) viewed voting as the function of electing representatives by casting votes in an election. In this vein, Okolie (2003) stressed that voting in elections for public offices is usually conducted using the ballot boxes. Voting, therefore, takes the form of thumbing in the ballot paper provided. Establishing the essence of voting, Hari and Choudhury (1997) stressed that it exerts influence over leaders through pressure. The leaders adjust their policies to gain votes since voting determines who will hold elective office. The vote, however, does not communicate the citizens' preferences to leaders or convey explicit information. Invariably, voting undoubtedly accentuates the significance of people's participation in the election process. In other words, it is the legal right and civic obligation of the citizens in a state. In this sense, voting is the legal, political, and social mechanism through which citizens can express their preferences in elections and exercise their interests and needs. It demonstrates political consciousness and citizens' participation (Ejue & Ekanam, 2011, p. 286). Furthermore, Ejure and Ekanam (2011) enunciated that Article 21 of the United Nations Charter on Human Rights indicates the following:

- Everyone has the right to participate in the government of their country directly or through freely chosen representatives.

- The people will be the basis of government authority.

Beyond the global recognition of civil liberty, the Nigerian Federal Republic Constitution of 1999 (as amended) in sections 77(2), 117(2), 132(5), and 178(5) also identified the conditions of voter eligibility and essence of participation in the election process. Essentially, voting as a right and civic responsibility is propelled by the need or interest to participate in the democratic process. Thus, when such a need or interest fails to exist for participation in the democratic process of election, voter apathy occurs. In this sense, Anderson (2017) defined voter apathy as a lack of interest in participating in elections by a particular group of voters. One side-effect of voter apathy can be low voter turnout on election day if voting is non-compulsory. Voter apathy also occurs when eligible voters do not vote in public elections.

Outside of election time, voters may seem disillusioned with the political process or politicians in general (Cloud, 2019, p.1). In other words, voter apathy is invariably the reluctance of eligible voters to vote in an election. In a more explicit sense, Hari and Choudhury (1997) highlighted forms of voter apathy evident in:

- Voter alienation is conceived as induced voter apathy among a proportional percentage of voters. For instance, it was the organizational failure of the Independent National Electoral Commission (INEC) that led to the disenfranchisement of 12 million eligible Nigerian voters who could not obtain their PVCs before the 2015 Presidential and National Assembly elections (Madubuegwu, 2015, p.172).
- Voter distrust is also conceived as voter disenchantment, reflecting the loss of confidence in the political system and process. As noted earlier, voter apathy is a global phenomenon that affects both developing and industrialized economies.

Regarding the United Kingdom, Verrall (2016) argued that the freedom to vote is a cornerstone of political democracy. However, for the last half of a century, voting has declined. In the 1950 UK General Election, voter turnout was 84 percent, whereas in the 2015 General Election, it was 66.1 percent. In the 2015 UK General Election, the Conservative Party won with a slim majority vote of 36.9 percent (11.3 million votes). This means that 11.3 million people voted for the interests of a total UK population of 64.7 million, i.e., 17 percent of the remaining 83 percent of the country. There was a closeness between those eligible to vote but did not vote (15 million) and those who could not (18 million). This worries our politicians because it undermines the incumbent government's legitimacy and indirectly indicates distrust and disbelief in democracy as a political idea. Furthermore, the Election Survey report (2019) examined five causes of voter apathy in the UK to illuminate why people do not vote:

- Lack of Interest: People do not vote simply because they are not interested.
- Lack of Knowledge: Many people who do not vote believe they lack enough knowledge about the government, the election process, or individual party policies.
- Many British people have had enough of the "political elite," whom they neither trust nor relate to.
- Safe Seat Residents: Many people who do not vote are nonetheless interested in politics and even support a political party, but do not vote because they feel their votes would be wasted.
- They Can't: Some people do not vote because they are not allowed to. Members of the House of Lords, most prisoners, and foreign citizens from outside the UK, Ireland, or the Commonwealth are among those who are not eligible to vote.

The most disenfranchised group, however, are those under 18. The move to lower the voting age has gained momentum since it was first put before Parliament in 1999. YouGov research from 2018 shows that public support for 16 and 17-year-olds' right to vote has increased from 20 to 34 percent since 2013, but still does not enjoy widespread favor. Interestingly, voter apathy, otherwise known as voter non-participation in the electoral process, is measured by the index of voter turnout. Thus, voter turnout has been identified in the extant literature as one of the core ways of measuring participation in any election (Blais & Dobrzynska, 1998). What, then, is voter turnout? Voter turnout is the extent to which eligible voters cast their votes on election day. It is measured as the percentage of votes cast in an election, including invalid votes (Abdurashid, 2016, p.1). Voter turnout is the percentage of registered voters who come out to vote in an election (Socialscientia Journal, ISSN: 2636-5979) (Regular. Volume 5. Number 2. June 2020 Page | 50).

In democratizing societies, voter turnout is the most common form of political participation (Mahmud, 2015, p.4). It implies that voter turnout determines the index of eligible electors who vote in an election. Similarly, voter turnout is usually measured as a percentage of registered voters who vote. The assumption is that the higher the voter turnout, the higher the level of voter participation and, by extension, the better the democratic quality of the election (Omotola & Aiyedogbon, 2012, p.57).

To this extent, the lower voter turnout reflects apathy among the electorate. Cameroon represents a peculiar case of reference regarding the phenomenon of voter apathy. As a developing economy, it has its history and challenges of voter apathy.

Again, democracy has failed to consolidate in the event of widespread voter alienation and disenchantment created by the failures of the election management body and violence of the election process. Also, the widespread non-involvement of eligible citizens in the elections affects, to an extent, the credibility of the exercise. It, therefore, implies that political parties and candidates that emerge victorious through the process characterized by widespread apathy do not enjoy the popular trust and mandate of the voting population. To this extent, democracy has failed to consolidate when the elected managers or administrators of the state lack the overall mandate and confidence of the electorate. Implicitly, the representatives or political parties elected by a fraction of the voting population to serve in government shall certainly pursue unpopular policies in the state. We may see policies (from this type of government) that need to reflect the plights of citizens and the development priorities of the state.

To this extent, democracy has again failed to consolidate in the event where voter apathy leads to the implementation of unpopular policies by the government and state. Subsequently, voter apathy alienates the citizens from civic enlightenment and obligation. Voter apathy excludes adult citizens from the values expressed and shared during electioneering events and party campaigns. Citizens conventionally become politically socialized through these informative channels to develop civic orientation and attitude towards participatory events of the state. This is because the viability of democracy or the democratic process is measured or assessed by the constructive involvement of the citizens in the political process. In other words, democracy fails to consolidate when the widespread incidence of voter apathy erodes the citizens' sense of civic responsibility.

Furthermore, voter apathy widens the gap between the governing elites and the citizens. As earlier indicated, it creates distrust and suspicion between the citizens and the constituted authority. Such an absurd situation hinders the governance process. It leads to unrest (in the form of popular protest against ill-advised policies and government actions), undermining the state's political stability. In the event of a failed process of social contract (stimulated by voter alienation) between the people and constituted authority, democracy has failed to consolidate. Voter apathy is a persistent issue in Nigerian elections. As earlier noted, it represents one of the daunting challenges of Nigeria's electoral democracy. It is a plague and a function of many variables that have persisted unabatedly in Nigeria's history, dynamics, and process of elections. Hence, it is established that voter apathy has continued to militate against efforts towards democratic consolidation in Nigeria. In this sense, it becomes pertinent to make recommendations about the findings of this study. Voter apathy is a menace that can be managed and reversed through plausible measures that are streamlined in the long and short term. Regarding long-term measures:

- There is a need to entrench a culture and practice of accountability and responsiveness in governance. To this end, the prevailing atmosphere of accountability in public sector service and responsiveness in governance towards various challenges, including poverty, insecurity, and youth unemployment, may gradually reverse the sense of voter distrust and disillusionment among millions of adult citizens towards state institutions and elections.
  A transparent and prudent election management system is also critical to reinforcing citizens' trust and confidence in Nigerian elections. The decisiveness and transparency in driving the electioneering process beyond the antics of opposition political parties and the interference of the ruling party and elites will certainly elicit public trust and confidence in election management and the electoral process in Nigeria.
  Decentralized structures and the voter education process will also bolster voters' confidence and enthusiasm for identifying with the electoral process. The Independent National Electoral Commission, Media, Civil Society Organizations, and Election Advocacy groups should shift their focus from voter information to constructively engaging citizens on the importance of voter participation. The content of such education should also change from the nature of elections to the implications of non-involvement in the electoral process.

A mechanism for monitoring and sanctioning political parties involved in undemocratic or unconventional practices has not only become necessary but also extremely expedient in restoring sanity to healthy competition, which will further encourage citizens' identification with party politics and the electoral process.

- An intense campaign for national consciousness should be undertaken by the National Orientation Agency and National Media Channels to inculcate a sense of patriotism and civic responsibility among Nigerians. This is also extremely important, given the euphoria of regional nationalism and suspicion. These long-term measures can be sustained through the following short-term measures:
    - Voter education and advocacy towards elections.
    - Neutrality and depoliticization of the security agencies before and after elections.
    - Emphasis on rules of engagement, neutrality, sanctions, erring personnel, and infiltration should be topical issues in Nigerian election security management.
    - Review specific provisions of the Electoral ACT in response to voter plights and civility in the political process.

Chapter 6 | Summary, Conclusion and Recommendations

6.1. Summary of Findings

This study has comprehensively analyzed EMBs in Africa, comparing them to their counterparts in other African countries. The aim was to provide a thorough explanation for voter apathy in Cameroon. Our hypothesis suggests that voter apathy is primarily a result of EMBs' inability to conduct free, fair, and transparent elections. Their lack of independence and autonomy has led to a lack of trust from voters, fostering disinterest and apathy.

Among the many findings of this research endeavor, the following arguments frequently popped up as mitigating factors for voter apathy:

<u>6.1.1. Polling Place Quality and Election Administration</u>

The administration of elections is a significant factor contributing to apathy, mainly when the election administrator is affiliated with the ruling party. In such cases, provisional ballots are more likely to be counted, and partisan influences become evident in the casting and counting of these ballots. This association between partisanship and election administration can sow seeds of doubt about the election's fairness. In elections overseen by NEO, where local devolved authorities and other civil servants played a crucial role, the quality of election administration was a significant concern. This led to voter distrust and apathy, underscoring the importance of impartial election administration.

Regarding the physical quality of polling places, including parking availability, location, and management and operation, this research found that low-quality polling stations tend to be located in low-income areas. In contrast, high-quality polling stations tend to be in higher-income areas. Thus, the incentive to vote was higher in high-income and low-income areas.

<u>6.1.2. The Effect of Waiting In Lines on Voting Day</u>

This work presents an exciting finding regarding the effects of election administration on voter behavior. It estimates the causal impact of lines on election day outcomes, revealing how decisions affecting internal polling place organizations influence voter behavior on election day. Thus, the results complement the existing work using diverse data sources—surveys (King, 2019; Stewart, 2013), administrative data (Herron & Smith, 2015, 2016), or cellphone pings (Xie et al., 2019) —to explore polling place wait times and line length. The magnitude of the effect is commensurate with related observational estimates in Pettigrew (2016) (that is, a 1% decrease per hour of waiting) and Highton (2006:24) (that is, a 3.5% decrease for each increase of 100 registrants per machine).

Lines make voting costlier for voters, thereby decreasing turnout. Since election administrators must finish serving queued voters before the start of counting, election-day lines can delay ballot counting and the reporting of results. This research finds evidence for both of these observable implications.

The figurative illustration below presents regression discontinuity results for turnout. Secondary data from polling centers just above the cut-off were observed to have 2.4 percentage points greater turnout than those just below the cut-off (95% CI: 1.1%, 3.6%). The average turnout below the cut-off is 77.9%, while just above is 80.3%. At the cut-off, long lines prevent 18 votes on average (95% CI: 9.6, 25.7).

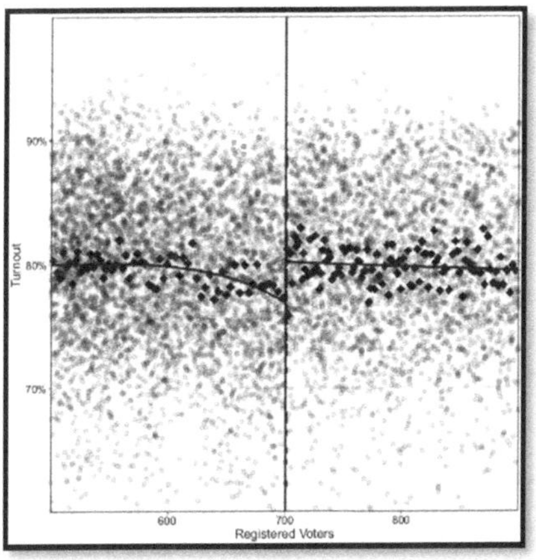

Figure 6.1: Discontinuity Plot—Turnout: Polling Centers above the 700-Registered Voter Cut-Off Have an Additional Stream, Leading to 2.4% Higher Voter Turnout Than Polling Centers below the Cut-Off. Dots Represent Individual Polling Centers. Squares Show Bin-specific Turnout Summaries.

Source: Agu, Okeke and Dike (2013)

While this turnout effect is consistent with a line-based mechanism, waiting- or time-related measures would provide more direct evidence (for example, time to check in, line length, and so on). Collecting such evidence would require an intensive data collection campaign. For instance, Stein et al. (2020:18) have reported detailed line-related data collected at a convenience sample of 528 polling places in 25 jurisdictions. Herron and Smith (2016) have carried out similarly detailed data collection at one polling place in New Hampshire. Collecting such data in a prospective regression discontinuity design would require a small army; for comparison, the adequate sample size for the time-based estimates presented below encompasses 4,243 polling centers. Direct line length and waiting time measures would require an impractical prospective design. Thus, this retrospective study relies on another time-based measure related to line presence.

6.1.3. Voting on Paper versus Voting with DREs

Another factor affecting the voting experience is the device used by voters to cast their ballots. Voters acclaim increased satisfaction when DREs are used in the voting process. This is, however, different in Cameroon, where voting is still conducted traditionally using paper, increasing the chances of ballot tampering and corruption. This research revealed that respondents believe the existence of security guarantees regarding electronic voting mechanisms can have a positive impact on voter confidence.

6.1.4. Partisan Differences

A correlation between voter confidence and party affiliation was also identified and dug into from aggregated data from several open-ended interviews to connect the two. The researcher found a positive relationship between voting for the 'winner' and confidence.

6.1.5. Electoral Communication and Timing of Elections

Electoral communication and information were found to be remarkably low. A whopping 70% of respondents indicated they were usually taken by surprise, per the electoral calendar. However, this variable is agreed to have seen progress with ELECAM compared to NEO.

Respondents also unanimously agree on the need for EMBs to dedicate more efforts to communicate and inform the population at all times, not just during election periods.

Similarly, the study found direct links between low voter turnout and political insecurity (threats to peace and security), with record-low numbers registered in the North West, South West, and Extreme North Regions, which have been affected by threats to peace and security since 2014. Apart from this, the timing of elections is seen as a variable of little concern.

6.1.6. The Socio-economic Environment

The research equally found that at the individual level, the propensity to vote is associated with several socio-demographic characteristics, particularly age and education. Similarly, it would be natural to assume that cross-national variations in turnout are related to socio-economic differences between regions, constituencies, and even political parties. When considered, the impact of the socio-economic environment affects turnout as it tends to be higher in more economically developed council areas, constituencies, and political parties than in less economically developed ones. Turnout also tends to be higher in smaller cities, but the relationship is not statistically significant.

6.1.7. The Role of Stakeholders in Promoting the Political Participation of Voters

6.1.7.1. ELECAM (Electoral Commission)

As the main protagonist and election organizer, ELECAM has a strategic role in determining the quality of an election. In addition to preparing for the administrative and logistical needs of the polls, this commission also increases voter participation. One of the most common strategies is providing political education to voters or prospective voters. Ideally, the socialization undertaken by ELECAM focuses on the election date and its aftermath. The socialization conducted in the 2018 election was limited. According to the Chairman of ELECAM, delivering information to the public conducted by his institution experienced several obstacles. The biggest was insufficient funds.

It impacted the implementation of electoral education campaigns, which required revision. All stages of the process were carried out within only three months. At that time, several education campaigns were conducted only five times in each chosen city, in rotation, by inviting local community leaders (ELECAM, 2019). In addition, according to the ELECAM Secretary, the problem was also constrained by geographical issues, as parts of the country were inaccessible at that time. The role of ELECAM, especially in the 2018 presidential elections, in disseminating information was vital. Unfortunately, most of the disseminating information tools (APS) and campaign tools (APK) were not provided by ELECAM since most of the information came from candidates or political parties.

Having new regulations in this light to provide an equal opportunity for every candidate to compete regardless of their financial status would be a game-changer in the future. The problem was that ELECAM had a budget that needed to be expanded to provide APK and APS. According to a top ELECAM official, the funding problem resulted in fewer education campaigns for the 2018 election compared to the previous municipal and parliamentary elections, where, as usual, each candidate was allowed to maximize their campaign to attract voters through banners, billboards, and posters.

6.1.7.2. Local Government Units

As one of the critical stakeholders in elections, local government units have consistently sought to promote the implementation of elections, from the neighborhood level, as minor government units, to the council areas. Their role has always been crucial in increasing the voters' political awareness and, thus, turnout. Strategically, councils serve as a swift and effective channel for providing information to the community. This communal institution becomes a strategic medium for disseminating information. The role of the heads of villages and quarters in mobilizing these voters is of prime importance, and it needs to be better harnessed. The councils cultivate national values among citizens, including promoting political awareness to enable voters to choose their future leaders. According to one Deputy Mayor, his council provided ten political education activities in the form of education campaigns to beginner voters in schools.

6.1.7.3. Political Parties

The political education process by political parties has yet to be effective. Most political parties work only when the elections are around the corner as a "boat provider" for candidates who will take part in elections. The stagnation of the political education process by political parties in Cameroon has not only affected voters but also internal political education and political regeneration within the party itself, often leaving these areas in disarray. A scribe of the SDF party in Yaoundé revealed to this researcher that most candidates his political party promoted were instant cadres with financial capital but little political experience. This is a political anomaly in which access to power is primarily granted to a group of individuals who are considered to have solid financial backing, without regard for their intellectual capacity to envision a vision for society, nation, and state. This means that the election legitimizes the investors who want to take power.

As the organizer of elections, a top ELECAM official admitted that many political parties only play a procedural role as candidate nominators when elections occur. They are less interested in providing political education to the public, which means voters do not have emotional ties with the ideology of these political parties.

6.1.7.4. Universities

Educational institutions are significant contributors to the success of local governance. Academics play a role in conducting studies and research on growing political issues. According to one Deputy Mayor in Buea, who also has an academic background, the role of universities in Cameroon in increasing political awareness among the citizens cannot be denied. This role is mainly limited to public lectures and seminars. The role of universities in improving the political education of the community is expected to be beyond just that. Universities can serve as incubators for policy and even nurseries for future leaders and noteholders.

6.1.7.5. Community Organizations

Community organizations are informal representations that emerge in society. In Cameroon, where the population is very heterogeneous, the role of these organizations is significant. The most prominent organizations are tribal organizations. There are at least two hundred big ethnic groups, and even groups with a smaller scope (sub-ethnics groups). The influence of these community organizations on voter participation cannot be underestimated. One Mayor from the Manyu division admitted that he made strides in the political build-up in Manyu because his wife held the Chairperson position of a significant community–tribal organization, and he was a prominent sponsor.

The role of religious groups was also seen to be very important. According to a respondent, the chairman of the ruling CPDM is considered a moderate religious leader, given that he went to seminary. This appeals to many religion-inclined voters who vote for him, even if they are not members or cardholders of his party.

Building political awareness takes a long time. The low level of voters' political idealism was also evident, as voters tended to vote for candidates based solely on pragmatic aspects, such as financial gain and other material benefits. In addition, in most cases, the low voter interest in suburban areas was triggered by voters' dissatisfaction due to low living standards and a lack of social amenities.

6.1.8. The Role of the Police and Security Agencies

The Cameroonian Police and other security agencies (including the Cameroonian Gendarmerie, army, and others) have historically played a pivotal role in elections in Cameroon. According to the Electoral Code (2006), police are legally mandated to provide security during election campaigns and fulfill various functions during elections. For instance, on election day, security officials are expected to mount roadblocks, guard individual polling stations, and escort ballot boxes from polling stations to collation centers. Despite their centrality in the election process, Cameroonians question the neutrality and professionalism of the security forces. During the 2018 presidential elections, there was a widespread view that the president, civil administrators, and politicians affiliated with the CPDM manipulated members of security agencies for electoral gain (National Democratic Institute 2007: 27). Various opposition organizations alleged that police officers turned a blind eye to electoral irregularities, while other members of the police force were actively engaged in stealing ballot boxes and denying opposition voters access to polling stations (International Crisis Group 2007:4).

6.1.9. The Role of the Judiciary

The Cameroonian judiciary has been called upon in pre- and post-election periods to adjudicate election-related cases. During the pre-election period, calls to implement electoral reforms have been a recurring theme in the judiciary, as well as disputes over political party primaries and a culture of candidate imposition, prompting many aggrieved candidates to seek redress in the courts. In the post-election period, losing parties and candidates file petitions with the Election Tribunals. Public confidence in the judiciary has increased significantly during and after the 2011 elections because of the judiciary's apparent autonomy in decision-making. As noted, Election Tribunals and the Supreme Court overturned most of the appeals made after the 2018 presidential elections, explaining each judgment on national television.

Although some commentators describe the court interventions as a perversion of democracy, citizens in regions with irregularities that were addressed saw the court actions as a democratic safeguard. To them, the courts provided democratic justice where the incumbent, ELECAM, and the security forces had fallen short.

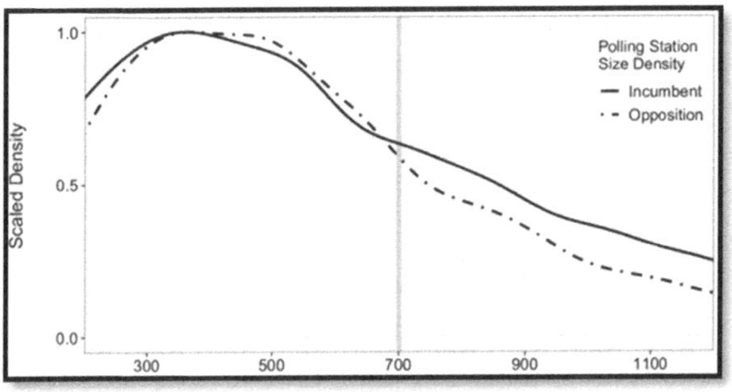

Figure 6.2. Polling Centers Just Over the Cut-Off Tend to Lie In Incumbent Strongholds; as a Result, Incumbent Supporters Are the Preponderance of Voters Experiencing a Lower Cost on Election Day

Source: Field Work, 2022

6.1.10. Vote Share and the Distribution of Election Administration Resources

While this finding does not directly relate to EMBs and voter apathy, it remains attractive to the study. Research gathered that while the presence or length of lines did not cause individuals en masse to change their vote choice, the vote share discontinuity favoring the incumbent reflects how registered voters are distributed across the country. Incumbent strongholds tended to have more significant registrants, leading to more dual-stream polling centers in those areas. As a result, marginal voters in opposition strongholds tended to face higher waiting costs than those in incumbent strongholds. Figure 6.2 (top panel) explores this idea by overlaying the density of polling center size—the running variable—by the opposition and incumbent strongholds. Constituencies with 90% or more vote share in support of the opposition or incumbent candidate in the 2018 presidential elections are strongholds. This figure reveals the source of the vote share effect: polling centers just over the cut-off tend to lie in incumbent areas, whereas those just under the cut-off more frequently lie in opposition areas. This provides depth to understanding voter trends and may help explain voter apathy in some areas and affluence in others.

6.2. Conclusions

Credible elections are today considered the cornerstone of an inclusive and sustainable democracy. The credibility of elections in many struggling democracies, such as Cameroon, has been compromised by flaws characterized by fraud and numerous irregularities that render the electoral process a farce, making the people's will meaningless and contributing to worrying voter apathy. This state of affairs has been attributed to the lack of a credible election management body to manage the electoral process in an unbiased, transparent, and independent manner. EMBs play a pivotal role in the electoral process and must adhere to specific minimum standards to ensure the ballot outcome is acceptable to all stakeholders. These minimum standards, comprising internationally accepted norms and practices, have been succinctly elucidated in this work. Using these standards, it has been amply demonstrated that the management of elections in Cameroon during the NEO/MINADT era was marred by numerous flaws and irregularities, as the electoral management institutions failed to meet the requisite international standards. It has been demonstrated that these institutions lacked the necessary legal safeguards for their independence, impartiality, and effectiveness, which ultimately led to unpopular elections marked by voter apathy.

The flawed nature of elections in Cameroon has stalled the drive for democratization and reinstated autocratic rule, masquerading as democracy. The electoral process has been subverted. Elections lost significance because more credible institutions needed to manage them in Cameroon. They became a mere ceremony through which the ruling elite validated their legitimacy without affecting the people's will.

The attempts of the government to remedy these problems through the creation of ELECAM are half-hearted and highly dubious because ELECAM still retains most of the significant structural and institutional weaknesses of its predecessors and fails to adhere, on many counts, to the minimum standards that have been set out. A careful examination of the significant facets of ELECAM's legislative and institutional framework has demonstrated that the government, and especially the Presidency of the Republic, still wields enormous and arbitrary powers over ELECAM and has multiple avenues of manipulating the institution to serve its whims and caprices. ELECAM was designed as an independent electoral institution; however, compared to similar bodies worldwide, especially the IEC of South Africa, one discovers that it lacks all the safeguards against interference and partiality. Despite its commendable strides to increase voter registration and turnout, it is highly doubtful that ELECAM can turn the tide of flawed elections and ensure transparent and credible ballot and popular elections.

6.3. Recommendations

Given that most Cameroonians have lost faith in the political (electoral) system and especially the institutions responsible for managing the electoral process, the sure way to rekindle their hope and inspire confidence in the electoral process is to conceive and design an EMB with all the necessary guarantees of independence, impartiality, credibility, and professionalism. This is indispensable for any hope of a peaceful transition and genuine democratization in Cameroon. Presently, ELECAM does not have these guarantees. In this light, the recommendations below are proposed to strengthen the institution and isolate it from any form of manipulation.

The legal framework of any institution, such as ELECAM, is pivotal for guaranteeing its effectiveness and independence. The legal framework of ELECAM needs to be reviewed to prevent arbitrary executive interference. ELECAM, as an independent institution, should be constitutionally established and its provisions entrenched. These provisions should outline the composition, selection, and appointment procedures for ELECAM members, their removal from office, the funding of ELECAM, and its accountability. These procedures must be transparent and inclusive, ensuring the independence and effectiveness of the institution. A law passed in Parliament can then set out further details about the institution that must conform to the stipulations of the Constitution.

The two-pronged structure of ELECAM, in which powers and responsibilities are shared between the EB and the DGE, is highly undesirable and should be abolished. The DGE of ELECAM needs to be scrapped, and all its powers and functions should be transferred to the EB. This way, the risk of any conflict of interest will be preempted, and the board can exercise the excessive powers conferred on the Director General more responsibly.

Appointment procedures of ELECAM members must be reviewed to render them more transparent, inclusive, and stringent. The role of the President of the Republic in the selection and appointment procedure should be very minimal. Since the independence of institutions in Cameroon is severely limited, the nomination of ELECAM members should be done by political parties represented in the National Assembly and civil society organizations. The president should make all appointments from such nominations, subject to parliamentary approval. This way, the president's ability to appoint party cronies, as has been the case before, will be put in check.

Regarding funding, ELECAM should be given the leeway to elaborate on its budget and submit it to parliament as an autonomous budget without prior approval from the government. A law should provide a minimum threshold budget that should be made available to ELECAM to improve the management process continuously, for example, by employing new technologies in election management to minimize irregularities. ELECAM should also be allowed to seek external funding. This would enhance its efficiency and guard against the possibility of the institution being starved of funds by the government. No effort should be spared in adequately funding the institution because it costs the state far more when elections are rigged and chaos and civil strife occur, as was the case in 1992. ELECAM should account for the funds entrusted to it to an independent authority, such as the Administrative Bench of the Supreme Court, and not the finance minister.

The procedure for removing ELECAM members from the office should include a review of any dismissal by an independent institution. The South African approach is recommended in this respect, and any dismissal of an ELECAM member for incompetence, misconduct, or breach of oath should be subject to the approval of two-thirds of the members of Parliament.

Provisions should also be made by courts of law to review such dismissals. In cases of physical or mental incapacity, the Senegalese approach, where a doctor designated by the National Order of Medical Practitioners determines such incapacity, should equally be adopted.

The terms and conditions of service of ELECAM members should be determined by law and not through a presidential decree, and provision should equally be made for a review of these conditions by a body created explicitly for that purpose. The term of office of ELECAM members should be limited in time to a maximum of two terms, which should not exceed ten years and should not coincide with the term of office of an elected government. This way, the President's arbitrary powers over the remuneration and re-appointment of ELECAM members would be significantly curbed, and the avenues for manipulation would be reduced.

ELECAM's mandate should be broadened to include registering political parties, delimiting electoral boundaries, overseeing candidates' and political parties' expenditures during elections, and leading the review of any bill concerning electoral legislation. It should equally be granted the power to make regulations governing the conduct of elections. This will ensure that the broader political landscape in which elections take place is leveled for fairer competition amongst parties.

ELECAM should report on its activities to Parliament through annual reports and any other such reports that Parliament may deem necessary. These reports should include information on the management of finances entrusted to it, information on the execution of its mandate and difficulties encountered, and projections for the future.

It is recommended that these reports be submitted and defended before a parliamentary committee is established. The committee can then seek clarification and further information on any pertinent issue before submitting the report to the Assembly's plenary for debate and approval by a simple majority.

ELECAM should also be required by law to report regularly to the public on its activities and enhance public participation. It should, for instance, conduct regular public assessments of its activities to obtain public opinion and perceptions of its performance. ELECAM should regularly inform the public about its activities by publishing its activity reports, as adopted by parliament, as well as newsletters, brochures, booklets, and pamphlets. If well-implemented, this will enhance the institution's transparency and public accountability.

The Constitutional Council's requirement to establish ELECAM's incompetence should be scrapped, and this power should be conferred on parliament. The Constitutional Council has not yet been established, and even if it were, its composition would render it highly inappropriate to discharge this responsibility impartially. MINADTs' role in any aspect of the electoral process should also be eliminated, given that it has hitherto been the chief architect of electoral fraud, and its involvement in the management of elections is highly suspected. Broader institutional reforms should be instituted because ELECAM cannot function effectively, even if well-insulated from manipulation, unless other institutions with which it is condemned to collaborate are more efficient.

Gathering from the responses to the questionnaires and interviews, the following recommendations are also made:

- Internet voting should be seriously considered and instituted, as this would enable even those eligible to vote but cannot make it to polling stations to cast their votes.
- Electoral education should be considered necessary by ELECAM and given the priority it deserves, as many eligible voters are unaware of the electoral calendar, registration modalities, and voting requirements.

Bibliography

1. Abdrashid, S. (2016). *Voter turnout trends around the world.* Sweden: International IDEA.
2. ACE The Electoral Knowledge Network. (2013). *ACE is the electoral knowledge network.* Retrieved September 11, 2015, from http://www.aceproject.org/ace-en/pdf/ei/view
3. Achen, C. (2001). Why lagged dependent variables can suppress the explanatory power of other independent variables. Paper presented at the annual meeting of the American Political Science Association.
4. Adejumobi, S. (1998). Civil society and democratic renewal in Nigeria. Paper presented at a conference on civil society organization organized by the African Centre for Democratic Governance (AFRIGOVT), Abuja, Jan 25–26.
5. Agbaje, A., & Adejumobi, S. (2006). Do votes count? The travails of electoral politics in Nigeria. *Africa Development,* 31(3). CODESRIA.
6. Agu, S. U., Okeke, V. O., & Idike, A. N. (2013). Causes of voter apathy and the survival of genuine political participation in Nigeria. *Mediterranean Journal of Social Sciences.* Milan, Italy: MCSER Publishing.
7. Ajayi, K. (2006). Security forces, electoral conduct and the 2003 general elections in Nigeria. *Journal of Social Science,* 13(1), 57–66.
8. Ake, C. (1996). *Is Africa democratizing?* Centre for Advanced Social Sciences (CASS) Monograph No. 5. Lagos, Nigeria: Malthouse Press Ltd.
9. Amdi, S. (2014). Democracy and elections in Nigeria: A study of voter turnout in the Fourth Republic. Ahmadu Bello University; Degree Project.
10. Antunes, R. (2008). *Identificação partidária e comportamento eleitoral: factores estruturais, atitudes e mudanças no sentido de voto* (Doctoral thesis, Universidade de Coimbra).
11. Anyang-Nyong'o, P. (1995). Discourses on democracy in Africa. In E. Chole & J. Ibrahim (Eds.), *Democratization in Africa: Problems and prospects* (pp. 29–42). Dakar: CODESRIA.

12. Anyangwe, C. (2013). Manumission from black-on-black colonialism; sovereign statehood for the British Southern Cameroons. In S. J. Ndlovu-Gatsheni & B. Mhlanga (Eds.), *Bondage of boundaries and identity politics in postcolonial Africa: The 'Northern Problem' and Ethno-Futures* (pp. 163–184). Pretoria: Africa Institute of South Africa.
13. Appadorai, A. (1974). *The substance of politics.* New Delhi: Oxford University Press.
14. Arrows, K. (1951). *Social values and individual values.* New York: John Wiley & Sons.
15. Arrows, K. (1986). Rationality of self and others in the economic system. *The Journal of Business*, 59(4), S385–S399.
16. Association of African Election Authorities (AAEA). (1998). *Charter of the Association of African Election Authorities.* Accra, Ghana: AAEA.
17. Autheman, V. (2004). The resolution of disputes related to election results. *Workshop on the Role of the Constitutional Court in Resolving Election Result Disputes* (pp. 1–21). Indonesia: IFES Rule of Law Conference Paper Series.
18. Ayittey, G. B. (1992). *Africa betrayed.* New York: Palgrave Macmillan.
19. Aywa, F. A. (2015). *Election management bodies in East Africa: A comparative study of the contribution of electoral commissions to strengthening democracy.* Johannesburg, South Africa: Open Society Foundations.
20. Ballington, J. (2001). *Youth and political participation: Trends or turnout.* Stockholm: International IDEA.
21. Barkan, J. D. (1997). African elections in comparative perspective. In United Nations Department for Development Support and Management Services (UNDDSMS), *Elections: Perspectives on establishing democratic practices.* New York: UNDDSMS.
22. Bayart, J.-F. (2009). *The state in Africa: Politics of the belly* (2nd ed.). Cambridge: Polity Press.
23. Beck, N., & Katz, J. (1995). What to do (and what not to do) with time-series–cross-section data in comparative perspective. *American Political Science Review*, 89(4), 634–647.
24. Bell, A., Fairbrother, M., & Jones, K. (2019). Fixed and random effects models: Making an informed choice. *Quality and Quantity*, 53, 1051–1074.

25. Bell, A., & Jones, K. (2015). Explaining fixed effects: Random effects modeling of time-series cross-sectional and panel data. *Political Science Research and Methods*, 3(3), 133–153.

26. Benz, M. (2007). The relevance of procedural utility for economics. In S. Bruno & A. Stutzer (Eds.), *Economics and psychology: A promising new cross-disciplinary field.* Cambridge, MA: MIT Press.

27. Berrebi, C., & Klor, E. F. (2008). Are voters sensitive to terrorism? Direct evidence from the Israeli electorate. *American Political Science Review*, 102(3), 279–301.

28. Birch, A. (1995). *The concept and theories of modern democracy.* London: Routledge.

29. Birch, S. (2005). Single-member district electoral systems and democratic transition. *Electoral Studies*, 24(2), 281–301.

30. Blais, A. (2000). *To vote or not to vote: The merits and limits of rational choice theory.* Pittsburgh: University of Pittsburgh Press.

31. Blais, A., Gidengil, E., Nevitte, N., & Nadeau, R. (2001). The evolving nature of non-voting. Paper delivered at the annual meeting of the American Political Science Association.

32. Bratton, M. (1997). *Democratic experiments in Africa: Regime transitions in comparative perspective.* New York: Cambridge University Press.

33. Bratton, M. (2008). Vote buying and violence in Nigerian election campaigns. *Electoral Studies*, 27(4), 621–632.

34. Center for Democracy and Development. (2019). Nigerian election trends. Abuja.

35. Chase-Dunn. (2003). Globalization from below: Toward a collectively rational and democratic global commonwealth. In C. E. J. (Ed.), *Globalisation: Critical perspectives.* New York: Nova Science Publishers.

36. Chiabi, E. M. (2011). Redressing regional imbalance in Cameroon: The lessons from the past. In P. Nkwi & F. B. Nyamnjoh (Eds.), *Regional balance and national integration in Cameroon: Lessons learned and uncertain future* (pp. 41–58). Bamenda: Langaa RPCIG.

37. Chigudu, D. (2012). *Perceptions of a free and fair election in Zimbabwe.* Saarbrücken, Germany: LAP Academic Publishing GmbH & Co. KG.

38. Chinsinga, B. (2006). Lack of alternative leadership in democratic Malawi: Some related issues ahead of 2004 general elections. *Journal of Nordic African Studies.*

39. Cloud, D. (2010). *Voter apathy: Definitions, statistics and causes.* New York: Palgrave Macmillan.

40. Consortium for Development Partnerships. (2010). *Governance and institution building in Africa.* CODESRIA.

41. Conteh, M. (2013). *An introduction to election managers and tertiary institutions in Sierra Leone.* Institute of Electoral Administration and Civic Education (INEACE) in collaboration with the University of Makeni (UNIMAK) in Sierra Leone.

42. Crawford, C. (2006). *Attack the messenger: How politicians turn you against the media.* New York: Rowman & Littlefield Publishers, Inc.

43. Crewe, I., & Denver, D. T. (1985). *Electoral change in Western democracies: Patterns and perspectives.* Hemel Hempstead: Harvester Wheatsheaf.

44. Crewe, I., Fox, T., & Alt, J. (1992). Non-voting in British general elections, 1966–October 1974. In *Issues and controversies in British electoral behavior.* Hemel Hempstead: Harvester Wheatsheaf.

45. Dahl, R., & Stinebrickner, B. (2005). *Modern political analysis.* New Delhi: Prentice Hall of India Private Limited.

46. Dalton, R. J. (1984). Cognitive mobilization and partisan dealignment in advanced industrial democracies. *Journal of Politics,* 46, 264–284.

47. Dalton, R. J. (1988). *Citizen politics in Western democracies: Public opinion and political parties in the United States, Great Britain, West Germany, and France.* Chatham, NJ: Chatham House Publishers.

48. Dalton, R. J. (2007). Voter apathy and revival of genuine political participation. ACE Practitioners' Network. http://aceproject.org/electoraladvice/archive/questions/replies/78797089

49. Delancy, M. W. (1989). *Cameroon: Dependence & independence.* Colorado: Westview Press Inc.

50. Downs, A. (1957). *An economic theory of democracy.* New York: Harper Collins Publishers.

51. Duverger, M. (1951). *Les partis politiques* (2nd ed., rev.). Paris: A. Colin.

52. Duverger, M. (1959). *Political parties: Their organization and activity in the modern state* (2nd English rev. ed.). London: Methuen & Co.

53. Duverger, M. (1984). Which is the best electoral system? In A. Lijphart & B. Grofman (Eds.), *Choosing an electoral system: Issues and alternatives*. New York: Praeger.
54. Duverger, M. (1986). Duverger's law: Forty years later. In B. Grofman & A. Lijphart (Eds.), *Electoral laws and their political consequences*. New York: Agathon Press.
55. EISA. (2003). *Principles of election management in the SADC region*. Johannesburg.
56. Endersby, J. W., & Krieckhaus, J. T. (2008). Turnout around the globe: The influence of electoral institutions on national voter participation, 1972–2000. *Electoral Studies*, 27(4), 601–610.
57. English, K. (Ed.). (2005). *The management of the 2004 electoral process: The power of the vote: Malawi's 2004 parliamentary and presidential elections*. Zomba, Malawi: Kachere Book Series.
58. Ethridge, M., & Handleman, H. (2012). *Politics in a changing world: A comparative introduction to political science*. New York.
59. Eyongetah, T., & Brian, R. (1974). *A history of the Cameroon*. London: Longman.
60. Falade, D. A. (2008). *Questions and answers on concepts, methods, issues and problems in social studies*. Lagos: Novec'kol.
61. Feldman, O., & Kazuhisa, K. (1991). Media use as predictors of political behavior: The case of Japan. *Political Psychology*, 12.
62. Filer, J. E., Lawrence, W. K., & Morton, R. B. (1991). Voting laws, educational policies, and minority turnout. *Journal of Law and Economics*, 34(2).
63. Flickinger, R., & Studlar, D. (1992). Exploring declining turnout in Western European elections. *West European Politics*, 15, 1–16.
64. Forje, J. W. (2008). Developing viable independent institutions for political and economic development in Cameroon. *Cameroon Journal on Democracy and Human Rights*, 2(2), 31–43.
65. Franklin, M. (1992). The decline of cleavage politics. In Franklin, Mackie, Valen et al., 1992.
66. Franklin, M. (1996). Electoral participation. In L. Leduc, R. Niemi, & P. Norris (Eds.), *Comparing democracies: Elections and voting in global perspective*. Thousand Oaks, CA: Sage.
67. Franklin, M. (2002). The dynamics of electoral participation. In L. Leduc, R. Niemi, & P. Norris (Eds.), *Comparing democracies 2: Elections and voting in global perspective*. Thousand Oaks, CA: Sage.

68. Gettleman, J. (2009, November 6). An international court prosecutor will seek an inquiry into Kenyan election violence. *The New York Times*, A6.
69. Geys, B. (2006). Explaining voter turnout: A review of aggregate-level research. Brussels: Universiteit Brussel.
70. Geys, B. (2006). Voter turnout: A review of aggregate-level research. *Electoral Studies*, 25(4), 637–663.
71. Ghana News Agency. (2011, August 14). Retrieved September 11, 2015, from http://www.ghananewsagency.org/
72. Goodwin-Gill, G. (1994). *Free and fair elections: International law and practice.* Geneva: Inter-Parliamentary Union.
73. Goodwin-Gill, G. S. (2006). *Free and fair elections.* Geneva: Inter-Parliamentary Union.
74. Gray, M., & Caul, M. (2000). Voter turnout in advanced democracies, 1950–1997. *Comparative Political Science Review*, 33(2).
75. Gray, M., & Miki, C. (2000). Declining voter turnout in advanced industrial democracies, 1950–1997. *Comparative Political Studies*, 33, 1091–1122.
76. Green, D., & Shapiro, I. (1994). *Pathologies of rational choice theory.* New Haven, CT: Yale University Press.
77. Grofman, B. (1993). Is turnout the paradox that ate rational choice theory? In B. Grofman (Ed.), *Information, participation, and choice: An economic theory of democracy in perspective.* Ann Arbor: University of Michigan Press.
78. Grumm, G. (1958). Theories of electoral systems. *Midwest Journal of Political Science*, 2(4), 357–376.
79. Güth, W., & Weck-Hannemann, H. (1997). Do people care about democracy? An experiment exploring the value of voting rights. *Public Choice*, 91(1), 27–47.
80. Gwaibi, N. W. (2015). Wrath from the gods: Traditional institutions and electoral politics in Bali. *Journal of Asian and African Studies*, 52(3), 324–345.
81. Hague, R., & Harrop, M. (2004). *Comparative government and politics: An introduction.* London: Macmillan.
82. Hall, S. (1982). The rediscovery of ideology: The return of the repressed in media studies. In *Culture, society and the media.* London: Macmillan.
83. Harding, S. (1993). Africa: The new frontier in voter participation. *African Affairs Journal*, 92(368), 555–567.

84. Heywood, A. (2004). *Political theory: An introduction* (2nd ed.). London: Macmillan.
85. Heywood, A. (2007). *Politics*. Basingstoke: Palgrave Macmillan.
86. Hoffman, D., & Patton, K. (1997). *Essential readings in comparative politics*. London: Harcourt Brace College Publishers.
87. Huntington, S. P. (1991). *The third wave: Democratization in the late twentieth century*. Norman: University of Oklahoma Press.
88. IIDEA. (2002). *A framework for the development of voter registration*. Stockholm: International IDEA.
89. IIDEA. (2006). *Engaging the electorate: Initiatives to promote voter turnout from around the world*. Stockholm: International IDEA.
90. IIDEA. (2006). *Introducing electronic voting: Essential considerations*. Stockholm: International IDEA.
91. IIDEA. (2006). *Political finance database*. Stockholm: International IDEA.
92. International IDEA. (2006). *Voter turnout since 1945: A global report*. Stockholm: International IDEA.
93. International IDEA. (2008). *Voter turnout since 1945: A global report* (updated version). Stockholm: International IDEA.
94. International IDEA. (2010). *Democratic accountability in service delivery: A practical guide to identify improvements through assessment*. Stockholm: International IDEA.
95. Inter-Parliamentary Union. (1994). *Free and fair elections: International law and practice*. Geneva: Inter-Parliamentary Union.
96. Inter-Parliamentary Union. (2006). *Free and fair elections*. Geneva: Inter-Parliamentary Union.
97. Jamison, E. (2007). Civil society and elections in Africa. *Democratization*, 14(3), 389–406.
98. Jennings, M. K., & Niemi, R. G. (1974). *The political character of adolescence: The influence of families and schools*. Princeton, NJ: Princeton University Press.
99. Jennings, M. K., & Stoker, L. (2004). Social trust and civic engagement across time and generations. *Acta Politica*, 39(4), 342–379.
100. John, C., & Damilola, A. (2014). *Political behavior and electoral studies*. Lagos: Zenith Publishers.
101. Johnson, J. (2009). The impact of electoral systems on women's representation. *Women's Studies International Forum*, 32(1), 19–28.

102. Joseph, R. (1999). *Cameroon's democracy experiment, 1990–1996.* Boulder: Westview Press.

103. Kalyvas, S. N. (2006). *The logic of violence in civil war.* Cambridge: Cambridge University Press.

104. Kavanagh, D. (1995). *Election campaigns: The new marketing of politics.* Oxford: Blackwell.

105. Katz, R. S. (1980). A theory of parties and electoral systems. *Baltimore: Johns Hopkins University Press.*

106. Katz, R. S., & Mair, P. (1995). Changing models of party organization and party democracy. *Party Politics*, 1(1), 5–28.

107. Katz, R. S., & Mair, P. (2009). The cartel party thesis: A restatement. *Perspectives on Politics*, 7(4), 753–766.

108. Kew, D., & Lopez, G. (2005). *The struggle for democracy in Africa.* New York: Routledge.

109. Lijphart, A. (1994). *Electoral systems and party systems: A study of twenty-seven democracies, 1945–1990.* Oxford: Oxford University Press.

110. Lijphart, A. (1999). *Patterns of democracy: Government forms and performance in thirty-six countries.* New Haven, CT: Yale University Press.

111. Linz, J. J., & Stepan, A. (1996). *Problems of democratic transition and consolidation: Southern Europe, South America, and post-communist Europe.* Baltimore: Johns Hopkins University Press.

112. Lipset, S. M. (1959). Some social requisites of democracy: Economic development and political legitimacy. *American Political Science Review*, 53(1), 69–105.

113. Lipset, S. M., & Rokkan, S. (1967). *Party systems and voter alignments: Cross-national perspectives.* New York: Free Press.

114. Lodge, T. (1999). *Consolidating democracy: Political participation and electoral systems in Africa.* Johannesburg: Wits University Press.

115. Mainwaring, S. (1999). *Rethinking party systems in the third wave of democratization: The case of Brazil.* Stanford, CA: Stanford University Press.

116. Norris, P. (2002). *Democratic phoenix: Reinventing political activism.* Cambridge: Cambridge University Press.

117. Norris, P. (2004). *Electoral engineering: Voting rules and political behavior.* Cambridge: Cambridge University Press.

118. Norris, P. (2008). *Driving democracy: Do power-sharing institutions work?* Cambridge: Cambridge University Press.

119. Norris, P., & Inglehart, R. (2003). *Rising tide: Gender equality and cultural change around the world.* Cambridge: Cambridge University Press.
120. Powell, G. B. (2000). *Elections as instruments of democracy: Majoritarian and proportional visions.* New Haven, CT: Yale University Press.
121. Putnam, R. D. (1993). *Making democracy work: Civic traditions in modern Italy.* Princeton, NJ: Princeton University Press.
122. Putnam, R. D. (2000). *Bowling alone: The collapse and revival of American community.* New York: Simon & Schuster.
123. Rosenstone, S. J., & Hansen, J. M. (1993). *Mobilization, participation, and democracy in America.* New York: Macmillan.
124. Sartori, G. (1976). *Parties and party systems: A framework for analysis.* Cambridge: Cambridge University Press.
125. Schumpeter, J. A. (1942). *Capitalism, socialism and democracy.* New York: Harper & Brothers.
126. Verba, S., Schlozman, K. L., & Brady, H. E. (1995). *Voice and equality: Civic voluntarism in American politics.* Cambridge, MA: Harvard University Press.
127. Wolfinger, R. E., & Rosenstone, S. J. (1980). *Who votes?* New Haven, CT: Yale University Press.

References

i. ACE Electoral Knowledge Network. (n.d.). Principles of election management. http://aceproject.org/aceen/topics/em/ema/ema01 (accessed 25/08/22) http://aceproject.org/ero-en/topics/electoral management/electoral%20cycle.JPG/view

ii. Cameroon-info.net. (n.d.). Various Presidential Decrees on ELECAM. http://www.cameroon-info.net/stories/0,27423,@,paul-biya-constate-la-mise-en-place-d-elecam.html (accessed 10/10/22)

iii. Decree No. 2008/463 of 30 December 2008 on the Appointment of Members of the Electoral Board of Elections Cameroon.

iv. Decree No. 2008/464 of 30 December 2008 on the Appointment of the President and Vice-President of the Electoral Board of Elections Cameroon.

v. Decree No. 2008/470 of 31 December 2008 on the Appointment of Officials of Elections Cameroon.

vi. Electoral Institute of Southern Africa. (n.d.). EISA documents and publications. http://www.eisa.org.za (accessed 12/07/22)

vii. Ezimiri, G., Nnamani, K. C., & Nnaegbo, O. (2016). Democracy at the crossroads: Ethno-regional power contestations and democratization in diversified Nigeria, 1960–2015. *South East Journal of Political Science Review, 2*(1).

viii. International Institute for Democracy and Electoral Assistance. (n.d.). Code of conduct for the ethical and professional administration of election. http://www.idea.int/publications/conduct/admin/part1.htm (accessed 15/08/22)

ix. Law No. 2000/016 of 19 December 2000 to establish the National Elections Observatory.

x. Law No. 2005-007 establishing the Commission Electoral National Autonome (Senegal).

xi. Law No. 2006.011 of 29 December 2006 to set up and lay down the organization and functioning of Elections Cameroon.

xii. Mack-Kit, S. (2007). Elections au Cameroun. Paris: Research International.

xiii. National Commission on Human Rights and Freedoms. (n.d.). The state of human rights in Cameroon (accessed 15/08/22).

xiv. Progressive Initiative for Cameroon. (n.d.). Press releases. www.picam.org (accessed 20/09/22).

xv. Remmer, K. (2010). Political scale and electoral turnout: Evidence from the less industrialized world. *Comparative Political Studies, 43*(3), 275–303.

xvi. Riker, W. H. (1982). The two-party system and Duverger's law: An essay on the history of political science. *American Political Science Review, 76*(4), 753–766.

xvii. Robbins, J., Hunter, L., & Murray, G. (2013). Voters versus terrorists: Analyzing the effect of terrorist events on voter turnout. *Journal of Peace Research, 50*(4), 495–508.

xviii. Scarritt Jr., & Mozaffar, S. (1996). The potential for sustainable democracy in Africa. Paper presented at the International Studies Association Conference, San Diego, 19 April.

xix. Schedler, A. (2013). *The politics of uncertainty: Sustaining and subverting electoral.* Oxford: Oxford University Press.

xx. Schumpeter, J. (1975). *Capitalism, socialism, and democracy.* New York: Harper and Row Inc.

xxi. Shugart, M. S. (2005). Comparative electoral systems research: The maturation of a field and new challenges ahead. In M. Gallagher & P. Mitchell (Eds.). *The politics of electoral systems.* Oxford: Oxford University Press.

xxii. Shugart, M. S., & Wattenberg, M. P. (2001). *Mixed-member electoral systems: The best of both worlds?* Comparative Politics. Oxford: Oxford University Press.

xxiii. Sklar, R., Onwudiwe, E., & Kew, D. (2006). Nigeria: Completing Obasanjo's legacy. *Journal of Democracy, 17*(3), 1000–115.

xxiv. Sources of electoral volatility. (n.d.). New York: St. Martin Press.

xxv. Takougang, J., & Krieger, M. (1998). *African state and society in the 1990s: Cameroon's political crossroads.* Oxford: Westview Press.

xxvi. Teixeira, R. (1992). *The disappearing American voter.* Washington, D.C.: Brookings.

xxvii. The Commission on the Remuneration of Representatives Act of 1994 (South Africa); The Constitution of Costa Rica, 1949.

xxviii. The Constitution of the Republic of Cameroon, 2008; the Constitution of the Republic of Ghana, 1992; and the Constitution of Kenya, 2010.

xxix. The Constitution of the Republic of South Africa of 1996; The Electoral Commission Act 1993 (Ghana).

xxx. The Electoral Commission Act of 1996 (South Africa).

xxxi. Tingsten, H. (1937). *Political behavior.* London: King and Son.

xxxii. US State Department. (n.d.). Report on the state of human rights in Cameroon (accessed 10/09/22).

xxxiii. Van de Walle, N. (1997). Economic reform and the consolidation of democracy in Africa. In M. Ottaway (Ed.), *Democracy in Africa: The hard road ahead.* Boulder: Lynne Rienner Publishers, Inc.

xxxiv. Van der Eijk, C. (2002). Design issues in electoral research: Taking care of (core) business. *Electoral Studies, 21*, 189–206.

xxxv. Van Ham, C., & Garnett, A. H. (2019). Building impartial electoral management? Institutional design, independence, and electoral integrity. *International Political Science Review, 40*(3), 34–56.

xxxvi. Van Ham, C., & Lindberg, S. I. (2015). From sticks to carrots: Electoral manipulation in Africa, 1986–2012. *Government and Opposition, 50*(3), 521–548.

xxxvii. Verba, S., & Nie, N. (1972). *Participation in America.* New York: Harper and Row.

xxxviii. Verrall, N. (2016). Behavior change: Voter apathy. Working document of the British Psychological Society.

xxxix. Wolfinger, R., & Rosenstone, S. (1980). *Who votes?* New Haven, CT: Yale University Press.

xl. Wright, J. G. (1977). Contextual models of electoral behavior: The southern Wallace vote. *The American Political Science Review, 71*, 497–508.

xli. Yamane, T. (1967). *Statistics, an introductory analysis* (2nd ed.). New York: Harper and Row.

xlii. Yorons, G. (2017). Electoral violence, arms proliferation and electoral security in Nigeria: Lessons from the 2015 elections for emerging. Retrieved from http//www.InNigeria.org/up/up-content/uploads/conference paper by Gani-Yorons.

xliii. Yusuf, A. (2012). Democracy and political apathy in Nigeria (1999–2011). *European Scientific Journal, 8*(2), 1857–7881.

xliv. African Election Database. (n.d.). Elections in Cameroon. http://africanelections.tripod.com/cm.html (accessed 21/09/22)

Printed at Repro India Ltd.